THE RUSSIAN RESEARCH CENTER

The Russian Research Center of Harvard University is supported by a grant from the Carnegie Corporation. The Center carries out interdisciplinary study of Russian institutions and behavior.

Russian Research Center Studies

1. *Public Opinion in Soviet Russia: A Study in Mass Persuasion,* by Alex Inkeles

2. *Soviet Politics — The Dilemma of Power; The Role of Ideas in Social Change,* by Barrington Moore, Jr.

3. *Justice in Russia: An Interpretation of Soviet Law,* by Harold J. Berman

4. *Chinese Communism and the Rise of Mao,* by Benjamin I. Schwartz

5. *Titoism and the Cominform,* by Adam B. Ulam

6. *A Documentary History of Chinese Communism,* by Conrad Brandt, Benjamin Schwartz, and John K. Fairbank

7. *The New Man in Soviet Psychology,* by Raymond A. Bauer

8. *Soviet Opposition to Stalin: A Case Study in World War II,* by George Fischer

9. *Minerals: A Key to Soviet Power,* by Demitri B. Shimkin

10. *Soviet Law in Action: The Recollected Cases of a Soviet Lawyer,* by Harold J. Berman and Boris A. Konstantinovsky

11. *How Russia Is Ruled,* by Merle Fainsod

12. *Terror and Progress USSR: Some Sources of Change and Stability in the Soviet Dictatorship,* by Barrington Moore, Jr.

13. *The Formation of the Soviet Union: Communism and Nationalism, 1917–1923,* by Richard Pipes

14. *Marxism: The Unity of Theory and Practice,* by Alfred G. Meyer

15. *Soviet Industrial Expansion, 1928–1951,* by Donald R. Hodgman

16. *Soviet Taxation: The Fiscal and Monetary Problems of a Planned Economy,* by Franklyn D. Holzman

17. *Soviet Military Law and Administration,* by Harold J. Berman and Miroslav Kerner

18. *Documents on Soviet Military Law and Administration,* by Harold J. Berman and Miroslav Kerner

19. *The Russian Marxists and the Origins of Bolshevism,* by Leopold H. Haimson

THE
RUSSIAN MARXISTS

& *The Origins of Bolshevism*

by LEOPOLD H. HAIMSON

If you can look into the seeds of time,
And say which grain will grow and which will not . . .
Macbeth, I, iii

HARVARD UNIVERSITY PRESS
Cambridge, Massachusetts
1 9 5 5

Distributed in Great Britain by Geoffrey Cumberlege,
Oxford University Press, London

This volume was prepared under a grant from the Carnegie Corporation of
New York. That Corporation is not, however, the author, owner, publisher,
or proprietor of this publication and is not to be understood as approving by
virtue of its grant any of the statements made or views expressed therein.

Library of Congress Catalog Card Number 55–10972
Printed in the United States of America

PREFACE

This book, which is intended to be the first in a series of volumes on the development of Bolshevism in Russia, attempts to cover a rather broad historical canvas. It is, in part, an interpretive essay on the evolution of the nineteenth-century Russian intelligentsia, an unique social formation in the intellectual history of Europe; it is more largely a study of the reception that Marxist ideology encountered, and of the transformations that it underwent, in the hands of this estranged group of Russia's nineteenth-century society. It is partly an analysis of the emergence of Bolshevism and Menshevism, the two opposing interpretations of Marxist doctrine — and Russian reality — around which most of the Russian Marxists ultimately coalesced; and partly an analysis of the early development of Plekhanov, Akselrod, Martov, and Lenin, the four figures who were chiefly responsible for the delineation of these two conflicting interpretations. These areas of Russia's nineteenth-century intellectual history have been explored in an effort to consider the whole complex of factors that entered into the development of the conception of man and of social reality to which the founders of Bolshevism and Menshevism ultimately gave voice.

The first part of the study traces the factors that were to exercise a long-lasting if not permanent influence on the image that Lenin, Martov, Akselrod, and Plekhanov held of the world about them and of their own positions and roles in that world. The first of these factors was the intelligentsia tradition to which these men fell heir, a tradition which encompassed not only the memory of a long and tragic historical experience but also a set of intellectual categories, a set of concepts and symbols, through which this experience was interpreted.

Contemporary studies of intellectual history tend to stress the existence of a common set of assumptions — of an intellectual climate — that characterizes most of the intellectual figures of an age, however conflicting their views may appear on the surface. What such studies sometimes fail to point out is that this common set of assumptions may be but a link in a cultural continuum. One generation of intellectuals lay their imprint on their successors, if only by defining the intellectual grounds on which the succeeding generation may challenge them. The "sons" will frequently deny the values that were held uppermost by their "fathers," but in this very process of denial they may hold onto the categories of analysis, and onto the definition of possible alternatives, that their despised predecessors maintained. Thus it was, as Carl Becker brilliantly demonstrated, that the prophets of the Enlightenment inherited so much of the medieval tradition. Thus it was, within a shorter historical perspective, that the eighteenth-century Empiricists were driven to Hume's solipsism, not for lack of alternatives, but because they drew on the same analytical tools (in their definitions of perception and of relations) as the Rationalist predecessors whom they had so confidently repudiated.

Such continuity was perhaps even more characteristic of the development of the Russian intelligentsia than of the experience of any comparable groups in the history of the West; for the members of the intelligentsia were held closely together, bound to one another, through most of the nineteenth century by their extreme alienation from the ruling forces in their Russian environment. In the first part of this book, I have outlined some of the elements in this intellectual tradition — some of the fundamental categories and symbols through the medium of which successive generations of the intelligentsia defined the nature of man and the character of Russia's historical development. I have particularly attempted to describe — and, in small measure, to explain — how so many members of the intelligentsia came to view "consciousness" and "spontaneity" as two opposing categories whose properties underlay the process of reality.

It was through the medium of this common set of categories and symbols that the future leaders of Bolshevism and Menshevism assimilated and interpreted the tragic experience of their intelligentsia predecessors. It was through the medium of these categories and symbols, and with this image of the past, that they interpreted the teachings of Marxist doctrine and apprehended the political, social, and economic forces in their contemporary environment.

Yet, even though Plekhanov, Akselrod, Lenin, and Martov were bred in the same intellectual tradition and indoctrinated into the same dogmas, their perceptions of and responses to men and events reflected, however subtly at first, certain crucial personality differences. In the biographical chapters of this book, I have attempted to describe the differences, as well as the similarities, in the personalities of the four men, and I have traced the reflection of these personality characteristics in those aspects of their orientations to the world about them that originally brought them together as well as in the aspects of their orientations that eventually drew them apart.

This is not to imply that the political behavior of Plekhanov, Akselrod, Martov, and Lenin has been considered solely a function of their personalities. What I have attempted to show is that implicit in the orientation of these men to reality was a set of perceptive and evaluative biases, which, given certain contemporary environmental conditions, would make them lean to certain kinds of political solutions rather than to others, and which would impel them to perceive more or less quickly and distinctly — and to respond more or less positively — than their fellows to various changes in the environment.

Although many of their specific views would continue to change as the world about them changed, Lenin and his *Iskra* colleagues had already developed certain relatively stable ways of apprehending, evaluating, and interpreting political phenomena at the time when they joined hands for the purpose of establishing an independent and powerful Social Democratic party in Russia. The second part of this study is largely an attempt to describe how, during the period in which the four men collaborated intimately, these modes of orientation were reflected in the image that each of them held of the various components of their Russian political and social environment and in the conceptions that they consequently drew of the position and role of Social Democracy. From this point on, the pace — as well as the focus — of the narrative changes, as we attempt to contrast Plekhanov's, Akselrod's, Lenin's, and Martov's perceptions of the various facets of their world — as well as to view these facets in the perspective of historical hindsight.

I have attempted to show that the particular views that each of these men voiced of the nature of the various interacting forces on the political map, and of the tactics and forms of organization that Social Democracy should consequently adopt, were interconnected, however implicitly, and that these complexes of views reflected certain as yet partly unspelled assumptions concerning the nature of man and the dynamics of the historical process. In this sense, one may say that each of the four leaders of Social Democracy had a world view, a complex of perceptions so interdependent that a major change in any one of these perceptions would compel a revision of the entire complex.

Even at the beginning of their association on *Iskra's* editorial board, certain profound differences were already perceptible in the world views of the four collaborators. At first, these differences remained largely buried, hidden as they were by the traditional categories and symbols to which the four men subscribed, and being of little political actuality as long as the authority of the autocracy appeared to remain unshaken. But as the forces of the opposition to absolutism came to life, these differences gradually came to the fore. In the last part of this work, we shall observe how, under the pressure of the changes on the political scene, Plekhanov, Akselrod, Martov, and Lenin came to recognize these differences. And we shall see that this slow and halting process of recognition — which accompanied the emergence of Bolshevism and Menshevism — marked a major breakdown in the intellectual and symbolic tradition of the intelligentsia, a breakdown which heralded the appearance of a new phase in the intellectual and social history of Russia.

Before closing this prefatory note, I should like to convey my appreciation to those who have helped to make this study possible. First, I wish to express my deepest gratitude to my teachers and friends, Michael Karpovich — who guided my first steps in the study of Russian intellectual history — and Margaret Mead, who did so much to stimulate and sharpen my interest in the field of personality and culture. I also wish to thank Merle Fainsod and Percy Corbett for their suggestions and unfailing support during the course of the completion of this study; William Langer, Barrington Moore, and Marshall Shulman for their many kindnesses in the past year; Mrs. Chase Duffy for her ever helpful editorial assistance and counsel; the Social Science Research Council, the Center of International Studies of Princeton University, and the Russian Research Center of Harvard University for their research grants; and last but not least, my wife without whom this work would probably not have been written.

Cambridge, Massachusetts   L. H.
July 1955

CONTENTS

ILLUSTRATIONS

Following page 134

The Ulyanov Family, 1878. Sovfoto

V. I. Ulyanov (Lenin), 1891. Sovfoto

Leaders of the Petersburg Union of Struggle, 1897. Sovfoto

G. V. Plekhanov

P. B. Akselrod, 1921

Y. O. Martov, 1921

PART ONE

The Origins

1

THE BACKGROUND

I was young, hotblooded, sincere, but not stupid; I loved, hated, believed, worked as hard and hoped as much as ten people. I charged against windmills, beat my head against walls. I did not measure my strength, did not pause and consider. Not knowing life, I assumed at once a burden so heavy that it crippled my back and my sinews. But this is how the life with which I fought takes revenge. I have injured myself. After thirty years, already a hangover; I am old, I have put on my housecoat.

Anton Chekhov, *Ivanov*

In the note of hopelessness struck by Chekhov's first play was expressed the broken spirit of an entire generation of the intelligentsia as Russia approached the last decade of the nineteenth century. The dreamy and slumbering mood into which many members of the intelligentsia chose to withdraw during the 1880's was an escape, a long-due withdrawal from the last two cruel decades of their lives. History appeared to have used those years to demonstrate to the Russian *intelligent* his unbridgeable isolation from the autocracy and the gentry above and from the ignorant, brutish peasantry below. It now seemed to him intent on proving his alienation from the growing forces of the future — from the impersonal new bureaucratic state and from the growing class of greedy businessmen and industrialists on whose shoulder the autocracy seemed content to lean. History appeared to have shown that this was the path, the inevitable pattern that had been traced through the past, present, and future, and that there was nothing the intelligentsia with its own mediocre resources could do to arrest, or even to deflect, the inevitable march of time.*

The intelligentsia had risen out of the old society of estates "as the very sign that this society was dying — that the old world of status had

* However inaccurate, this was the conception of Russia's historical position held by many members of the intelligentsia in the 1880's.

been outgrown." [1] Its birth had been precipitated by the attempt of the absolutist power, beginning in the seventeenth century, to superimpose with the aid of techniques and crafts imported from the West a modern bureaucratic state upon the old society of "medieval" estates.

The autocracy was intent on one basic goal — the maintenance and increase of its power at home and abroad. Blindly, fumblingly, it sought to extract from the West the manifest sources of its strength, while attempting at the same time to preserve the foundations of its traditional authority in the Russian land and even to elaborate upon them. It sought to borrow from the West its cannon and its war vessels, its foundries and its shipyards, as well as the skills needed to operate them; it even sought to borrow its manners and dress, its legal codes and moral treatises.

But at the same time, ignoring the social and economic foundations from which these Western institutions drew their vitality, the absolutist power attempted to strengthen its hold on its chief aid and chief rival in the pursuit of power — the landed gentry — keeping it in relative contentment with generous grants of lands and souls.

Parallel with the importation of the latest Western techniques and devices went, in the seventeenth, eighteenth, and the beginning of the nineteenth centuries, an expansion of socio-economic institutions of which the Western counterparts had, long since, taken the road to destruction. These centuries were marked by a steady extension of serfdom — until much of the peasant population of Russia was bound. And not only was the peasant tied to the land, but he was also subjected to the increasingly arbitrary authority of a landlord of the gentry class.

The spirit of this government-sponsored Westernization was symbolized by Peter the Great. With infinite energy Peter imported from Holland and England, from France and Germany, the cannonmakers, the sailmakers, the soldiers, and the dancing masters with whose aid he hoped to coach his gentry and his merchants into the ways of the West. At the same time, he attempted to draw on the medieval tradition of service to increase his power — to force the peasants to provide for the gentry and the gentry to support his state.

Not only did Peter and his successors increasingly tighten the bonds of the peasant folk to the land and to the gentry, but in order more easily to collect the money and recruit the men needed for the appurtenances of power, they strove to freeze the peasants' social and economic existence to the medieval communal institution of the *mir*. Even when more enlightened rulers, realizing the flimsiness of the edifice that was being built, attempted to strengthen its foundations by more thoroughgoing reforms, they were thwarted — thwarted by the opposition of the very gentry they had enlisted to help them in the renovation of the Russian state.

Thus Russia entered the nineteenth century a mass of largely enserfed peasants governed partially by a Westernized and already estranged nobility — a society so congealed as to hinder severely the growth of the bourgeois class on whose vitality and enterprise depended Russia's future political, social, and economic progress.

The preservation of this curious amalgam rested on keeping within safe bounds its contact with the West. But cultural contact can rarely be kept within predetermined bounds. There are always men so curious, so imaginative, or so unstable in temperament that they refuse to stop at the boundaries that society imposes and seek in foreign credos and foreign mores a rationale for dissatisfaction and the basis for a new faith. The rise of such a group was accelerated in Russia by the reign of Alexander I. Not only did the reign, dominated as it was by the Napoleonic wars, multiply for the sons of the nobility the opportunities for contact with Western thought, but it dramatically dashed their hopes for aid from above in remolding the existing world. Their disillusionment was great because their hopes had been great. Alexander, like his namesake in antiquity, had been viewed by them as a demigod, as a paragon of all the virtues, and when his later policies broke the promises he had made early in his reign to loosen, if not to break, the death grip in which the autocracy held the fate of Russia, they irrevocably lost, with only a few exceptions, their trust in the benevolence of "enlightened" rulers.

The disappointed young men were left to their own resources, and they now organized to force a change in the existing world. When in 1825 the tarnished hero disappeared from the scene and was succeeded on the throne by a reputed obscurantist and reactionary, they decided that the time to strike had arrived. But their revolt, the famous Decembrist uprising, succeeded only in exposing the dismal inadequacy of their strength and their isolation from society.

Marked as they were by this rapid succession of events — the "betrayal" of Alexander, the failure of the Decembrist revolt, the succession to the throne of that symbol of reaction, Nicholas I — the 1820's may be considered as the birth date of the Russian intelligentsia. These years saw the events that crystallized the feeling of total alienation from existing society which gave the Russian intelligentsia its peculiar and unique identity.

As Russia entered the 1830's, the more generous sons and daughters of the nobility (these children of the gentry were later to be joined by alienated youths from other social groups) plunged headlong into a new, exciting, rarefied universe — the universe of abstract ideas. And through the pursuit of abstract ideas, through the study and construction of vast philosophical systems (largely borrowed from the West), they sought to find a meaning for their existence, a sense and a purpose in the world about them.

One of the first systems into which many of the young members of the intelligentsia elected to pour their pent-up emotional fervor was the subjective idealism of Fichte, the doctrine that required the dissociation of the individual soul from material reality to permit its fusion with the purer world spirit. For most of these youths the discovery of Fichte, like their subsequent initiation in other philosophical systems, had the earth-shaking character of a religious conversion. For a few brief moments, they found in the ethereal doctrine of the German Idealist an answer to all their problems, a new order and meaning in the world, and they responded to this discovery with sheer ecstasy. The full quality of this feeling is recaptured in Turgenev's description of the all-night discussions that Bakunin used to hold with his friends during the 1830's.

> In listening to Rudin, it seemed to us, for the first time, that we had grasped that common bond, that the curtain had at last been lifted . . . Harmonious order was installed in all we knew, all the scattered facts became united, ranged themselves in order . . . Spirit breathed everywhere . . . Nothing remained senseless, fortuitous; in everything, an intelligent necessity and beauty was expressed. Everything acquired a clear and, at the same time, mysterious significance; every separate phenomenon of life rang out in harmonious order. And we ourselves, with a certain holy fear of adoration, with sweet quaking at the heart, felt ourselves to be instruments, living vessels of the eternal truth . . .
>
> Just imagine for yourself: five or six young men have gathered together . . . In every man's eyes there is rapture, his cheeks flame, his heart beats, and we talk about God, about truth, about the future of mankind, about poetry . . .
>
> And now the grey morning begins to appear and we disperse, moved, cheerful, honest, sober, with a certain agreeable languor in the soul . . . and we even gaze at the stars in a confiding sort of way, *as though they had become nearer and more comprehensible.*[2]

The satisfaction to be drawn from this immersion in the Idealist world view could scarcely last beyond the span of a winter morning. The abstract philosophical categories that were intended to make the world intelligible to the *intelligent* could only alienate him further from social reality; they could only make more unbearable the routine landowner existence, the routine careers of army officer or bureaucratic official that constituted the only recognized social roles open to him in the Russia of Nicholas I. And, during this period at least, every act, every gesture of the political authorities were calculated to exacerbate his feeling that he occupied no recognized place in the world. This was an age in which the very teaching of philosophy was eventually forbidden in the universities (1841); an age in which as moderate and socially prominent a critic of the regime as Peter Chaadaev could be placed under house arrest, and this on the ground that his writings obviously were the product of a "diseased" mind.

Yet, however arbitrary and barbarous the existing order appeared, no immediate prospects existed for altering it. To their complete alienation from the real world the intelligentsia of the 1830's and 1840's could respond only by as complete an immersion in the world of ideas. And the very intensity of this immersion, the very size of the gap that the world of ideas had to fill in their lives, meant that they could not afford to recognize those aspects of their personality and experience that might in the least upset the intellectual framework in which they were imprisoning themselves.* The *intelligent*'s search among the philosophical systems of the West for a reasonable and meaningful blueprint of his existence estranged him even from the experience of his own feelings: the more strenuously he sought to mold his image of himself in the light of some rarefied Western model, the more he felt compelled to suppress or deny the emotions and the memories that still bound him to his Russian environment. But, however suppressed or denied, these feelings and memories continued to govern much of his life. Beneath the abstract and elevated sentiments that he incorporated into his world view, beneath the thin shell of his supremely rational self-image, frequently ran darker and more turbulent emotional currents, which were all the more primitive and powerful because they were ignored. Commenting on this split between the *intelligent*'s intellect and his feelings — between his image of his identity and the real character of his personality and existence — M. Gershenzon, an acute twentieth-century critic, would observe:

> We have all become cripples, suffering from a deep split between our real self and our consciousness . . . We are being driven spasmodically by blind, chained, chaotic forces while our consciousness fruitlessly sheds its light on barren grounds . . . Like a run-away locomotive, it [our consciousness] rides far and wide, leaving our emotional life astray . . . Torn from its roots, it engages in fantastic games, and all its calculations are as incorrect and as impractical as would be those of an architect who draws up plans without regard for the laws of perspective or for the materials at his disposal.[3]†

* This was as true of the Slavophiles (who held onto an idealized image of pre-Petrine Russia) as it was of the avowedly Western-oriented majority of the intelligentsia of this period.

† It is true that certain features of this process of alienation is characteristic of the development of many intellectuals, particularly in societies undergoing rapid acculturation. Yet the extremeness of the feeling of isolation, of the sense of radical opposition combined with the condition of objective helplessness against the ruling political and social order, that underlay the formative years of the Russian intelligentsia is worth considering, for it gave its development a highly cohesive, and distinctive, character. While the term "intelligentsia" came into general use only in the 1880's, the members of the group to which the term would be applied were characterized throughout Russia's nineteenth-century history not only by certain intellectual attributes, but also by a whole complex of political and social attitudes. For this

In figures such as Stankevich and Bakunin the dissociation of the individual's intellectual life from the other aspects of his experience reached pathological proportions, but to a less acute degree it was present in the personality of others.

It is in this process of dissociation in the psychic life of the members of the intelligentsia, just as much as in their alienation as a "conscious" minority from the "unconscious" masses, it is in the contrast between the elevated sentiments that they could incorporate in their world view and the more undisciplined feelings that they attempted to suppress or ignore that we should look in part for the origin of the duality of *soznatelnost* and *stikhiinost,* consciousness and elemental spontaneity, the two basic conceptual categories under which so many of the intelligentsia were subsequently to subsume the conflicts in their own existence and the evolution of the world around them.

Divorced from social reality and driven by the pressure of their unrecognized and unsatisfied emotional needs, most of the young members of the intelligentsia expended their energy during the 1830's,* 1840's, and early 1850's, in the futile search for a philosophical panacea: they shifted repeatedly from one philosophy to another, from one intellectual god to another — from Schelling and Fichte to Hegel, from Hegel to the French Utopian Socialists, from the Utopian Socialists to J. S. Mill and to Comte.

The basic rhythm of these changes in intellectual climate was considerably more rapid than the tempo of the evolution of French and English thought, and it would continue to be so during the remainder of the century. For the problems that the Russian intellectual had to solve were incomparably graver than those of his Western confrère. His task was not merely to carve for himself a place in a world which, however dominated and monopolized by older and well-established authorities, remained in a sense meaningful — it was to make order out of chaos, to create for himself an identity out of the void. His problem was not just to find a set of values that could be systematically opposed to the smug and self-satisfied faith of his fathers — it was to search for new credos to substitute for the beliefs of a succession of older brothers whose spirit had broken, whose faith had been shattered or proven bankrupt, in the unequal spiritual (and later political) struggle against absolutism.†

---

reason, whenever I have had occasion to refer in this work to individual members of the group, I have used the Russian term *intelligent* rather than the deceptive translation "intellectual."

* In his clever essay on the intelligentsia of the 1830's, Milyukov systematically shows how the *Weltanschauung* of numerous members of the intelligentsia evolved in accordance with the unrecognized frustrations of their personal lives.

† The thesis expounded here implicitly contradicts Turgenev's approach in *Fathers and Sons,* which emphasizes the conflicts between generations. With the exception of Turgenev, most intelligentsia critics have analyzed Russian intellectual life in the nineteenth century in terms of a decade rather than a generational structure. Consider, among others, the studies of Milyukov, Ivanov Razumnik, and Ovsianiko-Kulikovskii.

The rapid and superficial shifts in ideology, the shallow changes in the organization of consciousness that marked the evolution of the intelligentsia during the 1830's and 1840's could not provide any substantial relief for the deep frustrations that underlay them. When more propitious political conditions arose, many in the intelligentsia were to abandon their characteristic introversion and turn outward to social reality. They would now seek to satisfy their emotional needs and to define — and confirm — their own identity through action in the real world.

By the late fifties and early sixties, the first signs of such a change in orientation appeared. Under the spiritual leadership of Chernyshevskii, Dobrolyubov, and Pisarev, a new generation of young Realists, who earlier in the decade had been content to "reorganize their consciousness" in accordance with the tenets of positive science, now felt impelled to transform the world in the light of these scientific principles.

This appearance of the intelligentsia on the social scene was accelerated by the upheaval into which the Russian state was thrown after the great fiasco of the Crimean War. The humiliating military defeat that the autocracy had suffered at the hands of France and Britain demonstrated the bankruptcy of the policy of containment of Western influences. The ruin of the absolutist edifice was accompanied by the death of its zealous defender Nicholas I.

The inauguration of Nicholas' successor, Alexander II, was not greeted with any great enthusiasm by the "enlightened" members of society. During his father's reign, Alexander had been a wholehearted supporter of reaction; for that matter, he would remain a conservative during the rest of his life. However, Alexander was a man of considerable intelligence and fortitude. These qualities served him in good stead immediately upon his accession to the throne, for they enabled him to perceive that radical reforms had to be instituted to save the state edifice, and impelled him to push these reforms through in spite of considerable opposition.

The most virulent evil to be eradicated was the institution of serfdom, which had steadily sapped the economic potential of the country and had kept the peasants pauperized and dissatisfied. In the face of vehement resistance by most of the landowning gentry, in the face of the more silent opposition of much of the officialdom, an Edict of Emancipation was finally proclaimed in February 1861.

The Act of Emancipation was somewhat emasculated by the time it passed through the hands of the reluctant Council of State. It gave the peasants less land and imposed upon them heavier redemption payments than had been hoped for by the intelligentsia and by the tsar's own liberal ministers. But in spite of its defects, it undoubtedly constituted, along with Alexander's subsequent reforms — the creation of the *zemstva* (district and provincial organs of rural self-government) and city assem-

blies, the changes in the judicial system and in the military establishment
— a considerable and very impressive measure of achievement.

Nevertheless, the net effect of the Emancipation was to exacerbate the
intelligentsia's opposition to the state power and to solidify its determination to follow the path of revolution. By the beginning of the sixties a
cocky and uncompromising mood had swept over the younger intelligentsia. In the writings of Chernyshevskii and his collaborators, which
began to appear at that time in the review *Sovremennik,* were expressed
an unlimited trust in the intelligence and acumen of the "men of the new
age" and an absolute confidence in the ability of a handful of such men
to remake the world in the light of rational principles.

In Chernyshevskii's *Chto Delat'?* (What Is to Be Done?), the idyllic
description of the future socialist Utopia that now became a Bible for
the intelligentsia youth, this confidence was expressed in the most ec-
static of phrases. And Chernyshevskii confidently maintained that such
a land of milk and honey would soon become a reality. The new order
would be built by determined, fearless, practical revolutionaries, "strong
personalities, who [would] impose their character on the pattern of
events and hurry their course, who [would] give a direction to the chaotic upheaval of forces [already] taking place in the movement of the
masses."

What youth of the intelligentsia could have helped being exhilarated
by Chernyshevskii's portrait of the "men of the new age" — or indeed
have failed to recognize in it his own likeness?

> Each of them is bold, unwavering, relentless, capable of taking
> matters in hand and of holding onto them tightly so they do not
> slip from his fingers. So far, such people are few in numbers but
> through them everyone's life is illuminated; without them it would
> be smothered, soured . . .
>
> Honest and good men exist aplenty, but those of whom I'm think-
> ing are rare specimens: they are like thyme in tea, like the bouquet
> of a fine wine; they are the source of strength and fragrance. They
> are the flowers of the optimates, the primal sources of energy, the
> salt of the salt of the earth!

This type of person might still be scarce, admitted Chernyshevskii, but
he already existed and was rapidly multiplying:

> It was engendered by the age; it is a sign of the age. Six years
> ago, one didn't see such people; three years ago, one despised them;
> but what one thinks of them now no longer matters. In a few years,
> in a very few years, people will call unto them for rescue, and what
> they say will be performed by all! [5]

In the frequent ideological shifts that marked the evolution of the
intelligentsia during the second half of the nineteenth century two con-

trasting modes of orientation may be discerned. The first of these — which was to become known in the history of Bolshevism as the "left" position — was now expressed in Chernyshevskii's chant of self-affirmation, in his insistence on the ability of a small elite to remake the world in the image of its consciousness. The second of these modes, which usually became dominant after the defeat of such gestures of self-affirmation, was marked by an effort on the part of the *intelligent* to give up his distinctive and yet unsatisfying identity in order to dissolve in — to fuse with — a potent and "life-giving" outside force, whether the peasant folk or the laboring masses. And at such moments in his life, these outside social formations were frequently viewed as potent, elemental, "spontaneous" forces, which governed the course of history by their instinctive strivings.

To say that the evolution of the intelligentsia moved in this fashion during much of the nineteenth and early twentieth centuries is not to deny that many members of the intelligentsia were predominantly inclined to one or the other position. Indeed, much of our story will be concerned with precisely such temperamental differences. But the statement does mean that the history of the revolutionary intelligentsia may be regarded as the product of the changing equilibrium between the self-affirmation of the intelligentsia left and the more adaptive position of the right.

When one considers the audacity and the confidence of Chernyshevskii's vision, it does not seem at all surprising that the younger members of the intelligentsia of the sixties rejected the compromise course that was being traced by the state power and that they elected instead to follow the path of revolution. But how were the thin ranks of the revolutionary intelligentsia to make this revolution and to establish their socialist Utopia? On this issue, the intelligentsia of the sixties were in substantial agreement: through propaganda and agitation they would enlist the support of the peasant masses, whose communal institutions already constituted a primitive economic and social foundation for socialism.* "Let us

---

* In 1861, a young writer, Mikhail Mikhailov, issued a manifesto "to the younger generation" urging his comrades to reject the Western model of state representative institutions and emphasizing that Russia, thanks to the communal traditions of its people, could and should follow its own path of development. "We have the fullest opportunity to escape the sorry fate of contemporary Europe," his manifesto affirmed. "We trust in our own fresh forces; we believe that we are called upon to introduce a new foundation in history, to utter our [own] words, and not to follow in the wake of Europe." For the complete text of Mikhailov's proclamation, see *Materialy dlya istorii revolyutsionnago dvizheniya v Rossii v 60kh godakh* (St. Petersburg, 1906), pp. 12–15.

The views advanced in Mikhailov's manifesto had been advocated originally by the small Slavophile circle in the 1830's and 1840's. They now became more and more widespread as the members of the intelligentsia digested the implications of the recent developments in Western Europe: the history of the revolutions of

give our lives to maintain equal rights in the soil, let us give our lives for the principle of the village community," Chernyshevskii wrote in the early sixties to Alexander Herzen, the herald of an older and already somewhat despised generation. The village commune would be Russia's salvation. It would enable Russia to bypass the miseries of capitalism and to enter without delay the joyful socialist era.

But how was this social program to be implemented? "Go to the people (*v narod*) . . . in the people lies your salvation," Herzen had advised the new generation in 1862. The intelligentsia youth picked up the slogan and heatedly debated its implications during the remainder of the sixties. By the end of the decade, two schools of thought were beginning to emerge. The first, inspired by the teachings of Peter Lavrov, emphasized that the intelligentsia should perform a primarily educational function, that they should concentrate their efforts on the development of the people's consciousness. A second school of thought, influenced by the writings of Michael Bakunin, was beginning to argue that the task outlined by the Lavrists was unnecessary and even harmful: the intelligentsia should appeal to the people's "feelings" and not to their "reason"; they should destroy the existing order by unleashing the revolutionary instincts of the peasant masses.

In 1873–74, spurred by a famine in the Volga region, many of the younger members of the intelligentsia finally decided to act, to go to the peasant villages and work for the peasant folk. But the mood with which these youths "went to the people" was already considerably different from the spirit of self-affirmation that had animated Chernyshevskii's "new men" in the preceding decade. The young men and women of the seventies were weighed down with the feeling of their own weakness; they were overwhelmed by a sense of their sins before the people, sins for their past comfortable existence "which had been born out of the sufferings of millions." As one of them later recalled, they "were striving not merely to realize specific practical goals but also to satisfy a deep need for a personal moral cleansing." [6]

Some members of the intelligentsia, under the influence of Lavrov, continued to insist that their mission was to educate the people so that it might develop a conscious socialist ideal out of its confused and diffuse collectivistic strivings. But even the Lavrists were careful to point out that their role would be as restricted as that of a midwife: the intelligentsia would not be bringing to the peasantry any ideas that it did not already instinctively hold; they would merely "instill in the people confidence in itself and enlightenment about its own aims." While they believed that, in order to fulfill this educational task, the intelligentsia

---

1848, the rise of Louis Napoleon to power through the mandate of universal suffrage, were not calculated to make the intelligentsia confident of the efficacy of representative institutions.

should create a strong propaganda organization, the Lavrists emphasized that this organization would fuse with the revolutionary minority of the suffering masses and would itself become a participant "in the *obshchina* and *artel* centers of the Russian people" (the agricultural and handicraft communal organizations of the peasantry). Thus, revolutionary propaganda would be made to "flow from within the habitual centers of the people's solidarity and not from the outside" and the eventual call to the revolution "would be sounded by individuals who would be the people's own on the basis of a long-standing, living solidarity." [7]

But to many members of the Narodnichestvo (the Populist movement), even the modest educational role that Lavrov advocated was no longer acceptable. For acting as guides meant to them striving for control, and the foremost desire of these young men and women was to fuse with the people, to imbibe their energy, their inner freedom and warmth. Consequently, they preferred to believe that the task of the intelligentsia was merely to "untie" — to loosen the revolutionary impulses pent up within the masses, to act as mere catalysts for the revolutionary explosion that would blow the existing order to bits and clear the way for a new world of freedom, equality, and justice. Rather than Lavrov's teachings, they chose to believe Kravchinskii's assertion (so reminiscent of Bakunin's statements) that the people were not lacking in socialist ideas, that all they needed from the intelligentsia was a further stimulant for their "rage." And instead of viewing themselves in the role of Lavrov's "conscious minority," many of them elected to identify themselves with Bakunin's brigands, those symbolic representatives of the destructive and yet creative energy of the people.[*]

Armed in the main with this credo of revolt (Lavrov's opponents chose to call themselves *buntari* from the Russian word for popular uprising, *bunt*), hundreds of young Populists "went to the people" in 1873–74. After "preparing" themselves for the completely strange life that was ahead of them by learning popular trades such as carpentry or shoemaking, these "raw youths" put on peasant costume and set out for the villages of Russia.

But the youthful agitators rapidly discovered that they could not arouse the people's "pent-up revolutionary energy." They were lucky if they shared the experience of their comrade, M. R. Popov, who later recalled that the peasants listened to his speeches as they did to the priest who preached to them about the Kingdom of Heaven, calmly resuming their existence after the sermon was over, as if nothing had hap-

---

[*] The evidence to be found in contemporary memoirs (Kropotkin's, Akselrod's, Kravchinskii's, etc.) indicates rather conclusively that by 1873–74 Lavrov's following was reduced to a small minority of the intelligentsia youth. This is also the conclusion reached by the leading authority on the history of the Narodnichestvo, V. Ya. Yakovlev: see V. Ya. Bogucharskii (pseud.), *Aktivnoe narodnichestvo semidesyatykh godov* (Moscow, 1912), pp. 160ff.

pened.[8] The unlucky ones were stoned out of the villages or turned over to the tsarist police by the indignant peasants. At the end of 1874, the government repression began in earnest, and within a year several hundred of the agitators were caught in the police nets.

The Quixotic spirit with which the youth of the intelligentsia had "gone to the people" and the response that they had encountered are humorously described in the memoirs of members of the movement. A. O. Lukachevich recalls how in the summer of 1874 he and a young comrade, having decided to conduct their "agitational activities" in Vladimir province took the train to a small town in the area. Upon arrival, they walked down a country road, and after a few hours' trudging, stopped "for tea and bread" at a village inn:

> After a short while we noticed that the innkeeper and his assistant were glancing in our direction with some sort of unfriendliness. We were asked where we were from, what we were doing. I answered that we were locksmiths and that we had been working in Kirzhatch.
> "So, you say, you have been working in Kirzhatch?"
> "We have."
> "And how many churches are there in Kirzhatch?"
> "Five," I answered, so to speak, in a flash.
> "You see what kind of locksmiths they are. There is only one church in Kirzhatch, and there never was more than one. Not only were you never in Kirzhatch, but you were never near the place!"
> The affair was reaching the point of scandal, but the innkeeper interrupted his assistant and, with a confidential air, advised the "locksmiths" to leave the inn before the incident reached the ears of the police.[9]

Chastened by this experience, Lukachevich returned to Moscow. This time, he decided to go to a district which he knew well and in which, he had been told, "successful" revolutionary propaganda was already being conducted. He succeeded in getting a job in an *artel* (a workers' coöperative) and in establishing personal relations with some of his fellow workers. Soon, he started to turn his conversations with the more intelligent of these workers to political and economic questions which he conscientiously attempted to link to their own personal experiences. The result was invariably disappointing! The workers would agree that conditions in their home villages were bad and that they were cruelly abused by government officials, but in the end they always came out with the answer that all this was their own fault because, to a man, "they were drunkards and had forgotten God."

The first waves of the go-to-the-people movement had broken against the wall of popular indifference and police repression, and the members of the intelligentsia began to reëxamine their credo on the basis of the gigantic fiasco that had occurred. The first attempts to evaluate the re-

cent experience followed the path of least resistance. If the first appeal
to the people had failed to evoke a response, it was not because the people were lacking in revolutionary instinct, chanted the *buntari*. If the
people had chased away the socialist propagandists, it was not because
they were lacking in collectivistic strivings, echoed the Lavrists. It was
because the intelligentsia had gone to the peasant masses with alien doctrines and schemes. It was because it had attempted to impose on them
Western socialist theories, preconceived, prefabricated plans of general
revolution. Kravchinskii wrote in 1878: "Five years ago we took off the
German dress and put on the peasant coat (*sermyaga*) in order to be
accepted by the people within its fold. Now we see that this is not
enough — the time has come to remove from socialism its German dress
and to put it in peasant costume." [10]

To the failure of these first attempts to break down the walls that
separated the intelligentsia from the people, the immediate response was
thus a call for a more radical abandonment by the *intelligent* of his
distinctive identity and program.

> We limit our demands to those which can be truly realized in the
> immediate future, that is to say, to the popular demands and desires
> as they are at the present moment — the transfer of all the land to
> the peasant labor estate and its equal division among them; the
> transfer of all social functions to the *obshchina,* i.e., complete self-
> administration; the division of the Russian empire into parts in con-
> formity with local desires.

This statement, introduced the first program drawn up by *Zemlya i
Volya* (Land and Freedom), the organization that set out in 1876 to
consolidate the various trends of the revolutionary Populism. Yet even
though the Populists now made every effort to adapt to the psychology
of the peasant masses, these masses continued to ignore their call. In
only a single instance did they provoke a peasant uprising, and, supreme
irony, they achieved this isolated success only because they told the
peasants that the tsar himself wanted them to seize the gentry's land and
that the nobility and local officials were trying to keep his decision secret
from them.*

Following this long series of fiascos, many of the revolutionary intelligentsia, at last, began to reconsider their stand. Interspersed among the
traditional statements of faith in the Populist tradition, signs of a new
spirit of self-affirmation are already apparent in the second program of
the Zemlya i Volya party, drawn in 1877: "The Party must refrain from

---

* The peasant unrest to which I am referring broke out in the Chigirin district
of Kiev province in 1877, as a result of the agitational activities of an energetic
group of Southern *buntari* led by Bokhanovskii, L. G. Deich, and Y. A. Stefanovich.
See "Dokumenty po Chigirinskomu delu," *Byloe,* December 1906, pp. 258–261.

coercing the economic and political ideals developed by history," stated
the theoretical section of this program. Yet, "because the development of
capitalism and the ever increasing penetration into popular life . . . of
the various plagues of bourgeois civilization [threatened] to destroy the
village commune and to mutilate . . . the people's world view," a revolution by force was to be undertaken "as soon as possible."

Owing to this feeling of the absolute necessity of forcing the course
of events — of making a revolution before it was too late — the authors
of this program proceeded to make practical recommendations that violated every vestige of the Populist tradition: Zemlya i Volya would
collaborate with the liberals; it would attempt to enlist the support of
army officers and state officials "so as to disorganize the state order"; it
would conduct a terroristic campaign, designed not so much to excite the
masses as to "annihilate systematically the most prominent and the most
hateful members of the government — and, in general, to eliminate the
people through whom the hateful aspects of the state order [were] upheld." [11]

The note of voluntarism and self-affirmation that seeped through the
pages of Zemlya i Volya's second program reflected, in some degree, the
sermons that a new prophet, Peter Nikitich Tkachev, had begun to
preach in 1875 in the Geneva journal, *Nabat*. In a manifesto drawn
the preceding year, Tkachev had warned the intelligentsia that it was
the only force capable of making a revolution. He cautioned his readers:

> Don't you understand that a revolution (in the usual sense of the
> word) differs from peaceful progress in that a minority makes the
> first and a majority the second? Don't you understand that a revolu-
> tionist always considers and should always consider it his right to
> call the people to an uprising . . . that he differs from a philosophi-
> cal Philistine precisely in the fact that he doesn't wait for the current
> of historical events to point out the minute, but selects it himself?

The time to strike was "now." It was "now" because Tkachev saw the
threat of capitalism looming over the horizon. Under its impact the village commune was beginning to crumble, and new classes of conservative peasants and affluent businessmen were being born:

> This is why we cannot wait. This is why we insist that a revo-
> lution in Russia is really indispensable, and indispensable right at the
> present time. We will not stand for any pause, for any temporization.
> It is now or very far in the future, maybe never! Now conditions are
> for us; in ten, twenty, years they will be against us . . .
> The problems of the future are fading; they are being relegated to
> the background. By this I do not mean to say that we must com-
> pletely abstain from resolving them. This would be blindness. But we
> must not inflate their importance so much as *to make them a barrier
> separating the revolutionary party from the present.*

Therefore, on the banner of the revolutionary party, a party of action rather than a party of reasoning (*rezonerstvo*), may be inscribed only the following words: struggle against the government, struggle against the existing order of things, struggle to the last drop of blood — to the last breath.[12]

For the next few years, Peter Tkachev was to repeat this refrain in more and more desperate tones until finally, in 1883, he succumbed to a mental illness from which he died two years later. Typical of his exhortations to the revolutionary intelligentsia to assume control over events, to take command of the chain of history, was an article in the first issue of *Nabat:*

Make [full] use of the minutes. Such minutes are not frequent in history. To let them pass means to permit willingly the possibility of a social revolution slipping away for a long time if not forever. Do not delay! . . . You have talked sufficiently about preparation . . . To prepare a revolution is not at all the job of a revolutionary . . . [A revolution] is prepared by exploiters, capitalists, noblemen, policemen, officials, progressives, and the like . . . Revolutionaries do not prepare; they make a revolution. Make it then; make it faster! Every indecision, every procrastination, is criminal . . . That is why we say: do not carry your thoughts too far ahead; stand firmly on the basis of a sober, thought-out realism. Do not dream, but act! Make a revolution and make it as fast as possible.[13]

Spurred on by the indifference of the peasant masses and by the efforts of the government to suppress its spirit and its life, the revolutionary intelligentsia turned to the path of "direct action," terrorism. The steadily rising emphasis on a terroristic campaign to overthrow the government caused a split in Zemlya i Volya and the birth of two rival organizations, the terroristic *Narodnaya Volya* (the famous People's Will) and *Chernyi Peredel* (the Black Partition), a diehard defender of the Populist tradition.

The program drafted at Lipetzk, immediately before the split, by leaders of the faction which was to become the Executive Committee of the Narodnaya Volya stated boldly that "the aim of the organization was the overthrow of the autocratic order, and the [intended] method — an armed struggle against the government." Such an open break with the past appeared too extreme even to the adherents of Narodnaya Volya, and the final program of this organization made the traditional bows to the Populist tradition. "The terroristic activity," it stated, "is aimed at breaking the charm held by the power of government, at giving direct proof of the possibility of a struggle against the government, at lifting in this way the revolutionary spirit of the people and its faith in the success[ful accomplishment] of the task . . ." But the document went on to declare: "In view of the oppressed state of the people, in view of the fact that the government, through partial appeasement, can hold up for a long time the general revolutionary movement, the Party must take upon itself the start of the overturn and not wait for the moment when the people will be able to act without its aid." [14]

According to its program, Narodnaya Volya was to conduct extensive propaganda and agitation among the laboring masses, the university students, the soldiers and officers of the army, and the members of the "possessing" classes. But owing to the concentration of all its available forces on the terroristic campaign against the government, these "outside" activities narrowed down in practice to the recruitment of new members and the gathering of material aid. This concentration of activity and purpose was directly reflected in the organizational structure of Narodnaya Volya, the final product of an organizational trend that had started in the days of Zemlya i Volya.

This evolution, which was characterized by a gradual tightening of organizational bonds and by an increasing differentiation of functions, cannot be explained solely in terms of the "objective conditions" in which the members of the intelligentsia had to act. It reflected just as much the changes in the premises that motivated their choice and definition of action, their image of themselves and of their relation to the world. The evolution of Zemlya i Volya and Narodnaya Volya bore witness to the revolutionist's mounting insistence on a specific and economical utilization of his strength and to his increasing identification, his increasing dependence — for his values, his discipline, his role, in short for his image of himself — on the model of the organization per se rather than on any reality outside its boundaries.

In the Executive Committee of the Narodnaya Volya, this evolution reached its culmination. This organization, like the future Bolshevik sect, demanded absolute commitments on the part of its members:

> Promise to dedicate all your spiritual strength to the revolution, give up for its sake all family ties and personal sympathies, all loves and friendships. If necessary, give up your life without regard for anything and without sparing anything or anybody. Do not keep any private property, anything your own that is not at the same time the property of the organization of which you are a member. Give all of yourself to the secret society, give up your individual will, submit to the will of the majority as expressed in the decisions of the society.[15]

These were the sternly monastic rules drawn up by the Executive Committee.

In the fall of 1879, the *Narodovoltsi,* harried themselves by the police agents of the autocracy, set out to destroy the very symbol of absolutism — the Emperor himself. After a relentless pursuit, marked by such daring attempts as the blowing up of a railroad train and the explosion of a bomb inside the very walls of the Winter Palace, the hunters killed their quarry on March 1, 1881.

The first of March was the day of Narodnaya Volya's greatest triumph, but it also marked the beginning of its downfall. The tide now began to turn, as the frightened liberal elements of society, who previously had sympathized with the Populist movement, rallied to the side of the new tsar. Even though the terrorists' ultimatum to Alexander III included among the conditions of peace only a general political amnesty and the calling of the people's representatives, the liberals now called on the government to make no concession to sedition. B. N. Chicherin, the grandfather of the first Soviet Commissar of Foreign Affairs and a typical representative of right-wing liberalism, wrote to Pobedonostsev, Alexander III's reactionary adviser:

> As long as a socialist party, striving for the overthrow of the entire social order, exists, exceptional measures will be indispensable. Only newspapers devoid of any political sense can dream at the present time of a return to a legal order. The most reasonable section of society understands that one cannot think of limiting the supreme power during an epoch of basic reorganization in which the entire social order is changing.[16]

After a short period of indecision, the new tsar took up the challenge, and this time the intended victim caught his pursuers. Within a few months, all the members of the redoubtable Executive Committee were captured by the tsarist police and sentenced to death or long imprisonment. (The sole exception was Vera Figner, who remained at large until 1883.)

Once again, the revolutionary intelligentsia was confronted with the spectacle of an alien and indifferent world, but this time they faced it with broken spirits and shattered dreams. No significant social force appeared, on the surface, to threaten the proud edifice of autocracy. At the beginning of the new reign, Alexander III's Minister of the Interior, D. Tolstoi, had insisted that "all institutional changes be reconciled with the basic foundation of the state order — the absolutist imperial power," and temporarily, at least, the modernized machinery of state power appeared to be achieving just this goal.

The net result of Alexander II's administrative policies and of the changes effected in these policies by his successor was to increase the authority of the state bureaucracy. This growth of a centralized bureaucratic state system — characteristic of almost the entire European continent in the last quarter of the century — was facilitated in Russia by two sweeping changes in the relationship among social classes. The first of these — the sapping of the economic strength of the landed gentry — was brought about by the weakening of the gentry's control of the land resulting from the reform of 1861, as well as by the rapid decline, from the end of the seventies onward, of the value of agricultural produce on the European market. The spendthrift nobility were rapidly losing their land; the drama of *The Cherry Orchard* was being enacted all over Russia.*

The capacity of the gentry to resist the encroachments of state power was further weakened by the rapid growth of a powerful rival for the government's favors — the industrial and business bourgeoisie. The rate of industrial and business expansion increased after the temporary recession caused by the Russo-Turkish War, and this development took place with the encouragement and under the control of the state. With the appointment of Bunge, the Ministry of Finances became a center of energetic and progressive economic policy; its stabilization of the currency, its protective tariffs, and its generous land and monetary grants won the support of most of the aggressive and ambitious members of the business and industrial bourgeoisie.

The intimacy of the connection between the Ministry of Finances and big business was furthered by the consolidation of the latter into pressure groups, the effectiveness of which as early as the 1880's and 1890's compared favorably with their counterparts in Western Europe and the United States.† The influence was reciprocal, as the government gained a high degree of control over the course of industrial development by manipulating credit and railroad rates. The result was that, on the surface at least, the big bourgeoisie gave the state a loyal support that did not waver until the eve of the 1905 Revolution. In view of these social conditions, it appeared in the 1880's that the tsarist regime might well be able to play off the conflicting interest of the big bourgeoisie and the gentry, to steadily increase its own power while pursuing this course, and to prevent the growth of any serious opposition in society.

The alliance between the autocracy and the most energetic forces of bourgeois society was a factor of decisive importance in the history of the Russian revolutionary movement. It helped maintain the psychological isolation of most members of the revolutionary intelligentsia. Already

---

* Between 1880 and 1895 the value of bread on the Russian market declined by 40 to 50 per cent, and in the last half of the century land sales by the gentry took place at the following increasing rate: 1859–1877, 517,000 desiatins sold; 1877–1896, 750,000 desiatins; 1897–1900, 1,978,000 desiatins. See B. Veselovskii, "Dvizhenie zemlevadeltsev," in *Obshchestvennoe dvizhenie v Rossii v nachale 20-go veka*, ed. L. Martov, D. Maslov, and A. Potresov (St. Petersburg, 1909), vol. I.

† These pressure groups held yearly congresses, attended regularly by the representatives of interested ministries. Usually organized according to industry and region, these congresses elected councils which functioned on a permanent basis. Typical of such organizations were the Organization of Mineral and Metal Industrialists of South Russia (founded in the 1870's), the Permanent Office of Steel Mills (1887), and the Congress of Petroleum Industry (1884). For further details, see A. Ermanskii, "Krupnaya burzhuaziya do 1905 goda," in *Obshchestvennoe dvizhenie v Rossii*, I.

walled off from the decaying society of estates, these men now felt compelled to oppose the growing force of capitalism, for the alliance of the big bourgeoisie with absolutism hardened their longstanding prejudices against the capitalist order and blinded them to the revolutionary potential of that offspring of capitalism, the industrial proletariat.

For an entire decade, the revolutionary intelligentsia would turn a deaf ear to the pleas of *Osvobozhdenie Truda* (Emancipation of Labor), a small group of newly converted Russian Marxists who were vainly pleading that capitalism was a progressive movement carrying the seeds of socialism. For an entire decade, it would refuse to heed the Marxist thesis that the proletariat was the one potentially conscious revolutionary force in the Russian land — this in spite of the fact that the working class had been the one group in the laboring masses among which the Populists' agitation had aroused some response.

Beginning in 1883, the doctrinal leader of Osvobozhdenie Truda, G. V. Plekhanov, advanced two fundamental theses, which were repeated in a steady stream of pamphlets and articles, only to be greeted as heresy by a large majority of the revolutionary intelligentsia. Plekhanov's first thesis, spelled out in *Nashi raznoglasiya* (Our Differences), an attack on the Populist movement written in 1885, was that capitalism was becoming the dominant economic form in Russia. "We must recognize," Plekhanov insisted, "that in this [economic] sphere the present as much as the future belongs to capitalism in our country." [17] Capitalism was not only inevitable, stated Plekhanov's second thesis; it was also a progressive and even revolutionary link in the chain of historical development. It carried within itself the destruction of the past and the seeds of the future, the end of the feudal order and the beginning of the new socialist era.[18]

The interests of the Russian bourgeoisie stood in irreconcilable conflict with those of absolutism. The bourgeoisie was still drawing some usefulness out of the existing order and some bourgeois elements were still unreservedly supporting it, Plekhanov admitted; but he affirmed with the absolute certainty of the abstract mind:

> Our bourgeoisie is now undergoing a significant metamorphosis. It has developed lungs which already demand the clean air of political self-government. . . . Its roots still lie in the grounds of the old regime, but its higher branches have already reached [a stage of] development which points to the necessity and inevitability of transplantation. The kulaks continue so far to enrich themselves, thanks to the predatory character of our state economy, but the big industrialists, businessmen, and bourgeois landowners already understand that the acquisition of political freedom is necessary to their welfare. The [present] political regime, suitable as it may be for some individual persons, has become unsuitable for the employer class as a whole.[19]

Not only did capitalism promise to destroy the "feudal" order, of which the autocracy was the expression, but it was also nurturing the industrial proletariat to maturity. Since the proletariat was the one social group capable of organizing a real socialist party and of leading the peasant masses to socialism, the free development of capitalism was, for the immediate future, the only truly revolutionary path,

The broad lines of the future had been traced by the objective laws of historical development. The task of the socialist intelligentsia was to aid the proletariat in delimiting its tasks on the basis of these laws: it was to make the proletariat a conscious revolutionary force capable of utilizing the inexorable march of history to its own advantage; it was to point out to the workers the necessity of winning the political rights that would make possible the free development of a socialist movement, and to convince them that the upper classes of society were too weak to overthrow absolutism without their aid. "Political freedom" would be "conquered by the working class or it [would] not be conquered at all." [20]

In this struggle for political freedom, the proletariat should assume the leadership of all democratic elements to obtain from the bourgeois revolution the best possible conditions for its own future development. The energy and resourcefulness displayed by the socialist leadership during this struggle would largely determine the length of the interval between the bourgeois and socialist revolutions.[21] If the proletariat managed to rally all the radical elements of society, if it succeeded, thanks to this accretion of strength, in gaining during the bourgeois revolution the most favorable political conditions for its own future growth, it would be in a position soon to lead the peasant masses to socialism.[22]

But while the proletariat was to lead the struggle for freedom, it should not sacrifice for this purpose its own class organization:

> The socialists must point out to the workers their own workers' banner, they must give them leaders from their own working ranks; in brief, they must see to it that a secret labor organization rather than bourgeois society assumes a dominant influence over the minds of the workers. In this way, the formation and growth of a Russian labor socialist party will be speeded up to a significant extent. And this party will be capable of gaining for itself an honorable place among other parties after having contributed, while still in its swaddling clothes, to the fall of absolutism and to the triumph of political freedom.[23]

After the conquest of political freedom, the labor party would undertake an energetic campaign of propaganda and agitation in the countryside. It would provide the minimum force needed to influence "the numerous benighted masses." "Under its influence and possibly under its tutelage, the surviving village communes [would] truly begin the transition to a higher communist form." [24]

In Plekhanov's eyes, this systematic program of action promised the best possible mobilization of the revolutionary potential of the age. Designed in accordance with the objective laws of social development rather than in opposition to them, it aimed to utilize for the profit of the proletariat the unique feature of Russia's historical position: the existence of a significant socialist movement "at a time when capitalism [was] still young." [25]

But in spite of the "simplicity, consistency, and completeness" of its propositions, this program was vehemently rejected by the vast majority of the intelligentsia of the era. The few remaining exponents of direct revolutionary action criticized it for its passivity, for the narrow practicality of its proposals. Their objections were summarized in an article by Lev Tikhomirov, a self-appointed heir of Narodnaya Volya:

> The plans of the new group are not practical; they are simply nearsighted. By themselves they may appear reasonable, but theirs is the same practicality that holds the liberals in a state of political impotence . . . This is not the way for an advanced revolutionary fighter to behave: he is required to move in front of others, to understand and feel, earlier than anyone else, when it is possible to cry "forward."
>
> No! It is not by holding onto the coat tails of a manufacturer that we will get the laboring masses anywhere. It is not for the bourgeois that we must attain a constitution; in general, it is not a constitution but popular power that we must attain. We must not deprive the peasantry of its land; we must not develop the proletariat, not implant capitalism, but increase the strength of the people economically, intellectually, and morally. [26]

At least Tikhomirov and his émigré supporters realized that capitalism was a living and growing force and that it threatened to become the ruling economic order. But in Russia itself, a large segment if not a majority of the intelligentsia, shutting their eyes to the all-too-conclusive evidence, went so far as to deny the very possibility of wide-scale capitalistic development — this during a decade marked by the doubling of the number of industrial workers and by the steady expansion of the big enterprises.*

Like infants who imagine that a wish has come true when they feel incapable of accepting its frustration, these Populists decided with the aid of specious economic arguments, that the curse of capitalist civilization would never come to pass, and they denied, therefore, that the

---

* According to Lenin's figures, the number of factories employing 1,000 or more workers grew from 86 in 1879 to 117 in 1894, while the percentage of workers employed in such factories rose from 32.8 to 39.5 during the same period. See V. Il'in, *Razvitie kapitalizma v Rossii* (2nd ed.; St. Petersburg, 1908).

seizure of power (of which they felt incapable) was needed to arrest its growth: "All hopes and fears on this account [were] futile." [27]

> The Narodnik party would gain a great deal [wrote Vorontsov in 1882] if the dualism which tears its world view to pieces was destroyed, and if its faith in the viability of popular institutions was united with a conviction in the historical impossibility of capitalist production in Russia.[28]

Such was the general tone of Populist publications during this period.

With this belief in the impossibility of capitalist development was frequently combined just as unreal a trust in the benevolence of the autocracy toward the "popular economy." Vorontsov and his supporters hailed the government's attempts to tie the peasants to the village commune. They refused to see that the state was interested in the commune only as an administrative and fiscal convenience, and that at the same time that it was preserving the façade of village life, it was destroying the last vestiges of peasant self-government.* Soothed by these beliefs, by these hallucinations of their tortured souls, a majority of the intelligentsia turned away from the futile pursuit of revolution and, in large numbers, dedicated themselves to the "small task," the modest task, of aiding the people of the villages in their day-to-day existence. Heeding the call of "practical men" like V. P. Vorontsov and Ya. A. Abramov, they flocked to the provincial and district zemstva. They became agronomists, veterinarians, doctors, and teachers, to help the people that one day were to fulfill their hopes.†

Other members of the intelligentsia, abandoning political and social activities altogether, turned to the pursuit of apocalyptic visions, or like so many of Chekhov's characters, wandered hopelessly, helplessly

---

* Cf. the creation in 1889 of *Zemski Nachalniki,* members of the gentry chosen to administer village life.

† This self-dedication to "small tasks" became known as *abramovshchina,* from the name of one of the initiators of the movement, Y. A. Abramov (1858–1906), whose journal *Nedelya* became its chief organ. V. P. Vorontsov defended the aims of the abramovshchina in the following terms: "The practical realization" of the strivings of the Narodnichestvo "as they have taken form in the post-reform period" requires, under the present Russian conditions "the intellectual uplift of the masses, which is, therefore, laid out as the chief task of the present moment" (*Nashi Napravleniya* [St. Petersburg, 1893], p. 7).

A few members of the intelligentsia, anticipating by more than a decade the rise of liberalism, condemned *Osvobozhdenie Truda* for its revolutionary exclusivism toward the bourgeoisie. At the end of the eighties, Mikhailovskii, Prizetskii, Dobrovolskii, and a few others opposed to Plekhanov's demand for an independent movement of the working class the formula of a united front of all progressive elements against absolutism. In No. 19 of *Volnoe Slovo,* a journal that this particular group published in Geneva during this period, Prizetskii asked that the old Narodnik formula — "the emancipation of the people is the concern of the people itself" — be replaced by the slogan: "All for the nation and every enterprise through the group in the nation that is most interested in it."

through the remainder of the era. How different the world looked to them from that universe of Turgenev's characters forty years before, in which even the stars had seemed comprehensible. "With heavy heads and lazy souls, without faith and without love, they roamed about, not knowing who they were, why they lived, or what they wanted."

2

THE MARRIAGE OF FEELING AND REASON

On a rainy summer evening in the year 1862, a twelve-year-old boy named Paul Akselrod was walking the twelve-mile distance which separated his native village of Shklov from Mogilev, the small Ukrainian town where he planned to take the examinations for entrance to the Gymnazium. As he walked, his mind struggled with boundless fears. Restlessly his thoughts jumped from the wolves, rumored to abound in the forest the road traversed, to the difficult examination ahead and the woeful inadequacy of his preparation for it at the little school for Jews in Shklov. And as he thought of his uncertain future, his fingers instinctively clutched the thirty-five kopeks in his pocket, all the money he had to feed and lodge himself if he did pass the examination. Yet he was determined to enter the Gymnasium and win the certificate that would open to him the doors of the university, the fabulous school where, according to his friends, "there were people who taught from their heads — not from books." * He was intent on escaping from a world of isolation, misery, and oppression, on outgrowing the painful memories of a childhood that sixty years later still retained a poignant immediacy. As he walked down that road, he was undoubtedly impelled by some of the very same images that flashed through his mind when, as an old man, he set out to dictate his memoirs — memories of the loneliness that had been his when, as a child, he played on the dirt walk in front of the parental *izba*, "walled off" from peasant children by the barriers of prejudice, and yet unable to partake in the companionship of Jewish playmates because his father, a tavern keeper, had set up residence far

* The details of this account are drawn from the sentimental reminiscences about his childhood and youth dictated by Akselrod at the age of seventy-three for his memoirs, *Perezhitoe i peredumannoe*, vol. I (Berlin, 1923). Although these recollections of feelings and moods experienced sixty years earlier may not be objectively accurate in every detail, they remain significant for our purpose, which is to establish, as precisely as possible, the image of himself and of the world about him that Akselrod, as an adult, cherished, an image into which necessarily entered his remembrances of things past.

from any Jewish settlement; memories of fear and anger when his parents scraped and bowed before the passing *pans* or trembled at the sight of officialdom; memories of the abject poverty his family had suffered when it moved to Shklov and was compelled to take refuge in the village poorhouse. There were pleasant memories too, memories of the kindness and interest shown by a Polish teacher at the school to which Paul had been sent by the Jewish community to fill the government quota and thus save more privileged children from the contaminating influence of the "goys" — memories of friendship and of precocious intellectual companionship with older schoolmates.

It was with these images of infancy and childhood that Akselrod came to Mogilev. To pass the examination, to complete his studies, he was ready to undergo any material deprivations; he was willing to subsist on weak tea and stale bread, willing to spend his nights in covered wagons and courtyards, for he was already certain that only the path of spiritual emancipation could lead him to the completeness and integrity of manhood.* Such faith could not be denied. Akselrod passed the entrance examination, and with the aid of a few enlightened members of the Jewish community, he began his studies at the Gymnasium. In the next few years, the works of the fathers of the intelligentsia kindled his imagination and his sensibility. Inspired by the pleas of Belinskii and by the heroic poses of Turgenev's heroes, Paul began to preach. In the name of enlightenment, he and his proselytes organized a literacy school for poor Jewish children. In the name of enlightenment, they strove to initiate the Jewish youth of the dormant provincial town to the spiritual heritage of the intelligentsia. Even when the orthodox members of the community organized a boycott, threatening him with the loss of all his sources of income, Akselrod persisted in his activities; for then, as in later life, he viewed his own development merely as a tool for the development of others.

It was when Akselrod was between the ages of seventeen and eighteen that this burning energy turned in a revolutionary direction. The immediate cause was reading the works of Lassalle. In the world view of the fiery German socialist, Akselrod found ample opportunities for identification; he found a romantic Messianism equal to his own and a definition of life under which he was able to subsume his long held feelings of the antagonism between poor and rich, peasant masses and gentry, subjects and oppressors. His recollections of the impression Lassalle made on him deserve careful scrutiny, for they illustrate some of the permanent aspects of his revolutionary temperament:

* Akselrod summarizes the significance of his childhood as follows: "On the basis of the impressions of the first years of my life in the countryside, I was partially prepared to worship everything spiritual and to scorn everything material and superficial" (*Perezhitoe i peredumannoe*, p. 29).

And here [wrote Akselrod some fifty years later] Lassalle is calling on the laboring class, on the oppressed and exploited masses, to unite their forces to struggle bravely for their emancipation. And not for their emancipation in the narrow sense of the improvement of their position, but with the goal of building the church of the future, of bringing to humanity general happiness, freedom, equality, general brotherhood, and of raising it to a new, infinitely higher level of civilization than the present one.

Grandiose perspectives were drawn in my imagination by reading Lassalle, and his conduct at trials and in labor meetings fired my imagination. I read with agitation his attacks against the procurator and his proud, wrathful addresses to the judge's chair in the name of the "fourth estate." The proud language and the authoritative tone of the statements of a "subject," a Jew at that, to the ruling power (for I so considered the procurator and the judge) made upon me an immeasurable impression and gave me a profound delight and satisfaction . . . *I decided to direct my strength toward the emancipation of all the poor and the oppressed of Russia.*[1]

How were the oppressed and the poor of the Russian land to be induced to build the church of the future? How were the Russian people to give birth to heroes like Lassalle who would lead them to a new heaven and a new earth? In Akselrod's mind, a scheme gradually unfolded of organizing an all Russian organization of university circles to recruit and train individuals dedicated to the task of educating the people and of guiding them to his vaguely conceived social revolution. Under the direction of the secret center of this organization "would be created little by little a whole army of people, united by a common ideal of ideological strivings and social goals, working for the emancipation of the people, and revolutionizing itself and its surroundings in the process."[2]

Possessed with this grand design, Akselrod left for Kiev in 1871 to recruit collaborators among the university students. But the scheme was a little premature. In 1871, the youth of the university towns of Southern Russia were still dreaming of legal work of cultural enlightenment or of Utopian colonies in the never-never lands of the Western Hemisphere. Even Andrei Zheliabov, the future leader of Narodnaya Volya, whom Akselrod met in Odessa, condescendingly referred him to the "useful constructive" work done by liberal men of substance such as Baron Korf. For want of disciples, the scheme had to be scrapped.

This was only the lull before the storm, and in 1872–73, Akselrod like many of the generous and enlightened youths of Russia, was swept by the tidal wave of the first go-to-the-people movement. Like the other young Populists, he answered Lavrov's call to pay his debt to the people; like most of them, he turned from Lavrov's "pale and moderate" program to the more revolutionary teachings of Bakunin, for Bakuninism prom-

ised a more "immediate fusion with the people," fuller and more unconditional than did Lavrism.[3] Paul prepared himself for the task ahead by
teaching in workers' artels and by learning a trade, and in 1874, he set
out for the countryside, a would-be carpenter and would-be revolutionary, determined to lead the peasant masses to revolution. While in
these gestures Akselrod's early revolutionary activities coincided with
the behavior of his generation of the Narodnichestvo, one could already
notice in them differences in tone that heralded the future.

To most members of the Populist movement, "going to the people"
had meant shedding an identity that spelled loneliness and estrangement
from the world about them; it had meant "fusing" with a great and
creative revolutionary force to which they were willing to entrust their
fate. To Akselrod the people never represented such a rescuing external
force. He prided himself on having risen from the people, and if he felt
it necessary to pay his debt, it was from a sense of filial duty. His emancipation, like the people's, was conceived purely as an emancipation
from ignorance and poverty, from servitude to gentry and officials —
and not at all from the weight of an oppressive identity; his victory, like
the people's victory, was to be achieved by *samodeyatelnost,* by a free
and independent display of initiative.

As the people's own, Akselrod was never afflicted by the conflict,
endemic to the psychology of the intelligentsia, between the desire for
self-affirmation and the urge to "fuse" with the masses. Consequently,
though he rejected Lavrism as a doctrine too condescending to the
people, he was not swept by the extremes of the Bakuninist fad. Although
he agreed that the intelligentsia should abandon the academies and go
to the people,* although he believed that "he didn't have the right to
dig into books and drink up new knowledge, [thus] ignoring [his]
debt to the people, at a time when this people couldn't even read," he
remained convinced of the utility of the study of "such masters of contemporary social science as Marx and Lassalle" and refused to see any
inherent contradiction between the task of bringing enlightenment to
the people and that of arousing their revolutionary impulses.

This feature of Akselrod's world view was illustrated in 1874 when
along with many comrades he took refuge in Germany to escape arrest

---

* The grounds for Akselrod's demand for the abandonment of academic pursuits
on the part of the intelligentsia are illustrated in an argument he had with Zheliabov
in 1872, at a time when the latter still considered that the intelligentsia could combine its revolutionary work with professional pursuits such as medicine. Askelrod
describes his position at the time in his memoirs: "I didn't agree with this [Zhelia-
bov's stand], feeling that a privileged position, even a professorship, would induce
distance from, rather than proximity to, the people, and would weaken its revolutionary tendencies. I insisted that the revolutionary intelligentsia select professions
placing it in an unprivileged position, directly furthering intimacy with the people
in day-to-day life, e.g., professions [such as] village teacher, doctor's assistant, or,
even better, handicraftsman" (*Perezhitoe i peredumannoe,* p. 104).

by the tsarist police. Partially as a result of Bakunin's teachings, the Russian colony in Berlin contemptuously ignored the German working-class movement, even though it was the most numerous and best organized in Europe. Indeed, how could they have done otherwise, for what possible resemblance existed between their romantic vision of the people as an explosive and spontaneous revolutionary force and the disciplined crowds of workers who peacefully assembled every Sunday and just as peacefully dispersed after all of the speeches had been delivered? But Akselrod did not join in his comrades' witticisms about the gatherings of the "sausage eaters":

> First of all, I was impressed by the mass character of these gatherings: several hundred people and sometimes crowds of one thousand or even more! Then, the composition of these gatherings. A circle of workers, real workers — in the audience, in the president's chair, and on the platform!
> And all these people freely and boldly speak about the government situation, pronounce themselves on the most difficult questions, criticize the government! The way in which, when they attacked the government, the orators looked down at the policeman guarding the meeting as if to defy him. And there he stood and listened.[4]

That representatives of the working-class masses should gather at a political meeting and defy authority was in itself a source of admiration and joy for one who, identifying with the sullenly suffering masses, still winced at the memory of his father's fright at the sight of a passing policeman. "Almost all of them," commented Akselrod on the attitude of his fellow refugees, "came from gentry or intelligentsia milieus in which feelings of dignity and independence were frequently found. While I . . . had grown at the very bottom of the people and from childhood had seen down-trodden, oppressed people, fearful of everything that stood above them." [5]

After staying in Berlin for several months, Akselrod decided to live in Switzerland, but he was not permitted to settle down. Inspired by the disorders in Bosnia-Herzegovina, the shiftless members of the Geneva emigration developed the wild scheme of sending Russian revolutionists to agitate among the Slavic inhabitants of that Turkish province. Akselrod was elected to seek the support of the comrades in Russia for this plan; reluctantly, he agreed to go.

The year 1875 was a difficult one for the revolutionary intelligentsia. Police raids were being conducted all over Russia; revolutionary circles were being effectively broken up and their members arrested or dispersed. As was to be expected, no one took any interest in the scheme of the Geneva dreamers. After brief visits to Kiev and Moscow, Akselrod went to St. Petersburg to consult with Sophia Perovskaya, Natanson, and German Lopatin, the revolutionary figures who a year later founded the organization Zemlya i Volya. To hide away such an "illegal" safely in the capital was no easy task, but his comrades suggested to Akselrod that he put up at the apartment of a sympathizer of the movement who still retained a respectable legal standing, a student at the St. Petersburg Metallurgical Institute named George V. Plekhanov.

> The youth produced an agreeable impression on me [recalled Akselrod]. He spoke well in a business-like fashion, simply and yet in a literary way. One perceived in him a love for knowledge, a habit of reading, thinking, working.
>
> He dreamed at the time of going abroad to complete his training in chemistry. This plan didn't please me . . . This is a luxury! I said to the young man. If you take so long to complete your studies in chemistry, when will you begin to work for the revolution? [6]

Everything about this young man aroused the curiosity of a Russian revolutionist: the neatness of his appearance, the curiously stiff courtesy of his manner, the rigid self-discipline. Every evening at about the same hour, Akselrod observed, Plekhanov and his roommate religiously retired to the privacy of their room and painstakingly quizzed each other on their lessons of the day.

What was drawing this young man to the Populist movement? What force was impelling this paragon of all conventional virtues, who, within a year, still neatly dressed and combed, was to become a celebrated revolutionist, hunted by every police agent in Russia? No obvious clue was provided by his background or by his social behavior. The son of a retired captain of Hussars who had become a conscientious gentleman farmer, Plekhanov had undergone the conventional preparation for a military career. Yet in 1874, at the age of seventeen, he had resigned from the Konstantinov Military Academy and matriculated at the St. Petersburg Metallurgical Institute, his first gesture as a "repentant nobleman."

To what elements in his early background could this decisive step be traced? In Plekhanov's case, the past is shrouded by the veils of reticence and fantasy, and the picture to be obtained of his childhood and adolescence is heavily blurred.[7] An overbearing, willful, irascible father; a gentle mother, worshiped by her numerous offspring;* a precocious, highly self-disciplined, overly self-contained youth, who even at the early age of ten years had dared to oppose his will to that of his despotic father† — that is all the tangible evidence that the biographer has to go

---

* Valentin Petrovich Plekhanov was married twice. From his first wife, he had three sons and four daughters. His second wife bore two sons and three daughters; George was her youngest son.

† Plekhanov's father, feeling that the reforms of 1861 had introduced an era of profound social changes, wanted him to study for the civil service, but George, who wanted to become an army officer like his older brother, won out.

on. Yet this conventional, industrious, self-disciplined youth became suddenly at seventeen the victim of an aroused and insistent sense of guilt. And at the moment when Akselrod met him, he was torn between his desire to pursue his intellectual endeavors, to continue to seek the rational borders of the universe, and an overpowering urge to fulfill his duty, to pay his "debt" to the people. For Plekhanov, as indeed for many of his contemporaries, this sense of indebtedness was much more than a conventional sentiment. It gave rise to a feeling of genuine anguish to which the usually reticent Plekhanov subsequently referred in describing his first confrontations with "representatives of the people." "When I met Mitrofanov for the first time and learned that he was a worker, i.e., one of the representatives of the people," he wrote of his first encounter with a Petersburg worker, "a mixed feeling of smallness and discomfort stirred in my soul, as if I had been guilty of something before him." [8] It was an unequal struggle. Everyone, everything, in Plekhanov's world called on him to redeem his "unpaid debt," and within a year he took the irretrievable step. On December 6, 1876, during a demonstration on Kazan Square, George V. Plekhanov committed himself to the cause of the revolution with a passionate address delivered to a crowd of young students, workers, and police spies.

The next three years of Plekhanov's career were marked by a rapid rise to the leading ranks of the Populist movement and by an outward conformity, even more faithful than Akselrod's to contemporary standards of proper revolutionary behavior. Beginning in July of 1877 upon his return from Germany where he had taken refuge after the Kazan Square demonstration, Plekhanov consistently spent winters in St. Petersburg, agitating among industrial workers, and the rest of the year in unsuccessful attempts at revolutionary propaganda among the people of the countryside. Although his revolutionary agitation among the peasants of Saratov province in the summer of 1877 and in the Don region in 1878 ended in dismal failure, he displayed in these enterprises a remarkable capacity for dodging the tsarist police. He was arrested during both of these journeys, but managed to convince the authorities by his cool and condescending behavior that he was not a revolutionary. Meanwhile he assumed a leading role in the organization Zemlya i Volya and became an editor of its organ.

But even in this period, one might have noticed in Plekhanov's adherence to Populism elements that sharply distinguished him from any of his collaborators. In two articles that he wrote for *Zemlya i Volya* in 1879, a sensitive critic could have discerned some of the features that Plekhanov was later to imprint on the development of Russian Marxism. The first of these articles, which sought to demonstrate the practicability of a socialist movement in Russia, was introduced by the following statement:

There was a time when to produce a social overturn was considered a comparatively easy business. One simply had to organize a conspiracy, seize power in one's hands, and then come down on the heads of one's subjects with a series of beneficial decrees. This was the teleological era of sociology. Just as in natural science all natural phenomena were explained by the will of one or a few gods during this phase, so [in social science] the course of social development was assumed to depend upon the influence of the legislative power.

When they became convinced that history is created by the interaction between people and government, [an interaction] in which the people have greater influence — the majority of revolutionists stopped dreaming about the seizure of power . . .

[Then, the revolutionists started to develop social systems, worked out to the smallest details, which were propagandized among the people.] These schemes did not take the laws of social development into account . . . These individuals did not know the limits to their own fantasies. They considered propaganda a metaphysical essence capable as a rule of modifying the course of history.

Only recently have socialists begun to pay serious attention to the elements of social overturns which are the product of the preceding life of society.[9]

From this rather Comtian interpretation of the evolution of social thought, one major maxim was clearly drawn: a revolutionist, in the formulation of his philosophy, should necessarily conform to the laws of social development: if he observed this rule, he could be certain of influencing the people; if he failed to do so, and remained blind to the "limits of his fantasy," he would be driven into a world of empty dreams. Thus, even at this early moment, Plekhanov discerned in the people the objective process of history, and so certain he was that the movement of the masses and the laws of social development were one that he complacently advised his followers:

When there is a chance to influence the masses through individuals won by your influence, do not hold them back, even if they are threatened with destruction. No one will be justified to reproach you, because no destruction of an individual has yet taken place in history in the interest, and before the eyes, of the masses without consequences . . . Individuals have died, but the masses know for what they have died . . . The struggles gave them an experience that they did not previously have; it illuminated, in its true light, the meaning of existing social relations.[10]

In keeping with his demand for realism, Plekhanov's defense of the Populist thesis that the triumph of socialism in Russia need not be preceded by the growth of capitalism was almost entirely based upon a "cold-blooded" analysis of "objective conditions." His arguments in the two *Zemlya i Volya* articles began with a quotation from Marx's discussion of the inevitability of capitalism in Western Europe, the strongest and most persuasive statement of the opposite view: "When some society or other has entered the path of the natural law of its development, it is in no position to skip over the natural phases of this development, nor to change them by decree; it can only facilitate and shorten its labors." * Accepting the validity of Marx's statement, Plekhanov immediately brought up the issue that it raised: Had Russia already entered the path of social development that led to capitalism? Obviously, the answer to this question hinged on the character of the socio-economic phase that had immediately preceded capitalism and carried its seeds. The immediate forerunner of capitalism in the history of Western Europe had been feudalism, which had destroyed the communal existence and institutions of the village and given birth to the individualism from which capitalism was born. But in Russia feudalism had never been able to destroy the village communes, Plekhanov argued, and these communal institutions were not afflicted with the contradictions that had characterized the development of feudalism in the West and led to its replacement by capitalism. There was, therefore, every reason to believe that the social principle of production represented by the village commune would constitute a solid objective foundation for a socialist revolution in Russia.

It was this same impelling urge to ground his world view on a solid objective foundation that drove Plekhanov to lay more emphasis than his fellow Populists on the revolutionary potential of the Russian industrial working class. From his activities among St. Petersburg workers, he drew the conclusion that "the question of the city workers belong[ed] among those that . . . [were] advanced independently by life itself at the point which *it* finds suitable, despite the *a priori* theoretical decisions of revolutionists." [11] Of course, Plekhanov's recognition did not lead him to abandon his "peasantism." The workers' revolutionary significance was tied to their emotional bonds to the land, and they were neatly categorized as the "most enlightened representatives of the peasantry." But in the very same breath, Plekhanov insisted that the revolutionists recognize the workers' existence as an independent objective phenomenon. He stated in criticism of the past efforts of his fellow Populists: "One should

---

* The prefacing of his own arguments by a frequently rather lengthy exposition of his opponents' views is characteristic of Plekhanov's polemical style. He displays in his articles the agility of a cat that plays with its victim before pouncing upon it. It is only when his adversary is "committed" that Plekhanov goes over to the attack, and gracefully, with the greatest of ease, tears his arguments to shreds. In this respect, Plekhanov's style of argument differed very sharply from Lenin's. In both speeches and writings, Lenin goes immediately to the attack, breaks up his opponents' statements into parts, from the very start literally surrounds them with his own interjections or statements, and hits out time and time again. Plekhanov's arguments have the economy and incisiveness of a rapier; Lenin's the brute strength of a club.

have dealt with the city workers *as a whole,* having *independent signifi-cance,* one should have sought for means to influence their entire mass, and this was impossible as long as one saw in the city workers only *a material* for the recruitment of individual persons." [12]

In the two facets of this early article about the working class were reflected the two fundamental and somewhat conflicting psychological needs that Plekhanov's world view was eventually to satisfy. First, there was a need for a consistent and all-inclusive system to which every aspect of experience had to be subordinated. But with this need went a fear of dissociation from the real world that impelled Plekhanov to demand that every idea in the system correspond to some objective correlative, that every thought and every action be grounded on some tangible segment of external reality. (See Plekhanov's statement on p. 53 below.)

How were these two conflicting needs to be satisfied? How was the revolutionist to grasp, beyond his own shadows, the noumenal world, the world of things in themselves? In this article on revolutionary propa-ganda among the workers, Plekhanov criticized his fellow Populists for their failure to deal with the working class "as a whole, possessing in-dependent significance." To be objectively justified, he asserted, "revo-lutionary propaganda would need to be directed toward encouraging strikes, which develop in the workers a sense of opposition to all privi-leged classes and a sense of their own class solidarity." [13] Here was the germ of Plekhanov's eventual solution, the identification of the socialist cause and of the socialist world view with the development of the con-sciousness of the proletariat. The revolutionists would hold onto their consistent and all-inclusive world view and yet maintain a firm grip on reality by joining their fate to that of a social class endowed with an outlook and strivings (*stremleniya*) potentially akin to their own. They would dedicate themselves to the development of the consciousness of this class until it fully mirrored their own world view. Then and only then, through the agency of this class, through this inherent component of social reality, would they seek to transform the map of the real world.

In this attempt to bridge the barrier that separated him from ob-jective reality, Plekhanov was groping toward a definition of political aims that closely approximated, at least on the surface, the goals toward which Akselrod was striving for opposite psychological motives. Ple-khanov was becoming concerned with the development of the people's consciousness because of a fear of estrangement from social reality — Akselrod was doing so on the basis of a natural identification with an inherent segment of this reality, on the basis of a feeling of communion with the masses that was conducive to an identification of their aims and their strivings with his own.

Akselrod's concern for the growth of the consciousness and initiative of the masses, a preoccupation which we originally observed in his comments on the German workers in 1874, gradually assumed a more articulated form. One of the precipitants was a clash with Tkachev, into which Akselrod was drawn immediately upon his return from Russia in 1875. It was an inevitable conflict — Tkachev's demand for the formation of a conspiratorial organization for the seizure of power, based on the principles of "centralization of power and decentralization of functions," his insistence that the people were incapable of revolutionary creativeness and that, consequently, only a conscious minority could "make" a revolution, ran counter to Akselrod's most cherished beliefs. Fifty years later, Akselrod was to find profound similarities between this doctrine and Bolshevism: "Doesn't Tkachev's 'revolutionary minority,'" he would say, "remind one of the Bolsheviks' 'carriers of revolutionary consciousness' opposed to the masses as the carriers of 'spontaneity'?" [14]

In answer to Tkachev's "Jacobinism," Akselrod now raised the banner of anarchism. Criticizing the "Jacobins" for considering the consciousness of the masses as a second-rate problem, he asserted in the journal *Obshchina:* "The anarchists do not regard the people as cannon fodder but as a force called upon to perform the great task of consciously breaking up the existing order and consciously establishing a new order on a totally new foundation . . ." [15] The only valid objective of a social revolution was spelled out in another passage of this extremely significant article:

> As federalists, we are striving toward the foundation of a social organization, from the bottom up, in opposition to a government which is tying the population from the top down, mechanically and by force. Such an organization can arise only as the result of a free federation of local groups on the basis of a solidarity of interests of which they are conscious. [16]

It was on these grounds that Akselrod criticized the centralized form of the party organization of German Social Democracy:

> The anarchists reject this principle [centralism], in favor of the widest possible autonomy [in each] section, and see in the maximum limitation of the authority of party administrative organs the indispensable guarantee of the development in the proletariat of individual and collective revolutionary consciousness and activism. [17]

For the rest of his revolutionary career, Akselrod firmly held onto this belief that the value of a socialist revolution would depend entirely on whether it was a reflection of the consciousness and activism of the masses. This consciousness and activism came first in his hierarchy of values — the revolution, second.

In February 1879 Akselrod returned to Russia, characteristically, in

response to the pleas of a workers' association, the *Severnyi Soyuz*, wh⟶
had requested him to become the editor of its organ. When this plan
fizzled out owing to the arrest of the leaders of the organization, Akselrod set out to organize an even more ambitious association of workers
in the South. But the times were inauspicious: terrorism was capturing
the imagination of the intelligentsia, and it was beginning to spread
even among the most enlightened representatives of the working class.
Akselrod was drawn into the debates on the terrorist question that were
raging within the ranks of the Populist movement, and in 1880 he con-
sented to relieve Plekhanov (who was being chased by the police again)
of the editorship of *Chernyi Peredel,* the organ of the anti-terrorist
faction.

It was their joint opposition to Narodnaya Volya that drew Plekhanov
and Akselrod into an intimate collaboration which was to last a quarter
of a century. Yet, ironically enough, behind their respective decisions to
oppose the People's Will, behind the very decision that brought them
together, lay profound differences in revolutionary temperament which,
twenty-four years later, were to draw them apart.

Plekhanov's antagonism toward the spirit that had arisen rapidly in
Zemlya i Volya during 1878–79 was instantaneous, almost automatic.
The moment terrorism appeared on the scene as a theory of political
action — as it did in March 1879 with the decision of the student A. K.
Solovev to assassinate the tsar — Plekhanov became convinced "that this
method of struggle was harmful to our immediate and most important
concern, agitation among the people on the basis of their immediate and
direct demands." [18] When three months later at the Voronezh Congress,
Andrei Zheliabov defined terrorism as a struggle to intimidate the tsarist
government into granting the constitutional rights without which no
serious mass agitation could be conducted, Plekhanov was his one irreconcilable opponent. He denounced terrorism as a rash and impetuous
movement, which would drain the energy of the revolutionists and provoke a government repression so severe as to make any agitation among
the masses impossible. He attacked the struggle for a constitution as an
illusory pursuit, harmful, if anything, to the revolutionary cause: Zheliabov was "merely pulling the liberals' chestnuts out of the fire";[19] even if
a constitutional regime were to be attained, the exhausted revolutionaries would be merely confronted by a new set of oppressors.[20]

These arguments failed to win the day, and Plekhanov left the
Voronezh Congress completely alone, yet absolutely convinced of the
correctness of his views. So absolute were his convictions on the issues
that had been debated that he was determined to abandon revolutionary work rather than compromise. Many years later L. G. Deich asked
him what he had planned to do when he left the Congress:

there to say: it was difficult," he said sadly. "But I have
̷dicine for everything — striving to accumulate more
̷if you [Deich and Stefanovich] had not returned from
̷reement with my views, but on the contrary as terrorists,
̷plit within Zemlya i Volya, to which I could never have
̷d not taken place, I would have dedicated myself com-
̷ience." That was precisely his answer.[21]

̷termination to abandon revolutionary work rather than
compromise with terrorism reflected the fundamental clash between the
new movement and the governing principles of his revolutionary faith.
In terrorism, he could not fail to see a reckless spirit of self-affirmation,
a recklessness which violated his rule that thought and conduct conform
to the guiding line of a universal, consistent, rational system, and a self-
affirmation which ran counter to the imperative that revolutionary action
be in accord with objective reality.

Against the dark forces of the government and the bourgeoisie, insisted Plekhanov, the revolutionist had to oppose an identity solidly
grounded upon a rational world view and supported by the "reality" of
the oppressed masses:

> A socialist "party" without foundations and influence among the
> people is nonsense, a staff without an army, *a negligible quantity in
> the course of the country's social life.* Its enemies would not have to
> take such a party into account; they would ignore its demands with-
> out any serious danger to themselves.[22]

Yet, it was precisely to this kind of "nonsense" that the Narodovoltsi were
turning. Rather than concentrating their efforts on consolidating their
support among the masses, they were recklessly expending all their
energy in the comparatively futile pursuit of a constitution. If they did
succeed in attaining a constitution, the immediate goal to which they
aspired along with the upper classes of society, the latter would immediately strike a bargain with the government. Exhausted and isolated, the
Narodovoltsi would be confronted by a new set of oppressors:

> The minute that the broken agreement between them [the upper
> classes] and the government is restored, another crust of bread will
> be thrown to the people. For the guardians of the "department"
> will be substituted the guardians of the *Zemskii Sobor*, and "order"
> will be restored to the general satisfaction of those interested in its
> preservation.[23]

For Plekhanov, opposition to the emerging terrorist movement had
been an automatic response; in Akselrod's case, it was a tortured decision, slowly arrived at. If Akselrod did not immediately become suspicious of the alliance with liberal elements in the struggle for political
freedom, it was because, as a son of the people, as a man certain of his

place in the world, he did not need to affirm himself against the dominant forces of society in order to maintain a sense of his identity. If he failed to regard terrorism as a necessarily reckless expenditure of energy, it was because he did not need to reassert continuously by his conduct his accord with objective reality.

Indeed, Akselrod had first thought it possible to combine the two conflicting tendencies in the revolutionary movement. Immediately upon his return to Russia in February 1879, he had wanted "a harmonious combination of the terrorist struggle against the government with propagandistic, agitational, and organizational activities among the people." [24] Thus, during the early phases of the struggle between Plekhanov and the Narodovoltsi, Akselrod was unwilling to commit himself fully to either of the two camps. But as the year 1879 drew to a close, it had become clear that the Narodovoltsi were willing to abandon all agitational work among the masses. And with their total engulfment in the political struggle, there began to seep through the statements of the terrorists an attitude toward the people that Akselrod was not ready to forgive. "Shall we take the initiative of anti-government action and of a political revolution — or shall we, as of old, ignore political activity, *waste our strength by pressing against the people just as fishes press against ice?*" rhetorically demanded the first editorial of *Narodnaya Volya*. Akselrod finally decided to oppose the Narodovoltsi, but not out of hostility against terrorism, not out of fear of the destruction of the revolutionary movement by "society." He answered the call of *Chernyi Peredel* because, as he explained in his memoirs, he conceived it as the goal of the revolutionary intelligentsia "to concentrate all its strength and all its resources on the development of the independent revolutionary activism (*samodeyatelnost*) of the masses in preparation for the socialist revolution . . . The Narodovoltsi considered such activity as useless, compared it to Sysiphian work. And this determined my choice." [25]

Through the collaboration of Plekhanov and Akselrod, two strands of revolutionary thought met and fused in *Chernyi Peredel*. As the reader pored over some of the pages of this short-lived journal, he could choose to see one or the other view reflected, depending upon the light — and the shade — that he himself brought to bear upon the page. On other pages, the respective emphasis of the two views were neatly balanced in skillfully counterpointed paragraphs. This basic ambiguity of the new journal was apparent in the very first statement of its program. History and the people, popular ideals and history — these concepts are repeatedily linked and equated in this statement of faith. Another key concept, "science," is inseparable from "the people" in statements made in *Chernyi Peredel*. The socialist program has two *raisons d'être*, two justifications. It is "the last word of science on social relations . . . the alpha and omega of progress in the economic order of society," but it is also the conscious expression of the strivings of the Russian people. In his call for the collective ownership of the tools and objects of labor, the socialist is, therefore, reconciling the reality of science with that of the existing world, the demands of the reasoning will with the strivings of the people. As Plekhanov contentedly stated, the socialist "expresses and generalizes the strivings of the people, and *not giving up the world view developed with science,* he can with full justification call himself a revolutionary Narodnik in the best sense of the word." [26]

√   Scientific socialism and popular strivings — these were the two foundations upon which the new party was to base its activities. As long as Plekhanov and Akselrod remained chiefly critics of the dominant trends of the revolutionary movement, as long as they were not confronted with the problem of wide-scale revolutionary organization for an immediate struggle, the double-edged character of this formula would not draw them apart. But already in the first issue of *Chernyi Peredel* a paragraph in an editorial comment on the subtitle of the new journal, "Organ of the Socialists-Federationists" — a subtitle for which Akselrod had been mainly responsible — indicated on which side of this formula Akselrod's chief sympathies lay: "As to the title "Organ of the Socialists-Federationists," it expresses our conviction that only the federative principle in the political organization of an emancipated people — only the complete removal of compulsion, upon which the present state is based, and a free organization from the bottom up — can guarantee a normal course of development to popular life." *

As we noted previously, the immediate reason for Akselrod's assumption of the editorship of *Chernyi Peredel* had been the effort of the tsarist police to capture Plekhanov and his close collaborators. This danger continued to grow, and after a few months, Plekhanov, Vera Zasulich, L. G. Deich, and Stefanovich left for Switzerland, at the insistence of other members of the organization. Akselrod, who was now left in charge, concentrated his attention on gaining support for *Chernyi Peredel* among the workers and university youth. He drew up a program for a Great Russian Society of Land and Freedom (*Velikorusskoe Obshchestvo Zemli i Voli*), which was ratified by the Moscow and St. Petersburg groups of Chernyi Peredel. Though the new program was welcomed and approved by the Chernye Peredeltsi in Russia, it was not so warmly received abroad. The delegate who had been sent with it to Switzerland returned with the news that the comrades in exile had flatly rejected Akselrod's project because of its reformist tendencies. "This is not Populism but Social Democracy, they told our delegate." [27]

* *Sochineniya,* I, 109. It is interesting to note that Akselrod selected this particular paragraph to indicate in his memoirs the revolutionary tendencies of *Chernyi Peredel,* which he had joined, we must recall, "in order to concentrate the energies of the revolutionary intelligentsia upon the development of the revolutionary *samodeyatelnost* of the people."

This development precipitated Akselrod's own departure, and he left Russia in June 1880, intent on reëstablishing harmony with the Swiss group.

Were the comrades in the emigration justified in considering that the new program reflected the spirit of Social Democracy? Certain passages in this project tend to indicate that they were and that Akselrod was taking at this time a crucial step toward Marxism. To be sure, Akselrod's draft was introduced by the conventional Populist statement that the village commune (*obshchina*) would constitute "the point of departure and the basis for the development of a socialist order in Russia." But the next few sentences already suggested that Akselrod's faith in the adequacy of the Populist credo had begun to waver, for he found it necessary to state that the socialist order was rapidly approaching in the West and that the revolution in Western Europe would herald the coming of socialism in Russia: "Bourgeois society cannot long survive in Russia side by side with a socialist West." How could a reader avoid inferring from this argument that the village commune did not constitute an insuperable obstacle to capitalist development; how indeed could he fail to deduce that this capitalist phase was coming in Russia even though its reign would be shortened by the triumph in the West of no other group than the industrial working class?

This emphasis on the role of the industrial proletariat in the socialist revolution was even more apparent in the section of the program devoted to immediate demands. This discussion of the bases for agitation was also prefaced by a Populist article of faith: "It is highly necessary to encourage and strengthen the tradition of the village commune among the peasantry in order to facilitate the socialist overturn." But the specific proposals which immediately followed were concerned predominantly with unglamorous and unorthodox topics such as wages, hours, and working conditions. The author's preoccupation with these problems obviously indicated an implicit belief that Russia was entering a phase of development characterized by a clash between capitalists and workers; it indicated, even if Akselrod did not choose to say so, that he was no longer certain that Russia could skip over the capitalist phase of development.[28]

The matter-of-factness, the lack of theoretical explicitness of this document was characteristic of Akselrod's conversion to Social Democracy. It was marked by no dramatic gestures, by no great theoretical upheavals, but rather by a rising response to the accumulating evidence of immediate experience. And it was the evidence of this experience, the evidence advanced by his revolutionary activities among the working class, rather than the imposing edifice of Marx's theoretical formulations, that impelled Akselrod toward Social Democracy.*

* Thus, the 1880 program to which his comrades in Switzerland reacted so strongly was, for Akselrod, no real break with his past. His very return to Russia

The differences between Akselrod and his collaborators proved to be short-lived. By the time of his arrival in Switzerland in June 1880, his comrades were themselves beginning to undergo a process of conversion to Marxism. However, the pattern of their conversion was significantly different from the one that Akselrod's had assumed, a difference that was particularly striking in the case of Plekhanov.

According to the recollections of his wife, the first blow to Plekhanov's faith in Populism was inflicted, significantly, by a book, Orlov's *Obshchinoe Vladenie v Moskovskom Uezde* (Obshchina Ownership in the District of Moscow), which he read during the year 1880.[29] To explain the ferment that this specialized and rather obscure economic study produced in him, we must bring to mind again the dynamic components of his revolutionary world view. Plekhanov had erected under the cover of his Populist faith a consistent, complete, and closed system. So effectively sealed had been the system that the impact of Plekhanov's experiences during the first five years of his revolutionary life had not affected it at all. But this imposing logical edifice has been predicated entirely upon the existence of an objective phenomenon, the village commune, a phenomenon which gave Plekhanov the confidence that, independently of his will, the social development of Russia was moving in the direction of his wishes. And now, suddenly, in the impersonal scientific language of statistics, Orlov appeared to have demonstrated that the foundation upon which Plekhanov had erected his faith was undergoing a rapid process of internal disintegration. (Plekhanov had assumed that the village commune was free of internal contradictions, and thus an objective basis for the socialist revolution. See above, page 34.)

As his faith began to crumble, Plekhanov resumed his studies in political economy, concentrating on the classics of Marxist literature. His doubts grew as he pondered over Marx's and Engels' arguments. "Our knowledge is inadequate," he told his colleagues with a newfound humility; "what do we know basically? . . . we lack a great deal . . . we must study." [30] A note of hesitancy now hedged even his pledges of allegiance to peasantism, as for example, in this statement of September 1880:

> We do not deny in the least the significance of revolutionary work in our industrial centers. Such a denial is impossible for us, if only

---

had been a response to the call of a working class organization, and some of the proposals to which his comrades so strenuously objected had been included in a program drafted in 1879 for another association of Russian workers, the Union of Southern Russian Workers (*Yuzhno-Russkii Rabochii Soyuz*) which Akselrod had attempted to organize after the breakdown of the *Severnyi Soyuz*. The program that he drafted for that organization included demands for universal suffrage, freedom of speech and meetings, reduction of the work day, and minimum wages among its proposed "bases of agitation."

because we are in no position to determine in advance from which segments of the laboring masses the main forces of the social revolutionary army will be recruited when the hour of economic revolution strikes in Russia.

At present, the industrial development of Russia is negligible and the term "laboring masses" covers the meaning "peasantry." This is why, when we speak of practical activity, we have in view chiefly the economic existence, the needs and the demands of the peasantry . . . But while we are occupied with our [revolutionary] enterprise, Russian industry is not standing still . . . Need is tearing the peasantry from the land and pushing it to the factory, to the plant . . . In this connection, the center of gravity of economic questions is shifting in the direction of industrial centers.

The distribution of our forces must conform to this organic process. Fortified in the factory and in the countryside, we will take a position in accord not only with the contemporary situation but also with the entire course of the economic development of Russia.[31]

The process of conversion to Social Democracy, which took place in 1880–1882, narrowed the gap between Plekhanov and the Narodovoltsi. He became a centralist, sympathetic to the necessity of the political struggle. He now began to view this struggle as an operation required to aid the birth of capitalism under conditions most favorable to the socialist cause, a position midway between the fatalism of legal Marxists like Ziber (who denied the utility of revolutionary activities) and the willful indeterminism of the Narodovoltsi. Though he disagreed with the Narodovoltsi about the significance of the coming revolution, he became amenable to a *rapprochement* with them, under the conviction that his influence combined with the pressure of the very objective conditions which had converted him to Marxism would drive them to the camp of Social Democracy. These expectations did not come to pass, for the more desperate the cause of the Narodovoltsi became, the more they enveloped themselves in the web of their omnipotent fantasies.* In 1883 a final break took place (whether instigated by Plekhanov or whether he was reluctantly driven to it is not clear),[32] and the Chernye Peredeltsi organized an independent Marxist group, the famous *Osvobozhdenie Truda,* or Emancipation of Labor.

Between 1883 and the end of the decade, a stream of pamphlets and articles in defense of Marxism flowed from Plekhanov's pen. These writings contain observable psychological features identical to those which

* After the assassination of Alexander II, the *Narodovoltsi* abandoned the aim of using the terrorist struggle to force the government to call a *Zemskii Sobor.* They now dreamed of seizing power under the illusion that all progressive elements in Russia expected them to. And they held on to this fantasy, even when only a single member of their executive committee, Vera Figner, remained at large. For a fascinating account of this real flight from reality, see L. G. Deich, "O sblizhenie i razryve s narodovoltsami," *Proletarskaya Revolyutsiya,* no. 8, 1923.

had marked his Populist phase, the same equilibrium between determinism and indeterminism, the same imposed balance between the revolutionary will and the objective reality of the masses. Plekhanov's revolutionary temperament impelled him to direct the course of history along a rational path, with the aid of those ideas "revolutionary in content [which] constitute a sort of dynamite for which no explosive in the world will act as a substitute." [33] But, as we have noted, this drive was kept in leash by the fear that reckless self-affirmation, imperious attempts to make the world conform to his own self-image, would relegate the revolutionist to irrevocable isolation. "The Social Democrat fears as much as it is possible to fear falling into isolation," stated Plekhanov, "and consequently [he dreads getting into] a false position in which his voice would stop reaching the masses of the proletariat and become a voice crying in the desert." [34]

No man could afford to oppose or even disregard the inexorable laws of history. No man could safely oppose his will to objective reality, for the laws of social development could act "with the overwhelming force and the blind cruelty of laws of nature" when they were not taken into account.[35] "We do not want to go against history, but we do not want to stay behind it one single step," stated Plekhanov in 1883, and in all his discussions of revolutionary activities, he attempted to conform to this maxim, to find objective grounds for the demands of his will.

Plekhanov's theory of revolution was a reflection of this need for balance. He insisted that in the revolutionist's world view "the desirable flow out of the necessary." He insisted that the revolutionist accept the objective laws of social development. For however strongly it asserted itself, the revolutionary will could never succeed in deflecting the course of history, in "forcing society" to skip over one of the natural phases of its development. But the revolutionary could and should "reduce and facilitate the labors of society," and he could and should see to it that the birth of a new phase of development takes place under conditions most favorable to the revolutionary movement. Such were the immediate tasks of "the socialists convinced of the historical inevitability of capitalism in Russia." [36] "To a significant extent [the Populist movement] places its faith on the likelihood of the complete omission of one of the phases of social development," Plekhanov admonished his opponents, "because it does not understand the possibility of shortening the length of this phase." [37] Such a possibility really existed, because the socialist movement had developed in Russia at a time when capitalism was still wrestling with the bonds of the old feudal order, but it would remain only a possibility unless socialists utilized the contemporary "lack of influence of the bourgeoisie over the minds of the Russian workers to develop *rapidly* an independent labor party led by its own secret organizations of workers." [38]

From this assumption, Plekhanov deduced the role that history had assigned to the revolutionary intelligentsia. It was "to work actively to develop and consolidate the class-consciousness of the proletariat." Alone, the intelligentsia lacked the talents, the energy, the ties, and the wealth required to influence seriously the course of history. If it attempted to acquire these assets through a union with the upper classes of society, the latter would inevitably betray it. The intelligentsia's only real chance was to tie its fate to that of the proletariat. "We point out to it the industrial workers," stated Plekhanov, "as the one intermediary segment capable of 'fusing' it with the 'people.'" [39]

How did Plekhanov conceive of the consciousness that was to be developed in the proletariat? He always regarded the proletariat as an instrument, as an instrument of reason, of history, of his will. Consequently, there was never present in his world view the emphasis on free development, on free maturation, that Akselrod attached to the idea of proletarian consciousness. Instead, Plekhanov emphasized all the factors he felt were needed to make the proletariat an effective revolutionary force, alienated from the existing order and mobilized to struggle against it, as he himself was. The proletariat should gain "a clear understanding of what it [was] striving for." [40] It needed knowledge to become the leading class, for without knowledge there was no strength.[41] It needed organization to consolidate it into an effective fighting force able to "attack its foes at the right moment and to utilize even the most insignificant victory to ease its further activities." [42] "Only organized revolutionary forces seriously influenced the course of events." [43]

This emphasis on conflict in the development of proletarian consciousness Plekhanov attempted to justify on the basis of the inexorable conflicts among social forces. It would be folly, he argued, for the socialists to place any confidence on the continued good will of their liberal allies, once the struggle against absolutism ended: "In politics, only he who cannot count on anything more serious will rely on the gratefulness of yesterday's friends and today's enemies." [44] It would be just as great a folly to count on the weakness of the bourgeoisie. Although the latter was quite willing to take up such a tune, the socialists would be quickly and disastrously disillusioned [45] if they became enthralled by it. To fuse with bourgeois parties "would constitute an act of political suicide for the Russian socialists, because in the case of fusion, it would not be the liberals who would adopt their program, but they [the socialists] who would have to adopt the liberal program." [46]

Through the development of its consciousness, the proletariat was to become a force capable simultaneously of supporting capitalism in its struggle against reaction and of opposing the very same capitalism in its struggle against the workers' revolution of the future. But the relation between proletarian consciousness and the class struggle was not a one-way affair. The very fact of the struggle would greatly aid the development of the workers' consciousness: "Only by going through the severe school of the struggle for particular patches of enemy territory does the oppressed class acquire the constancy, the audacity, and the development needed for a decisive battle. But once these qualities have been acquired, it can look on its opponents as a class finally (and forever) condemned by history; it can no longer doubt its own (future) victory." [47]

The fundamental dualism that underlay the formation of Plekhanov's world view was also characteristic of V. I. Lenin. Lenin, like Plekhanov, attempted to reconcile the imperious demand of his will to mold the world in his own image with an insistence that the revolutionary adapt to the requirements of an objective reality external to the will, external to the self. But here the similarity ended, for unlike Lenin, Plekhanov acquired a genuine and deep-rooted confidence that the laws of history were inexorably moving the world toward the rational order with which he had identified himself. Lenin never succeeded in gaining this confidence. The continuous conflict created in his personality by the clash between the will to master and the principle of reality was reflected in the image of a world in flux. His revolutionary career was marked by repeated attempts to extend the area of his control until he reached and vainly pressed against insuperable obstacles. Usually, these obstacles rose to his view only *after* their successful resistance to his pressure, and only *post facto* was he willing to regard them as objective conditions, as foundations of reality against which he had to pause, at least momentarily.

Out of Plekhanov's dualism, on the other hand, emerged a static integrated world view which reflected a secure belief that history would conform to the image of his wish: "The Social Democrats are convinced that the natural logic of things, that the natural development of contemporary relations must lead to the political and economic defeat of the bourgeoisie." [48] And: "Let our *intelligenty* go to the workers; *life itself will make them revolutionaries.*" [49]

The note of absolute confidence which rings through these phrases was to pervade Plekhanov's thought from the 1880's onward. For him there was no doubt that "the Social Democrat [was] swimming along the current of history." [50] Lenin, who never managed to gain this confidence, was to reverse the metaphor and insist that to seek his identity as well as the laws of history the revolutionist should swim *against* rather than *with* the current.

Plekhanov's need to impose on the external world an order corresponding to the rational scheme with which he had identified himself impelled him during a portion of his revolutionary career to join hands with Lenin and to see in Lenin a confused reflection of himself. It was his confidence in the capacity of forces outside his control to bring this rational order about (a confidence that he would draw from his image of the irresistible transcendent forces of history) that made the bond which tied him to Paul Akselrod. Akselrod had never felt the alienation from existing society which had given the initial impetus to the revolutionary development of both Lenin and Plekhanov. From the very beginning of his career he had identified to his satisfaction with a people which, he believed, would mature to consciousness and throw off the bonds of ignorance and oppression imposed by external forces, as he himself had done.

Because Akselrod succeeded in externalizing completely the elements of conflict in his world, he never had to cope with the conflicts between contradictory impulses that plagued Lenin's life, and to a much lesser extent, Plekhanov's. His antagonism toward the dominant forces of external reality could rise to great heights, and the hostility he attributed to these forces rose along with it. But because his image of external threats was always counterbalanced by a confident identification with the people, these threats never aroused anxiety, they never impelled him to deny his feelings or to tighten his control over his supporters. Since his was a personality securely rooted in the external world, his own self-affirmation combined naturally with a trust in forces outside of himself, and the free expression of his feelings could run together with a confidence in the determining influence of history.

During the second half of the 1880's, Akselrod gradually developed, in response to the antagonism that Russian radical circles continued to express toward Osvobozhdenie Truda, a hostility against the intelligentsia equal to their own.* With greater intensity than ever before, he now called on the proletariat to cease being "cannon fodder in the hands of the wealthy and of the educated," [51] to speed up the growth of its own intelligentsia and to organize it into an independent force, which "instead of dragging at the tail of so-called intelligentsia circles" would "direct all its efforts, all its energies toward the formation of a single independent labor union or labor party in the full sense of the word." [52] But for the reasons that we have discussed, this greater insistence on self-affirmation and independence of action on the part of the proletariat in the face of a hostile world did not prevent the whole-hearted conversion to a belief in the determining role of objective conditions that Akselrod underwent through the agency of Plekhanov and Marxism. Only three years after he had called for the formation of an independent labor party, Akselrod would caution some of his younger comrades: "We drop from

* In his recollections of this period which were published in *Letopis' Marksizma* (*Gruppa Osvobozhdenie Truda,* VI, 1928), Akselrod acknowledges freely the reactive character of his hostility toward the intelligentsia, a hostility which, as we shall see, was to pale considerably during the succeeding decade.

sight [the fact] that the final blow against the enemy regime will be dealt mostly by a force or an event outside the control of the acting party . . ."[53]

Thus it was that while Plekhanov's confidence in the proletariat grew out of a faith in the determining forces of history, Akselrod's confidence in these determining forces was born out of a faith in the proletariat.

3

THE RISE OF A NEW FAITH

In the year 1891, a severe drought blighted the black earth regions, the "bread basket" of eastern and southeastern Russia. In the preceding decades, the pauperized but rapidly multiplying peasantry had been compelled to dig farther and farther into its reserves of grain, and now, as the crops turned to dust, it was faced inevitably with the specter of hunger. Famine swept over the land, and in its wake came an epidemic of cholera.

The famine exposed the bankruptcy of the imposing state edifice. The foundering tsarist bureaucracy, which had sucked the countryside dry for so many years, now proved itself incapable of transporting available supplies to the stricken regions. At first the government attempted to hide the scope of the disaster from "society," but as the news trickled from the villages to the district and provincial *zemstva* and from the zemstva to the cities, government spokesmen were forced to reveal their utter helplessness in the face of the emergency.*

In contrast to the government bureaucracy, the zemstva and the hastily formed welfare committees of "society" turned with great vigor to the administration of relief and medical aid. The active and constructive role that the Populist intelligentsia played in these organizations was a long step toward the restoration of its self-esteem. Its work in the zemstva during the preceding years had laid the foundation of a new sense of identity, purpose, and belonging. Not only had this work thrown like-minded members of the intelligentsia together in ever-rising numbers, but it had brought them into intimate contact with liberal elements of

---

* When Vishnegradskii, the Minister of Finance, admitted that the government did not have the resources to aid the famine-stricken region, society laid the blame at his own policy of excessive grain exports, a policy followed ruthlessly in the interest of financial stabilization. In this respect, the famine of 1891 offers a striking parallel to the famine of 1932–33. For fuller discussion, see Maslov, "Razvitie zemledeliya i polozhenie krestian do nachala 20go veka," in *Obshchestvennoe Dvizhenie v Rossii*, vol. I.

the gentry. Through the agency of the provincial zemstva, the intelligentsia assumed the direction of the social and economic services which the zemstva performed, and it expressed in these activities a confidence born in part from its increase in numbers.* It strove at the same time to solidify its ties with those elements of the gentry that were prepared to voice dissatisfaction with the government's economic policy. (In 1891 the government had signed a trade agreement with Germany distinctly unfavorable to Russian agricultural interests — this at a time when the price of grain on the European market was already severely depressed.)

Confident of its own strength and of the support of "society," the intelligentsia renewed its demands for basic changes in the economic and political physiognomy of the state. Most of its older members remained faithful to the Populist program, and some of them continued to rest their hopes on reforms from above. But even among the adherents of Populism, a majority now called for an alliance between the intelligentsia and the progressive elements of the bourgeoisie in order to win a constitution. They organized for this purpose a People's Rights Party (*Partiya Narodnogo Prava*). Its program (prefaced by a severe criticism of the apolitical tendencies of the past) aimed "to unify all the opposition elements of the country and to organize an active force, capable of achieving by all the appropriate moral and material means the destruction of absolutism and the gain by everyone of the rights of man and citizen." [1]

But the dreams of the "reformers from above" just as those of the "partisans of a united front of society" were soon to be dashed to the ground. In 1894 the death of Alexander III, the corpulent defender of the policy of "absolutism, nationalism, and orthodoxy," brought to the throne a young man rumored to be more sympathetic to liberal views. Hopeful of a change in government policy, a number of zemstva used the medium of their addresses to the throne to complain of the "rule of bureaucracy" and to demand the "establishment of legality" as well as a greater participation of the zemstva in local affairs. Even though only one of these addresses (that of the Tver Zemstvo) had veiledly alluded to the need for a constitution, Nicholas II's stinging answer made it quite clear that no changes in the existing order were contemplated by the new tsar: "It is known to Me that recently in zemstvo assemblies have been heard the voices of people carried away by senseless dreams of participation by zemstvo representatives in the affairs of internal administration. Let everyone know that I, who am dedicating all My strength to the

---

* The growth of professional groups reached respectable proportions by the middle of the nineties. These groups, organized through the zemstva, utilized conventions, such as the Moscow Congress of Naturalists and Doctors in 1894 and the Kiev Congress of the same organization in 1896, to arrive at a consensus on questions of national importance. See N. Cherevanin, "Dvizhenie Intelligentsii," *Obshchestvennoe Dvizhenie v Rossii,* I.

welfare of the people, will preserve the foundation of Absolutism as strongly and as undeviatingly as did My lamented late Father." [2]

Nicholas drastically reduced the autonomy of the zemstva and peremptorily subjected the authors of the offensive Tver address to administrative exile. A few months later, he made plain the nature of his dedication to the people's welfare by sending a telegram of congratulations to the *"molodtsay fanagoritsy,"* expressing his "highest appreciation" to the "brave" soldiers of the Fanagoroskii regiment for their bloody repression of the strikes in the city of Yaroslav. The strike of the Yaroslav workers, the shots fired by the "brave Fanagoritsii," the tsar's telegram of congratulations — destroyed the intelligentsia's last remnants of faith in the autocracy; and the liberal elements of "society," which had recoiled from a head-on clash with absolutism after the tsar's rebuff of the Tver Zemstvo, were alienated as well.

The Yaroslav strikes also heralded the appearance on the historical scene of the industrial proletariat, the new social force whose revolutionary character Plekhanov and his associates had so vainly emphasized during the preceding decade. But these strikes were even more significant in another respect. They marked a turning point in the evolution of Marxism, which ever since the famine had been competing with increasing success against Populism for the minds and hearts of the younger generation of the intelligentsia.

For the majority of the younger members of the intelligentsia, the famine of 1891 had marked a decisive break with the past. It had exposed the bankruptcy of the existing political order and the utter helplessness of the peasantry. Contemptuous of the tattered Populist faith of their elders, they enthusiastically turned to the credo that had predicted the events that had now come to pass, to Marxism, which had affirmed that the autocracy was doomed and that the wave of the future was not to be found in the villages. They installed a new idol in the temple of their faith—capitalism, the force that was bringing to life the bourgeoisie and the proletariat, the only really progressive social groups in Russian society. It seemed to them that the eventual triumph of socialism, which they, like other "advanced elements" in Russia, took almost completely for granted, could only come about through the further development of capitalist society. Only the growth of capitalism — and that of its agents, the bourgeoisie and the proletariat — could insure the eventual downfall of absolutism and the establishment of a constitutional order. And, what seemed of most immediate importance, only capitalism could pull Russia out of the state of economic and social backwardness which — rather than the blunders of government policy or the alleged shortage of natural resources — was the "chief cause" of the periodic famines that were ravaging the Russian land.[3]

Bitterly, the champions of Populism complained that the younger generation had abandoned the service of the "people" for the service of "capital"; bitterly, they assailed them for "deserting" the peasantry and actually aiding in its pauperization. V. Vorontsov expressed the "hope" that the views of the Marxists were based on deficiencies of an intellectual rather than of a moral nature, but, he added, "it might well be that the material interests of the intelligentsia, as members of the privileged classes, [carried] more weight than feelings of a higher nature." [4]

The complaints of their elders succeeded only in spurring the young Marxists to seek with greater diligence for evidence to confirm their own beliefs and expose those of their Populist opponents. With a feverish intensity, rarely equaled before or since, they investigated all the phases of Russian life and all the fields of social science.

> In their circles, they argued night after night about "surplus value," about the "theory of markets," about "the differentiation of the countryside." Research studies dedicated to the peasant economy, to industry, to handicrafts and cooperation were read and reread until they were worn. Dry statistical tomes, which had been until then the reserved domain of the specialists, were now studied with fascination by hundreds of young people.[5]

The evidence they sought of the growth of capitalism was to be found everywhere: in the increased tempo of industrial expansion, in the differentiation of land ownership among the peasants, in the migration from the villages to the cities which had developed as a result of the famine, in the break by the industrial workers of the cities of their former ties with the countryside.*

Because Marxism was the only revolutionary vision of the future that could demonstrate its roots in contemporary reality, because it was the only doctrine based on faith in the proletariat and (to a lesser extent) on the bourgeoisie, the only two social classes that were not completely discredited, it easily gained possession of the minds and hearts of the young members of the intelligentsia. By the mid-1890's, the movement had reached its height. Into the Marxist ranks poured individuals of the most varied sympathies and outlooks: determinists and indeterminists, champions of "consciousness" and persons ready to be swept by "spontaneity," future Revisionists like Peter Struve and Tugan Baranovskii as well as future Bolsheviks like L. B. Krasin, D. B. Goldendakh-Ryazanov, and Yu. M. Steklov.

* According to A. V. Pogozhev, a sample of 1,263 families studied in the district of Moscow during the period of 1883–1893 indicated that 82 per cent worked in Moscow industries all year around and 12 per cent went home to the countryside in the summer time. According to the same source, the famine of 1891 broke most of the remaining ties with the land (*Uchet chislennosti i sostava rabochikh v Rossii*, p. 101). See also D. Koltsov, "Rabochie v 1890–1904 gg.," *Obshchestvennoe Dvizhenie v Rossii*, pp. 183–229.

Even though the range of converts was so wide, a dominant note was struck by the Marxist literature of the period, a note of determinism. It was all too tempting for the young Marxists to be exhilarated, at least for a while, by the discovery that their diagnosis was correct and the Populists' erroneous, and consequently to rest their confidence entirely on the rationality of the historical process which was proving them right.

Such an emphasis on the inevitability and rationality of the current of history was expressed in the writings of young Marxists like Peter Struve.* It was even to be found in the contemporary works of George Plekhanov, the "grizzled" leader of orthodox Marxism. Plekhanov's pronouncements of this period contained, to be sure, elements of revolutionary activism. Their main impact was, nevertheless, to encourage the Marxist youth to ride confidently the wave of historical development in the expectation that a rational apprehension of the ruling laws of society would automatically bring the fulfillment of their desires.

The opening paragraph of "The Tasks of the Socialists in the Struggle against Famine," a pamphlet intended to outline the current tasks of Russian Social Democrats stated:

> In Russia, as in the entire civilized world, contemporary socialists base themselves on a scientific investigation of contemporary life and only on a scientific investigation. They study the course of historical development and without thinking anything up, without adding anything themselves, they take it as the starting point of their strivings, which in its own right represents only the conscious expression of the unconscious, blind, historical process . . . In our attitude toward the present famine, we must base ourselves on reality as it is and as it will be. It is not logic which must follow the demands of our feelings, but our feelings which must conform to the demands of logic.[6]

Plekhanov's study of historical materialism, which he published legally in 1895 under the pseudonym of Beltov and which was consequently more widely circulated than his pamphlet on the famine, expressed even more confidently the belief that the process of historical development would *necessarily* reflect the laws of human reason. Dialectical materialism, he stated, affirms:

> All that is reasonable in the human mind — i.e., all that is not illusory, but is a true reflection of reality, will necessarily become reality . . .
> "I am a worm!" says the idealist. "I am a worm as long as I am ignorant," states the materialist dialectician — ; "but I am a God when

---

* About his attitude toward socialism in this period Struve subsequently commented: "Socialism, however it be understood, never inspired any *emotions*, still less a passion in me. It was simply by way of reasoning that I became an adept of Socialism, having come to the conclusion that it was an historically inevitable result of the objective process of economic development" (Peter Struve, in *Slavonic and East European Review*, XII, 577).

I *know"* [emphasis in text]. *Tantum possumus, quantum scimus!*
[Our powers extend as far as does our knowledge!] [7]

Plekhanov's view of Marxism as the conscious expression of the ruling
laws of objective reality was universally accepted among the young.
Even Lenin, the most voluntaristic representative of the new generation,
made the identification of Marxism with social science the opening note
of the critique he directed against the Populists in 1894:

> As long as we do not have another attempt to explain scientifically
> the development of a social formation . . . an attempt which installs
> an order into the corresponding facts as well as materialism has been
> able to do . . . [and] which will succeed in giving a living picture
> of a given formation along with a rigorous scientific explanation of
> it, the Marxist understanding of history will be the synonym of social
> science.[8]

For most young Marxists, the emphasis placed on determinism meant
more than an identification of Marxism with science or reason; it involved the emasculation of its revolutionary content. Peter Struve's
"Critical Remarks on the Economic Development of Russia," published
legally in 1894, were typical in this respect of the mood of the new generation. Although this study questioned as fundamental a Marxist axiom
as the inevitability of revolution and offered in its place a gradualist
theory of social change, although it praised the progressive character of
capitalism almost unqualifiedly, few of the young Marxists voiced any
criticisms of it. Even the famous keynote statement of the work, "Let us
admit our lack of culture and go to the school of capitalism," a phrase
which was subsequently identified with the Revisionist position (and
which Struve himself would eventually describe as an "apology of capitalism"), did not perturb most of his contemporaries. Martov, then one
of the "activists" in the Social Democratic movement, comments about
his attitude at the time: "The call for 'going to the school of capitalism'
did not disturb me personally. I interpreted it in a purely sociological
sense and did not, therefore, attribute to the author the idea of the political hegemony of capital in the emancipation of Russia." [9]

The transformation of Marxism into a deterministic economic science,
primarily concerned with the demonstration of propositions such as the
progressive character and inevitable triumph of capitalism in contemporary Russia, was encouraged by the changes that had taken place,
beginning in the early nineties, in the rules of government censorship.
When Struve's "Critical Remarks" and Plekhanov's "Monistic Interpretation of History" successfully passed the censor, it became evident that
any Marxist studies could be published legally providing that they emphasized the deterministic rather than the revolutionary aspects of the

doctrine. A stream of articles and pamphlets written in this vein consequently began to pour from the printing presses. This literature was to become known as legal Marxism; its pattern had become crystallized as early as 1893. Lenin's wife and collaborator stated:

> Vladimir Ilyich arrived in St. Petersburg in the autumn of 1893 . . . At that time the problem of markets interested all of us young Marxists. Among the Petersburg Marxist circles a special tendency was already beginning to crystallize. To the representatives of this tendency, the processes of social development appeared as something mechanical and schematic. Such an interpretation of social development completely neglected the role of the masses, the role of the proletariat. The revolutionary dialectic of Marxism was stowed away somewhere, and only lifeless "phases of development" remained.[10]

As we already have observed, a movement's view of reality, the image its members hold of their role in society, tends to be reflected, in large measure, in the organization of their activities. This continuity was to be observed in this as in other periods of the history of the intelligentsia. In the first flush of victory, the young Social Democrats had been content to entrust their fate to the historical process which had demonstrated the validity of their expectations and the flimsiness of the Populists' dream. They were convinced that they had acquired in dialectical materialism the true science of social development, the key to a process which would unfold in conformity with laws as reasonable and as progressive as the science that had discovered them.

Because of their trust in the rationality of history, because of their confidence that, to quote Plekhanov's phrase, all that was reasonable in the human mind would necessarily become reality, most Social Democrats conceived during the early nineties that their chief, if not their only, function was to impart to the more advanced workers the consciousness and understanding of the laws of social development which they themselves had gained. Plekhanov proclaimed:

> The indispensable condition of the victory of the proletariat is the consciousness by them of their position, of their relation to the exploiters, of their historical role, and of their social and political tasks. The new socialists consequently consider it as their chief, not to say their only, obligation to aid the growth of this consciousness of the proletariat, which they call, for short, its class consciousness.[11]

The development of class consciousness demanded by Plekhanov was viewed in this period as an intellectual endeavor, as an assimilation of the principles which brought meaning and order to the flux of social reality.

Social Democratic circles sprang up in the big cities of Russia —

study groups in which young members of the intelligentsia strove to impart to the more advanced workers the revelation contained in the teachings of Marx and Engels. Some of the young Marxists were more successful than others in this work of enlightenment. But with almost complete unanimity, they appeared satisfied at least for the moment to confine their efforts to drawing into the movement, through this path of knowledge, a labor intelligentsia, an elite of workers.*

Plekhanov had taken pride in the fact that the class struggle of the proletariat would be at the same time a struggle against its intellectual slavery.[12] This dedication to the workers' intellectual emancipation became, in the early nineties, the almost exclusive concern of Plekhanov's disciples. Strikingly absent in their view of social reality was any sense of urgency, any feeling that time might run out for Social Democracy. They discounted, in effect, the ability of any other social force to threaten their eventual triumph or even to grapple seriously with them for control of the historical process. Their credo affirmed that the bourgeoisie was their only possible rival for the fruits of the future, and the bourgeoisie was showing in its conduct signs of glaring weakness, of striking inferiority to the proletariat. Was not the bourgeoisie scraping servilely before the autocracy, when it was overwhelmingly clear that its interests demanded the overthrow of absolutism? Was it not showing itself incapable of developing a political ideology and movement of its own, thereby impelling its most advanced members to join the ranks of Social Democracy? How could a social formation so devoid of rationality constitute a serious threat to the party of Marx and Engels? †

Because they shared this belief in the preponderant strength of the proletariat, those of the Social Democrats for whom the overthrow of absolutism loomed as the most immediate task of the movement failed to

* Lenin's propaganda activities during this period appear to have been slightly more oriented toward action than those of most other Social Democrats. Krupskaya comments in her memoirs: "Most of the intellectuals of those days badly understood the workers. An intellectual would come to a circle and read workers a kind of lecture. For a long time a manuscript translation of Engel's booklet, *The Origins of the Family, Private Property and the State,* was passed around the circles. Vladimir Ilyich read with the workers from Marx's *Capital* and explained it to them. The second half of the studies was devoted to the workers' questions about their work and labor conditions. He showed them how their life was linked up with the entire structure of society and told them in what manner the existing order could be transformed. The combination of theory and practice was the particular feature of Vladimir Ilyich's work with the circles. Gradually other members of our circle also began to use this approach" (*Memories of Lenin,* I, 9–10).

† *Ibid.,* 405. Plekhanov's contemporary writings evidenced an equal contempt for the bourgeoisie and an equal faith in the strength of the proletariat: "The Russian proletariat shows the most certain signs of political awakening. Politically, it has already outgrown the bourgeoisie. It has arrived earlier than the latter at the idea of political freedom . . .

"The other [new social class], the backward one, the bourgeoisie — will be forced under the threat of ruin to become conscious of its own interests" (i.e., of the necessity of political freedom).

stress in their program the need to maintain the independent identity of the proletariat in the struggle for political freedom.

Even Akselrod did not deem it imperative to qualify thus his insistence that the labor movement become the lever for bringing into action all the other opposition forces in the country.[13] And young Martov, who had proclaimed in the opening statement of the manifesto of the Petersburg group of Emancipation of Labor that the immediate goal of Social Democracy was the attainment of political freedom and its chief task the organization of the labor party, nonchalantly added in the next paragraph: "It doesn't matter whether this task can be fulfilled until such time as the overturn is completed." [14]

Although the members of Martov's Petersburg circle were more oriented toward action than the majority of young Social Democrats, they reflected, in all essential respects, the prevailing spirit of the period. The six cocky university youths who founded the organization in 1893 defined its purpose as the ideological integration of existing Social Democratic groups and the strengthening of Social Democratic cadres in the intelligentsia, particularly among students. They were satisfied that they could achieve these aims by the publication and distribution of illegal Marxist literature.

Such were the manifestations of the "circle spirit" of the early 1890's. So great and so rapid had been the triumph of Social Democracy that its young champions appeared satisfied to view it (as they viewed themselves) as an aristocracy of the intellect. This elite, recruited from the most advanced members of the intelligentsia and the working class, was apparently to sit back at least for the present and preside over the unfolding of the omniscient and omnipotent process of history.

Isolated outbreaks already forewarned that the proletariat might not consent to wait for the dialectic of history to decide its fate. Since the famine, the peasants had been flocking to the cities. As the labor supply swelled and the market for consumer goods contracted owing to the pauperization of the masses of consumers, wage rates steadily deteriorated and unemployment became rampant. By 1893, strikes and disorders were breaking out in St. Petersburg, Egorovsk, Kharkov, and Rostov. By 1894, they had spread to Tiflis, Minsk, and Vilno.

Most Social Democrats had remained oblivious to these signs, but they could not afford to ignore the huge wave of strikes which overran the textile industry in 1895. Over forty thousand workers were involved in many towns and cities, principally in Western and Central Russia — in St. Petersburg and in Moscow, in Ivanovo Voznessensk and in Yaroslav, in Orel, Samara, Minsk, Belostok, Vilno, and Roslav.[15]

The year 1895 marked a turning point in the history of Russian Social Democracy. It impressed on the Social Democrats, whose vision had been dimmed by dogmatic assumptions, the fact that the outbursts of the

√

workers' revolutionary energy would not necessarily conform to the patterns laid down by theory. The workers demonstrated in these strikes that they were driven by needs and demands of their own. They demonstrated that if the Social Democrats wished to absorb the labor movement they themselves would have to go to the workers rather than wait for the workers to come to them. The problem that now confronted Social Democracy and the psychological and social issues it was to raise differed in no essential respect from those which had plagued their Populist predecessors. Reality had again shattered the fine web of theory, exposing the breach between the ignorant masses and the intellectual elite which had idealized them, the gap between the immediate demands and needs of these masses and the ideology of the intelligentsia.

By now it was clear that Social Democracy could not afford to ignore the problem that reality had thrust forward. In the preceding year, labor circles had begun to appear in St. Petersburg which rejected any collaboration with the intelligentsia. These "intransigeants" (*dikii*) embodied the threat that faced the Social Democrats — the danger of a permanent split between them and the labor movement.[16] Gone was the faith in the magical efficacy of the historical dialectic. Gone was the exclusive trust in the "study circles" and the intellectual elite they were designed to create. A drastic change in the tactics of Social Democracy was overdue.

A rather brief mimeographed pamphlet was chiefly responsible for delineating the path that was to be followed during the next few years. Its main thesis was that Social Democracy would eventually be in a position to lead the class struggle of the working class in the political sphere only if it concentrated now on the organization of the economic movement which had "spontaneously" arisen. The Social Democrats should shift the focus of their activities from propaganda to economic agitation, assuming the leadership of the workers in their day-to-day conflicts with the employers: "Abstaining for the time being from presenting the masses with wider tasks, Social Democracy was to leave it to the experience of the struggle itself to confront the workers no longer with individual employers but with the entire bourgeois class and the government power which stood behind it, and on the basis of this experience, to widen and deepen its agitation."[17]

This pamphlet, which played so influential a role in molding the new tactics of the young Marxists, was appropriately entitled *Ob agitatsii* (About Agitation). Its author was A. Kremer; its editor Martov, the revolutionary pseudonym of Y. O. Zederbaum, the young man who two years previously had defined his revolutionary role as that of a propagandist of Social Democratic ideas among the intelligentsia. From this moment on, Martov was to be a leading figure in the history of Russian Social Democracy and to play a decisive role in the development of the two opposing tendencies in the movement — the theme with which this study will be primarily concerned.

Let us pause, therefore, to see what sort of man this young intellectual was, who at the age of twenty-two was already making so considerable a mark upon the Russian revolutionary scene.

4

THE MAKING OF A HERO

Among Lenin's notes on the Second Congress of the Russian Social Democratic Labor Party there is a remark, probably jotted down in a fit of bad temper, to the effect that one-third of the delegates present at the Congress were Jews.* Lenin's remark alluded to the major role Jews were playing in the Russian revolutionary intelligentsia, a role out of all proportion to their numerical representation in the population. By the beginning of the twentieth century this high proportion of Jewish leaders and followers had become characteristic of the entire gamut of Russian revolutionary movements; it was as true of the peasantist Social Revolutionaries as of their great opponents, the Social Democrats.

The causes of this phenomenon lay deep in a cultural tradition that had been largely uprooted in the West but that had held fast in the backward Russian empire. In the face of an isolation born as much out of their own ethnocentrism as out of the prejudices of the outside world, the Jews had been faced with the problem of maintaining their identity and finding a meaning for the strange universe into which the Lord had seen fit to throw them. This identity they could not seek in the land on which they stood, the houses in which they rested, or in the tools they carried, for all these were parcels handed out to them by a hostile world — parcels that could be withdrawn as easily as they had been granted. There was but one thing the Jews could safely cling to — the spiritual tradition of their fathers; it was on the foundation of this spiritual tradition that the *shtetls*, the Jewish communities of Eastern Europe, were built. As a result, the rabbis became the recognized heads of the *shtetls*, and their houses of worship became the social centers of Jewish life.

* It was at this 1903 Congress of the Russian Social Democratic Party (the standard abbreviation of which is RSDRP) that the original split between Bolsheviks and Mensheviks took place. This split was aggravated by the desertion from Lenin's camp of a number of delegates, led by Martov, Akselrod, and Trotsky, all Jews.

This spiritual tradition upon which Jewish community life was based and upon which rested the authority of its ruling elite was secular as much as it was religious. Its principles and their ritualistic expressions encompassed all phases of Jewish life, and therefore the authority of the rabbis was not limited to the religious sphere alone but extended to all significant areas of existence. It would be a distortion to infer from this that Jewish community life was characterized by the superiority of the spiritual over the temporal, in the medieval sense of the phrase. The rabbis were viewed as the masters of all significant knowledge, and their leadership was attributed to their superior intellectual ability and to their assimilation of the spiritual tradition contained in the Great Books (the Torah, the Talmud, etc.) rather than to direct unmediated contact with the Deity. The spiritual tradition of Jewry was thus founded ultimately on reason, and the authority of its ruling elite rested on its capacity to rationalize the accepted body of doctrine and ritualistic practices and to interpret conduct in day-to-day life in terms of this doctrine.*

Since the realm of the spirit had become identified with the essence of Jewish life and the concerns of day-to-day existence with the debasing contacts in an alien and despised world, the ideal of the "good life" necessarily came to involve a divorce from material reality, an estrangement from mundane care, which permitted the spirit to roam freely in the rarefied atmosphere of abstract principles.

Ironically enough, these very features of its traditions and life fatally exposed the Jewish elite to the temptations of the external world. They had, in effect, cut themselves off from the living, sensual, concrete aspects of Jewish life. When a group equally alienated and equally preoccupied with the life of the spirit was born in the world of the Gentiles, and when this group was ready to welcome the members of the Jewish elite into its ranks, no earthly bounds or ties remained to hinder their flight.

Such a group was born with the Russian intelligentsia. Like the Jewish intellectual elite, it was estranged from the existing world; like them, it sought its identity in the life of reason and rested its hopes on the fine webs of theory. This spiritual affinity acted as a magnet for the sons and daughters of the guardians of the Jewish intellectual tradition, and by the end of the nineteenth century many of them were breaking their original ties and joining the ranks of the revolutionary intelligentsia.[1] Their participation in the life of the intelligentsia accentuated cer-

---

* It was against this dominant tradition that the Hassidic movement revolted. This movement, born among the poorer and less educated Jews, opposed to the intellectual primacy of the ruling groups of Jewish life, an equalitarian credo based on the idea of a direct unmediated mystical contact with God. The Hassidic movement reached its ascendancy at the end of the eighteenth and beginning of the nineteenth century and rapidly declined thereafter.

tain of its features. They raised the taut emotional fervor of its discussions; they heightened its already obsessive preoccupation with fine intellectual distinctions and nuances. And thus the Congresses of Russian Social Democracy came to resemble the *shules* of Jewish orthodoxy.

It was in the bosom of an already partially estranged family of the Jewish elite that Yuri Ossipovich Zederbaum was born on November 24, 1873. His father, who worked at the time for a Russian commercial company in Constantinople, was the son of A. O. Zederbaum, the founder of the first Jewish newspapers in Russia and an intellectual figure of some note. Yuri's father followed in these footsteps, and during his residence in Constantinople worked as the part-time Turkish correspondent of *Petersburgskya Vedomosti* and *Novoe Vremya*, two leading St. Petersburg journals.

Yuri's mother was a Viennese by birth, and until the family left Turkey at the outbreak of the Russo-Turkish war of 1877–78, the child was accustomed to the sound of two tongues — French, the language in which his parents addressed him, and New Greek, the Constantinople popular dialect used by the numerous servants. The first detailed childhood memories cited in Martov's memoirs[2] refer to his life in Odessa, the sunny cosmopolitan city on the shores of the Black Sea to which his family moved when he was four. Odessa was a thriving commercial center, crowded with various nationalities and religious groups — Greeks and Great Russians, Ukrainians and Armenians, Jews, Catholics, and Greek Orthodox. Thus the Jews in Odessa were one of many minority groups, and since Yuri's parents were not religiously inclined, he grew up during these early years knowing he was neither Orthodox nor Catholic, but without a distinct feeling of Jewishness, with "no sense of belonging to some particular kind of non-Russian people."[3]

Odessa was a glittering and colorful city, a Bagdad among Russian towns, and yet the childhood world of Martov's memoirs is gray, dimmed by a sense of loneliness. Was this due to the absence of his father, who had left Odessa for St. Petersburg to assist A. O. Zederbaum in the publication of his Yiddish newspaper, or to the fractured leg which had left Yuri with a limp and kept him from sharing in the active games of other children? Whatever the causes, one draws from the memoirs the image of a prematurely reserved and ingrown child withdrawn into a universe of fantasy and dreams, far away from this large household of female relatives and servants.*

* Yuri enjoyed little companionship with his older brother, who was sickly and remained bedridden until his death in the early 1880's. Of his younger siblings Lydia, the oldest, was five years younger than he, and Yuri did not develop a close relationship with her, or with his younger brothers, until they reached their early teens. By then Yuri had already begun to "discuss" his revolutionary views with his younger brothers and sisters, and three of them, Lydia (born in 1878), Sergei (born

From the distant adult world, the child would sometimes overhear phrases he painstakingly attempted to interpret to himself. He learned of the assassination of Alexander II through such vague echoes as the servants' comment that "the nobles killed him because he freed the peasants" and remarks dropped in his mother's living room about the madmen who had dreamed of gaining freedom by throwing bombs. It was in the same blur that he became aware he was a persecuted Jew in a land of Gentiles.

In 1881, a few months after the tsar's assassination, a pogrom was loosed in Odessa. The household was warned of the impending disaster a few days before it took place. Those were days of mounting agitation and anxiety among the servants, of visits by the august chief of police and the strong armed doormen of the house with offers to guard the unprotected household. It was difficult for Yuri to understand what was happening, and apparently no one attempted to explain it to him. "The news that, as Jews, we were candidates for some sort of 'pogrom' and threatened with injury did not easily find room in my consciousness," he wrote in later years. "I don't remember whether I asked my elders for the causes of this event. Most likely I did not, because, in general, I asked very little and attempted to think everything out for myself until I arrived at some satisfactory answer." [4]

The day of the pogrom arrived. Systematically, block by block, street by street, the mob broke into the homes and shops of Jews, leaving destruction behind it. As the news of its approach reached the threatened household, Martov's paternal uncle, who was waiting for them in the living room, began to fondle his revolver nervously. The hysterical servants begged Yuri's mother to permit them to hang ikons at the windows and to paint crosses on the mirrors, but she adamantly refused. The pogrom never hit the house. By the time the mob reached the street on which the Zederbaums lived, its fury was spent and it retreated before the police, which as usual had intervened only at the last moment.

Martov never forgot these scenes. Deep within himself, however strongly he attempted at times to deny it, he would always remember that even though his thoughts and feelings, his ideas and his social background might in every crucial respect duplicate those of his companions in the intelligentsia elite, he remained, like the poorest and least educated of his brethren, an oppressed Jew in a hostile world.

in 1879), and Vladimir (born in 1883), eventually became active figures in the Menshevik wing of Russian Social Democracy. For accounts of their political careers, see G. Aronson, "Martov i ego blizkie (K 30-letyu smerti Martova)," *Protiv techeniya*, vol. II (New York, 1954); S. Ezhov (Sergei Zederbaum's revolutionary pseudonym) and K. I. Zakharova, *Iz epokhi "Iskry"* (1900–1905 gg.) (Moscow, 1924); and V. Levitskii (Vladimir Zederbaum's pseudonym), *Za chetvert veka. Revolyutsionnye vospominaniya* (Moscow, 1926).

This recognition, which had come so traumatically, could not easily be rationalized in young Zederbaum's mind. It could not be rationalized, as it had been in Akselrod's case, by an identification with the oppressed masses, for Yuri had been brought up as one of the privileged few; neither could it be balanced by a positive sense of the rich Jewish cultural tradition, for his parents had denied the value of this tradition in their efforts to assimilate. Jewishness was therefore to become in Martov's mind a weakness in his armor, a handicap with no compensatory rewards, and much of his subsequent hostility against the Bund may perhaps be attributed to this fact.*

The wound that had been inflicted on Yuri's soul was not allowed to heal. Shortly after the Odessa pogrom, his father had the family join him in Petersburg, and there Yuri entered a Gymnasium. Apparently, the school selected was a poor choice, for the nine-year-old child was thrown into contact with unusually brutal, "uncultured" youths and with prejudiced teachers. Martov recalled subsequently:

> We, the few Jewish students, were confronted on all sides by a spontaneous view of ourselves as an "inferior" race rather than with anti-Semitic hatred. The others, sons of petty bourgeois Jews, carried this burden passively, attempted to survive unnoticed . . .
> I, who had been brought up in a Russified and liberal milieu, was incapable of surrendering without a struggle. Acerbated by the whole order of school life, my sensitiveness became a disease.[5]

Up to this moment, Yuri, who had been educated by governesses, had always conducted himself as an unusually studious, diligent, and obedient child. But now, overnight, he became a rebel, clashing head on with his environment, meeting violence with violence, answering insults with insults. His school marks dropped, and within a few months he was on the verge of expulsion. His father, whom, characteristically, he had kept in the dark about what was happening, accidentally discovered his precarious position. After quizzing Yuri, he called on the school director. Thereafter, the boy was treated less harshly, and his outward behavior improved.

The armistice which had been concluded enabled Yuri to withdraw again into the world which, since childhood, had been his chief source of nurture, a world of fantasy and imagination. This world of his had been filled with Jules Verne's visions of man's conquests of distant and glittering spaces — 20,000 leagues below sea-level, millions of miles

* The Bund was a Jewish Social Democratic organization, born in the late 1890's. Its platform insisted on the autonomous organization of Jewish workers in the RSDRP. Martov clashed violently with the Bund representatives when this issue arose at the Second Party Congress. There was greater acerbity in his polemical tone during these discussions than in that of any other members of his camp.

away in interplanetary space. It now became populated with the creations of Turgenev, Lermontov, Schiller, Victor Hugo, and George Sand, with the heroes of sensibility and romantic self-affirmation who had dared to oppose their vision to the gross and senseless world.

Other heroes soon began to grip the imagination of the fourteen-year-old boy. Through Herzen's memoirs and tales about the Narodovoltsi, works he found lying in his father's study, he was introduced to the revolutionary tradition of the intelligentsia. The Russian revolutionists and the heroes of the exotic West blended in his mind, and his first dreams of revolution, his first visions of the struggle for emancipation were born. Thus, he acquired a new and shining armor. It buttressed him in his isolation in Tsarskoe Selo, the town of tsarist flunkies and clerks to which his family moved in the succeeding year. It fortified him against the anxieties which arose when, upon the family's return to St. Petersburg in 1889, their right of residence in the capital as privileged Jews was questioned by the police.*

The Zederbaums received a last minute reprieve, and Yuri was permitted to enroll again in a Petersburg Gymnasium. Many of the students at his new school were from intelligentsia families; for the first time in his life, he found himself among congenial youths who welcomed him into their ranks. For many adolescents of his milieu, this might have seemed part of the expected pattern of things, but for young Zederbaum the solidarity of youth that now was opened to him came as an important and tremendously rewarding experience. He who had come to accept loneliness as natural discovered that, even in the world of his contemporaries, there were individuals who shared his ideas, his feelings, his values. The passion with which he now entered into these comradely associations was never to desert him. For the rest of his life, political and intellectual relationships were to constitute a brotherhood in which his feelings of love and affection would be freely invested.

Membership in this brotherhood of young students was meaningful to him in yet another respect. It provided the mold for the development of his revolutionary ideas, the confidence to support his vision of turning the existing world upside down. With a few of his chosen companions, he now began to draw, in high seriousness, plans for their future revolutionary careers and to discuss the "practical ideas" contained in the few illegal revolutionary pamphlets to which they could get access.

Their parents and professors had long since compromised themselves by making the inevitable concessions to "reality," and the only

* During the reign of the obscurantist Alexander III, only a few Jews of high social status were allowed to reside in St. Petersburg. The Zederbaums' right of legal residence was apparently based upon the father's degree from a higher educational institution. For some unknown reason, it was temporarily revoked in 1889.

models available to these youngsters in the existing world, their only sources of counsel and aid, were the older radical students of the university. But even with these representatives of the adult world their encounters were frequently strained, for the university students were often reluctant to give the sixteen- or seventeen-year-old boys the recognition they demanded. Martov in his memoirs gives an amusing account of one such slight that he and his classmates suffered when they attempted to participate in a demonstration conducted by a few radical workers and university students during the funeral of the liberal writer Shelgunov. As the procession paraded through the streets of St. Petersburg and on to the cemetery, the students in charge of the demonstration repeatedly urged Yuri and his companions to go home. But the youngsters refused to move out of the ranks, even when they were reminded of the risks involved. "Some [of the university students] even brought a note of anger into their arguments," Martov recalled. "They explained that students and workers had the right to run risks, but that we, who were hanging to our parents' coat tails, should not carry the fulfillment of our civic duties to the point of depriving ourselves of the right to enter higher educational institutions." But the more their pride was wounded, the more Yuri and his young friends remained obdurate, and they stayed in the procession until it reached Shelgunov's tomb. Only then did they go home, running through open fields to escape the attention of the police spies.[6]

For Yuri and some of his companions, initiation into the revolutionary camp became identified with the attainment of adulthood, with the capacity to confront the existing world on equal terms. The inextricable way in which the concepts of revolutionist and adult became fused in his mind was expressed in his first gestures upon graduation from the Gymnasium. During this period, students of the Gymnasium were denied entrance to the Imperial Public Library of St. Petersburg, a prohibition Yuri resented considerably. As soon as he passed his final examinations and was allowed to drop the Gymnasist's uniform, he flew to the library, haphazardly seized all the books that contained in their titles some vague reference to socialism, and for two weeks, hardly budging from his chair, he indulged in a glorious reading spree.[7]

Admission to the University of Petersburg in the fall of 1891 marked another step in this initiation. In the halls of the university, his older comrades pointed out to him the bearded and somewhat disheveled figures of third and fourth year students already celebrated for their illegal activities. When he and a few friends organized a study circle, one of these august figures, the Narodovolets N. D. Sokolov, took the little group under his wing. This was in 1891, the year of the famine and of the first triumphs of Marxism in Russia, and most of Martov's young friends were self-consciously plodding through "weighty scientific tomes," since the fashion now dictated that to become an effective revolutionist it was necessary to acquire the knowledge "needed for the development of a solid theoretical world view." [8]

Consciously, young Zederbaum espoused these worthy principles, just as later in his revolutionary career he would stress the importance of discipline and organization. These were, in his mind, the serious-minded and responsible gestures required to deal with the real world. He chose to enter the natural science faculty, and he made real efforts to read serious scientific works. But his heart led him in more romantic directions. Soon his interest in science subsided, and he returned to his reading and dreams about the glorious deeds of the Narodovoltsi and the great upsurges of the French revolutionary masses. While his comrades were concerning themselves with "fundamental" questions — the historical role of the proletariat and the special features of the historical process in Russia — Yuri preferred to read over the speeches of his heroes Robespierre and St. Just. Later he would guiltily recall the romantic views of this period of his youth — "this primitive Blanquist conception of revolution as the triumph of abstract principles of popular power valid for all times, resting firmly on the support of the 'poor,' not embarrassed about means." [9]

The same spirit of romantic exaltation was expressed in Yuri's first literary endeavor, the introduction to an illegal publication. It was filled with quotations of Robespierre and St. Just and, to quote his own later evaluation of it, "was completely deprived of moderation and accuracy." [10] The same spirit was reflected in his expectation of an immediate peasant revolt and in his proposal to create a revolutionary organization with ties among the workers and soldiers which would direct an uprising in St. Petersburg to coincide with the peasants' march on the capital.

The revolutionary activities of his group led inevitably to a police crackdown, but Yuri welcomed his arrest, the last act in his initiation to revolutionary adulthood. As the eighteen-year-old youth was driven to his police interrogation, he apparently felt no fear, only an exultation over the realization of a childhood dream: "Seeing myself in an old-fashioned, unwieldy coach, between two of the *most real* gendarmes, I finally experienced, so to say, an aesthetic satisfaction. One cannot be eighteen years old and not feel a need for a romantic context for the serious situations of life." [11]

This arrest would normally have had no serious consequences, since it was Yuri's first. The case was complicated, however, by the fact that a member of his circle named Rizenkampf had broken under police interrogation and made a detailed confession about the activities of the group. Yuri remained in prison for several months, and, upon his release, was expelled from the University of St. Petersburg and deprived of the right to enter any other institutions of higher learning.*

The grueling experience of political interrogations and his friends' decision to boycott their comrade Rizenkampf because of his confession to the police had convinced Yuri that in the code of revolutionary behavior the demands of organizational rules and discipline should overrule all personal feelings, that emotions should play no role in the conduct of a responsible revolutionist. In the months following his release from prison, he was to become convinced that as reasoned a discipline should govern his revolutionary world view.

The peasant uprising he had so hopefully awaited did not come to pass. Instead of rising against their oppressors, the ignorant muzhiki in various regions of Russia turned their anger against those of the intelligentsia who had dedicated their lives to aiding the oppressed. From Astrakhan, from Tsaritsin, from Saratov, the news filtered to the capital that the peasants were attacking and killing helpless doctors, doctors' assistants, and veterinarians. (A cholera epidemic was then raging in Southeast Russia, and the helpless peasants decided that the doctors and nurses who were inoculating them were actually trying to infect them.)

---

* The account given in Martov's memoirs of Rizenkampf's subsequent history throws considerable light on the nature of his attitude toward discipline and organization in revolutionary activities, as well as on the significance these activities held for his comrades in the revolutionary intelligentsia.

When Martov learned that Rizenkampf had broken under the pressure exercised upon him by his mother and by the police authorities, his first impulse was to forgive. He met Rizenkampf in the street a few days after his release and impulsively threw his arms around him. "But, my little pigeon, I nailed you on the cross," Rizenkampf exclaimed. "I will thank you never to mention this incident again," Yuri answered him. His comrades did not share his generous feelings, however. They told Rizenkampf that, while they held nothing against him personally, it was their concerted opinion that he did not possess the mettle required of a revolutionist. They demanded that he abandon forthwith his revolutionary activities and leave St. Petersburg.

Rizenkampf bowed to their decision and entered a university in the provinces. But he was incapable of keeping away from revolutionary activities, and in 1895 he returned to Petersburg on a mission for his local revolutionary circle. When his former comrades informed him that they stood on their previous decision, Rizenkampf answered that since Martov had been the chief victim of his youthful error, he would bow to his decision and to it alone. The intervening years had changed Martov's view of the episode. It now appeared to him legitimate that the concerted view of the members of his organization and its disciplinary laws should overrule his own emotional inclinations. Consequently, when his comrades told him of Rizenkampf's statement, he sat down to the unpleasant task of writing him a note expressing his complete agreement with his comrades' decision. He never had to mail this note, as Rizenkampf committed suicide that evening. A comrade later told Martov that he had observed Rizenkampf pacing nervously in front of his house that fateful evening, apparently trying to collect the courage to come up and confront him. His nerve apparently failed him, for after a half-hour's indecision he left without having seen Martov; a few hours later, he shot himself.

How was one to understand the events that had come to pass? Disillusioned, Yuri began to seek the answers in the heavy tomes he had so shamefully neglected to study. With his friends, he now pored over the dry statistics of *Das Kapital* and over the works of Plekhanov and Akselrod that Potresov brought back to Russia in the fall of 1892 from a visit abroad. The gigantic theoretical edifice of Marx's classic, the sweeping and incisive generalizations of Plekhanov, the concrete argumentations of Akselrod quickly swept him and his friends off their feet, and soon they were ready to dedicate their lives to the cause of Marxism, to dedicate the activities of their group to the goals set by Plekhanov and Akselrod. To mark this unanimous decision, in the winter of 1893 they renamed their circle the Petersburg Group of Emancipation of Labor (*Petersburgsaya Gruppa Osvobozhdenii Truda*).*

How was the group to implement most effectively the goals to which it had dedicated itself? It could, of course, offer its services to one or several of the study circles which were striving to indoctrinate the advanced workers of the capital. But this seemed too modest an activity to these ambitious young men. Martov later recalled:

> We instinctively felt that circle propaganda alone threatened to leave Marxism out of the main current of the revolutionary movement and that it should be supplemented by some sort of work designed to spread our ideas more widely among the working class and to exercise political influence over democratic circles, which were in a state of fermentation.
>
> We came to the conclusion that to simply offer our services as propagandists to a Petersburg Social Democratic group — which had appeared, even to us, as the most natural thing to do — would be unreasonable. Instead of this came the idea of providing propaganda ourselves by the publication of a series of pamphlets and thereby . . . aiding in the establishment of ties between Petersburg and other cities in which there were labor circles, on the one hand — and on the other, influencing circles of young students, and in general those milieus in which the battle between Marxism and the *Narodnichestvo* was raging. [We hoped] thereby to strengthen the cadres of Social Democracy.[12]

In the months following the formation of the Petersburg Group of Emancipation of Labor, the groundwork of Zederbaum's adult political philosophy was laid. The events of the previous months had made him aware of the need to discipline his feelings with the aid of his critical

---

* In his memoirs, Martov was to define this change of orientation as a triumph of consciousness over spontaneity. Of his first wavering in the summer of 1892, he wrote: "I no longer remember whether it was on the basis of readings or of comradely conversations, but my attitude toward spontaneity strongly changed at this time. Very little was left of my naïve *buntarstvo* [spirit of revolt]" (Martov, *Zapiski sotsial demokrata*, p. 137).

intelligence. This lesson was now reflected in his first actual publication, a historical foreword to a speech of Jules Guesde put out by the Petersburg Group (his earlier literary effort had not been printed because his comrades objected to its demagogical character).

Yuri's preface consisted of a dialectical interpretation of the evolution of Russian revolutionary thought: The Narodnichestvo of the seventies, the thesis of this dialectical pattern, had been grounded on the idea of a social revolution achieved through a popular uprising. Its antithesis had been the attempt of Narodnaya Volya to bring about a political revolution through the efforts of "critically minded people" and without the aid of the masses. Social Democracy was to constitute the synthesis of this pattern of development, for it aimed to achieve a social revolution by following the path of political reorganization and through the agency of a *conscious* working class.

From Yuri's interpretation of the revolutionary past a specific moral, a statement of imperatives was to be drawn by his fellow revolutionaries: A social revolution could not be based on the strength of the spontaneous revolutionary impulses of the masses. Neither could it be made by an isolated minority of conscious intellectuals. Only a synthesis of these two forces — a combination of revolutionary energy and consciousness — could successfully carry it through.

The statement left a number of important questions unanswered, however. What, for example, was Yuri's conception of a "conscious" working class? It was clear that by "consciousness" he meant some sort of synthesis between revolutionary impulses and "critical mindedness," but he did not make clear the role that Social Democracy should play in the development and preservation of this synthesis. History was soon to ask for an answer to these questions; it was soon to demand whether in the development and in the evaluation of revolutionary consciousness, the chief responsibility, and therefore the chief authority, should lie with the individual or with the party leadership.

At this crucial stage, Yuri's revolutionary career was temporarily disrupted. In the spring of 1893, he was forced to return to prison to serve the remainder of the sentence for his previous offense. For five months he was imprisoned in a fortress, and this imprisonment was infinitely difficult for him to bear. During his previous incarceration, his mind had fed on intoxicating adolescent fantasies. This time it became the victim of hallucinations which it could no longer control. During the long nights in his prison cell, a steady stream of images flashed through Yuri's mind. As he lay on his cot, scenes of recent weeks, pictures drawn from his readings of the previous day came to him, and he could not shut them out of his mind.

The ordeal ended in May 1893, but Yuri's release from prison was qualified by a sentence of two years of administrative exile from Petersburg and other university cities. On the advice of his friends in the movement, he decided to spend those two years in Vilno, an industrial and commercial center at the border of Poland and Lithuania. Vilno was reputed to have an active Social Democratic movement, and a few weeks after Yuri's arrival he was invited by local Social Democrats to head a study circle of garment workers. The leadership of this circle was his first direct encounter with the type of Social Democratic organization that was prevalent in this period, and it did not take him long to diagnose its inadequacy. The revolutionary movement had signified for him an opportunity to enter with a sense of purpose a world from which he had always felt alienated; he now discovered that the Vilno Social Democrats were for all intents and purposes operating in a vacuum. Their propaganda was detached from the lives of the workers to whom it was directed. The only effect of their activity was to enable the Jewish craftsmen who went through their study circles to realize their desire for a petty bourgeois existence. "By teaching these workers Russian," he observed, "we were making it possible for them to leave the very class whose collective self-consciousness they were supposed to express." [13]

By the spring of 1894 most of the active Social Democrats in Vilno had become convinced that the movement had reached a turning point. All members of the local working class capable of doing so had passed through the study circles, and the only result had been to tear this labor elite away, materially and spiritually, from other workers.

A new path had to be traced. It was discovered, thanks to the experiences of the industrial strikes of the preceding year. In 1893 a strike movement had started among Vilno artisans for the limitation of hours and labor. Because A. Kremer, a local Social Democrat, had the idea of appealing to a forgotten statute of the reign of Catherine II which limited the work-day of artisan workers, the movement had had a legal foundation, and the authorities were compelled to remain neutral. Mutual aid funds and societies of opposition were organized in numerous Vilno factories. In a matter of months, almost the whole local garment industry was involved. The movement petered out after the complete failure of a general strike for higher wages in the fall of 1893, but its lesson was not to go to waste, for it now spurred the Social Democrats to turn to economic agitation.

> We decided [Martov later recalled] that the center of our activity should be transferred to the sphere of agitation and that all propaganda and organizational work should be subordinated to this basic task. By this was implied agitation on the basis of the day-to-day economic needs of the laboring masses which brought the proletariat into conflict with its employers. There was no talk of agitation on the

basis of other social interests . . . or on the basis of cultural questions, because we instinctively followed the path of least psychological resistance. We took the average worker as he was at that time,
limited to a local and shop view, failing to bridge the gap separating
this view from the social life of other classes.

But we were convinced that once they were drawn into a social
struggle on the basis of these day-to-day economic interests, the
masses would be prepared by the very process of this struggle to
assimilate wider social and political strivings and thus put into contact with other classes, brought to self-definition in relation to them.
Therefore, we didn't doubt in the least that by this new path we
would arrive at the formation of a social democratic labor movement.[14]

The fundamental change in policy that had occurred was based on
the frank recognition that a gap separated the workers from the Social
Democratic intelligentsia, a gap which could be bridged only by profound changes in tactics and organization. The reforms that now took
place reflected this recognition of the independent reality of the working-class movement, for they assumed that a sound Social Democratic
movement could be born only out of the fusion of the Social Democratic
center with the workers' own "spontaneous" economic organizations.
Permanent ties were to be created between the Social Democratic center
and the workers' societies of mutual aid and defense funds by instituting
regular meetings between the leaders of these organizations and the
representatives of the center. Further, active participation in working-
class organizations rather than intellectual development was now to be
the criterion of admission to the study circles. The teachers in these circles, in turn, were to adapt themselves to the level of their new pupils
by bringing their training closer to real life and by presenting their
courses in Yiddish rather than in Russian.

The Vilno Social Democrats firmly believed that they had found the
key to the next phase of the development of Social Democracy. To provide a guide for organizations in other Russian cities they drew up a
statement of their new "line": this statement, *Ob agitatsii,* was drawn up
by Kremer, the local Social Democratic leader, and edited by Yuri
Zederbaum under the pseudonym of Martov, which was henceforth to
be his revolutionary "nom de guerre."

The pamphlet encountered violent objections from a number of
quarters. The most vigorous opposition came from the workers already
in the circles. For these workers, the circles had been the one available
means for intellectual development. Consequently, they felt that the
shift to agitation would deprive them of their only opportunity for
spiritual enlightenment. An anonymous statement of this position attacked the new tactics with arguments that subsequently became stand-

ard in one section of the Social Democratic movement. One of the basic goals of socialism, it stated, was to develop critical thinking in individuals. Yet the proponents of the new tactics aimed to use the workers as cannon fodder for the revolution; they were attempting to maintain them in a state of half-ignorance in order to assure their own mastery over them. The intelligentsia should consider itself, the pamphlet piously concluded, as the servant rather than as the master of the masses.

While the working-class members of the circles attacked the new line because of its exclusive concern for the interest of the Social Democratic organizations, a number of Martov's Petersburg comrades condemned it on precisely opposite grounds. Intent on the development of a vast political movement for the overthrow of absolutism and feeling that the rise of such a movement would depend entirely upon the active leadership of Social Democracy, these young men wished to undertake immediately the creation of an all-nation party organization which would concentrate its activities on the political scene. Consequently, a serious disagreement arose when Martov suggested to his comrades during a visit to St. Petersburg in January 1894 that they should dissolve their group and join existing Social Democratic organizations to activate propaganda and agitation among the workers. Even though Martov accused them of Blanquism, his friends held on to their goal of forming a coördinating center of existing Social Democratic organizations in order to speed up the birth of a permanent party.

The partisans of the new line shared the belief that the working class should eventually enter the political arena, organized as an independent Social Democratic party. But they were confident that the workers would naturally, "spontaneously," grow into conscious Social Democrats on the basis of their *own experience* of the economic struggle. The opponents of the new program did not share this trust in the efficacy of natural growth. Impressed with the political stupor of society, they expected that only the active revolutionary consciousness and will of the Social Democrats could shake the progressive classes out of their lethargy and successfully lead them to the overthrow of absolutism.

The two opposite grounds from which the program of *Ob agitatsii* was attacked were to crystallize into two positions between which Russian Social Democracy would oscillate in succeeding years. The partisans of "spontaneity" gathered in one camp, the advocates of "consciousness" in the other.

The subsequent development of Social Democracy was to be complicated further by the fact that the slogans around which the two camps coalesced contained fundamental ambiguities which it would take years to unravel. Did "spontaneity" and "consciousness" stand for mutually exclusive, *instant* affirmations of feelings and the reasoning will? Or could "spontaneity" develop into "consciousness" by a harmonious, *continuous* process of growth? Even though this issue was already implicit in the controversy over the new tactics, it was to take almost a decade before it became clear to the Social Democrats. In the intervening period, individuals who would eventually return opposite verdicts on the question were to join hands under the illusion that they stood for the same values and for the same goals.

Ob agitatsii was clearly an embryonic attempt at a reconciliation of some of these actual and potential differences. It aimed to give birth to a "conscious" Social Democratic party; yet it traced the path to this ultimate goal through the "spontaneous" experience of the workers. It visualized this path as a process of growth of the workers' consciousness; yet it aimed to entrust the supervision of this growth to the leadership of a center of "conscious" Social Democrats.

Interestingly enough, Martov, who had been one of the authors of this attempted synthesis, was himself to oscillate during the succeeding years from one side of the equation to the other. For he was himself a divided man. His feelings bent him toward a preference for the free and uncontrolled growth of the Social Democratic movement. But his disciplined will hardened in his contact with adverse reality, would make him periodically aware of the need to control the development of the movement and keep it away from "the path of least resistance." At a crucial moment in the history of Russian Social Democracy, it was to attract him to Lenin, the hard-headed realist, who stood for the belief that in this world "a man had to keep his heart between his teeth."

5

THE PATH OF LEAST RESISTANCE

Martov's term of administrative exile expired in 1895, and in the spring of that year, he returned to Petersburg determined to convert the Social Democrats of the capital to his new program of action. To his surprise, his proposals were now sympathetically received not only by his young contemporaries but even by the *stariki*, the more mature members of the movement, who were called "old men" because they were all of twenty-five to thirty years old. Conferences were held between the *molodye* (the young ones) and the stariki to discuss a fusion of the two groups; Martov and Yukhovskii proposed to the stariki leaders, V. I. Ulyanov, Krzhizhanovskii, and V. V. Starkov:

> the creation of a labor organization founded on agitational circles, each of which was to constitute the gathering place for the best *spontaneous* fermentations at various points of the labor world and the center of agitational activity on them.
> By making use of various causes for dissatisfaction, the organization was to formulate and motivate the presentation of demands in every clash between the masses and the employers, and as far as possible, it was to present to the masses proposals of struggle for this or that economic or legal improvement, even before the masses expressed strong dissatisfaction.[1]

All of the molodye enthusiastically endorsed the new tactics advocated by Martov; most of the stariki also supported them, although with some reservations; and along the lines that Martov had proposed, a new "all-Petersburg" Social Democratic organization was formed: the Union of Struggle for the Emancipation of Labor (*Soyuz Borby za Osvobozhdenie Truda*). This change of attitude was largely the product of the new spirit in the air. The labor movement was coming to life, and it now appeared that unless the Social Democrats coped successfully with the workers' outbursts of energy the latter might well run amok, sweeping before them the thin layer of the Social Democratic intelligentsia.

The Social Democrats were thus in agreement on the need to conduct economic agitation in the Petersburg factories; yet incipient differences already existed among them concerning the path that this agitation should follow.

Vladimir Ulyanov (the future Lenin), an outstanding figure in the circle of the stariki, was as vigorously opposed as Martov to what he called the old "laboratory technique of the development of class consciousness," and just as convinced that the Social Democrats had to come to grips with the "spontaneous working-class movement." But Ulyanov also believed that this "spontaneous" working-class movement could not *naturally* grow to political consciousness and organization, that it could do so only under the active leadership of Social Democracy.*

Ulyanov's differences with the molodye extended to still another issue. He was already convinced that one of the chief instruments required for the development of Social Democratic consciousness among the rank and file of the movement, and for the replacement of their local, parochial point of view by a wider and more inclusive world view, was the foundation of a nation-wide Social Democratic *organization*. Since Ulyanov believed that this nation-wide organization would itself play a critical role in the development of Social Democratic consciousness, he obviously could not entrust its development to "the path of spontaneity," to a process of natural growth. The urgency that Ulyanov attached to this organizational task was intensified by a fear that at their current stage of development existing Social Democratic groups were singularly vulnerable to the inroads of absolutism. The arrest of a few key figures, he felt, might mean the collapse of entire organizations; yet the danger of such arrests was steadily rising, for the Social Democrats were being compelled to abandon their old conspiratorial caution in conducting economic agitation among the workers.

Ulyanov's fears were largely substantiated. The new tactics of the Social Democrats did enable the tsarist police to track down their activities, and in December 1895 and January 1896, the *Okhrana* suddenly pulled in its net: Ulyanov, Krzhizhanovskii, Starkov, Vaneev, Malchenko, Martov — almost all the major figures in the Petersburg movement —

* Lenin faithfully followed this line of thought in his agitational pamphlets and leaflets. These pamphlets were usually didactic demonstrations of the general political significance of particular economic grievances. Step by step, the reader was led to a political conclusion which was not explicitly stated but left to his own formulation. See, for example, the conclusion of the pamphlet *O shtrafakh* (On fines), written in jail in 1896: "The workers will understand that the government and its officials are on the manufacturers' side, and that the laws are drawn up so as to facilitate the exploitation of the worker by his employer . . . When they understand this, the workers will see that they possess only one means for their protection — to unite for the struggle against the manufacturers and the unjust order upheld by the law."

were suddenly arrested and jailed. The arrests were not followed by a breakdown of the Petersburg organization, but they did lead to the assumption of its leadership by the most youthful and enthusiastic advocates of the economic struggle. The result was still what Ulyanov had feared: for the next few years, Social Democracy was to follow the road of least resistance — the path of "spontaneity."

In all fairness to the Economists (the advocates of the "economic" struggle), the tactical program originally outlined in *Ob agitatsii* could not possibly have been achieved. By 1896–97 it had become obvious to the Social Democrats that the struggle of the proletariat against economic exploitation could not lead to the overthrow of absolutism; it could not be expected to arouse the lethargic bourgeoisie and peasantry to political consciousness. Yet without the aid of these social classes, the proletariat would be too weak to bring about a successful political revolution. To Plekhanov and Akselrod and to their few followers in Russia it appeared that the way out of this dilemma was to widen the content of Social Democratic agitation so as to include political slogans and demands calculated to appeal to all dissatisfied social groups.

But this approach was unacceptable to the young leaders of the Union of Struggle. Even if the emphasis that these new leaders placed on the independent development of Social Democracy had not prejudiced them against adopting such an approach, the spirit reigning among their followers would have precluded it. The strike agitation of 1895–96 (and particularly the strikes in the summer of 1896) had indeed resulted, as Martov and his comrades had hoped, in the rise of a spirit of class consciousness and class solidarity among Petersburg workers; it had also made many workers aware of their conflict with a government which had so clearly taken the side of the employers during the strikes.[*] But these two years of struggle had also had psychological repercussions which Martov had not foreseen. They had aroused in the rank-and-file members of the Social Democratic movement a bitter and enduring hostility toward "society" as a whole and the bourgeoisie in particular; they had taught the "conscious" workers that in a world dominated by selfish forces, they should rely on their own strength and their own strength alone.

It was too much to expect that the rank-and-file Social Democrats

[*] Stated an editorial of *Rabochaya Mysl* (no. 2, 1897), during the period when this journal was published by the Committee of Labor Organization of the Petersburg Union: "The government is not ashamed to place itself openly on the side of the capitalists. With the aid of the police and the army, weapons in hand, it is attempting to force the workers to submit again to its unbearable strap . . . therefore, we will have to struggle against two foes, the factory owners and their protector, the government" (Quoted in K. M. Takhtarev, *Ocherki Petersburskogo rabochego dvizheniya 90-kh godov*, 93).

should accept the idea of a political alliance, if only a temporary one, with the very social groups against which they were fighting so bitterly in the struggle for their daily bread. And for what purpose? To gain some political rights asserted to be necessary for the further growth of their movement? But had experience not already shown by this time (1897) that the way to gain concessions was by a show of their own strength? Had not the government been compelled by the reality of their power, by the pressure of their strikes, to grant the workers a substantial portion of their demands? *

The labor journal, *Rabochaya Mysl,* argued:

> There is no aid but mutual aid, no means of protection but *self-protection:* life will point out no other way than *self-emancipation.* Enough of the lie that the labor movement develops because there already is political freedom. No! Real freedom develops out of the fact that the labor movement has moved forward and irrepressibly strives forward.
>
> The truth is that every strike, every mutual aid fund, every labor union will become legal when it becomes a matter of habit, when it is immaterial whether it is permitted or forbidden. The question of organization is not one of law but of the imperious demands of life.[2]

Thus, to Akselrod's proposal of the formation of a coalition of dissatisfied social groups to overthrow absolutism, the Petersburg Social Democrats opposed the vision of an organized and mobilized working class *forcing* the government, even if it was an autocracy, to take the workers' views into account, just as now it was taking into account the demands of the employers. Intoxicated with the early successes of the economic struggle, they confidently predicted that although the workers could count only on their own strength, their united efforts could sweep away all the obstacles encountered in their struggle for emancipation. "In our struggle against . . . [the capitalists], we have but one weapon — unity and friendship. Nothing will stand up against the united workers," stated the sixth issue of *Rabochaya Mysl.* "Unity among the workers, the consolidation of their strength can achieve everything. They [the workers] will take all of production into their hands and become their own bosses." [3]

The Petersburg Union of Struggle had been completely overhauled since 1895, in order to facilitate its fusion with the labor movement. In the Committee of Labor Organizations created to represent the factory agitators and propagandists, and in the newspaper *Rabochaya*

---

* The strikes had frightened Count Witte into pushing through the law of June 2, 1897, which reduced the legal working day to 11½ hours. Owing to legal loopholes and lack of proper enforcement this law rapidly became ineffective. See D. Koltsov, "Rabochie v 1890–1904 g.g." in *Obshchestvennoe dvizhenie,* I.

Mysl, the rank-and-file partisans of the economic struggle had acquired a highly articulate voice.

Even if the young leaders of the Petersburg Union had wanted to widen the political program of the organization, they would not have succeeded, for their own control of the movement was threatened. In the pages of *Rabochaya Mysl* and at the meetings of the Union, the partisans of the "spontaneous" movement had started to attack the very notion that the development of the labor movement should be guided according to any prearranged theoretical or organizational schemes. They insisted that the theory and practice of Social Democracy should itself be the outgrowth of the self-consciousness (*samosoznanie*) and independent activity (*samodeyatelnost*) of the workers. "It is not *Rabochaya Mysl* which creates a specific state of mind among the workers," proudly stated its editors. "On the contrary, it is *Rabochaya Mysl* which is created by the workers' state of mind and reflects their thoughts." [4] To the theory that the leadership of the Union should guide the development of the movement, they opposed the view that this leadership should act merely as the reflection of the opinions of its followers. They also criticized the predominance of the intelligentsia in the existing leadership: "We must select [our leaders] from among our comrades," stated a document of the period, "because only the workers can honestly and conscientiously fulfill the demands of their comrades — of their class." [5] If Social Democracy was truly to become the expression of the consciousness of the working class, its leadership should be composed of workers.

Although some of the editors of *Rabochaya Mysl* were themselves members of the intelligentsia, they attributed the continued political preoccupations of their adversaries to their sick intelligentsia consciences. Political ideals, they insisted, were extraneous to the nature of the labor movement and the average worker would not rise to their defense. He would fight and fight heroically — but only for his economic interests, for his right to existence. This argument, spelled out in the manifesto of *Rabochaya Mysl,* ended with the inevitable conclusion:

> The economic struggle, the struggle against capital on the grounds of day-to-day basic interests, strikes as the instruments of this struggle — this is the motto of the labor movement . . . Let the workers conduct this struggle, knowing that they are fighting not for some future generation but for themselves and their children; let them understand that each victory, every inch seized from the enemy, is one more step climbed on the stairway leading to their own welfare; let the existing forces call the weak to the struggle and place them in their own ranks, without counting on any external aid. Victory is ahead, but the upper hand will be held by the fighters only if their motto is: *the workers for the workers.*[6]

The leaders of the Petersburg Union attempted to appease *Rabochaya Mysl*. They proposed the organization of a "labor fund" that would include all the active elements of the proletariat and act as a check on the activities of the Social Democratic leadership. When, in February 1897, the old leaders of the Union were released for a few days before being sent to Siberia, this organizational plan was submitted for their approval. Ulyanov vehemently criticized the project, and according to Martov's recollections, the other stariki supported him wholeheartedly:

> Insofar as the day-to-day practice of the Union had previously consisted of the leadership of the workers' professional struggle, the proposed organization would cramp these leading ranks in all attempts to widen the scope of their revolutionary work and to take it out of the wrapping of the purely trade-union struggle . . . [Since] we considered the concentration of the strength of the party on the latter as just a strategic scheme, leading by the surest path to a direct struggle against absolutism, we greeted the project with skepticism, and supported Ulyanov.[7]

The remaining *politiki* (advocates of the political struggle) in the Social Democratic leadership reluctantly agreed with the substance of these criticisms and they made one last effort to stem the tide of Economism. Believing, like Ulyanov, that the one step which might turn the movement back to a more enlightened political direction was the consolidation of existing Social Democratic groups into a nation-wide organization, they convoked an all-Russian congress, which met in Minsk on March 1, 1898.*

The congress announced the formation of the Russian Social Democratic Labor Party (*Rossiskaya Sotsialdemokraticheskaya Rabochaya Partiya*, or RSDRP), and it assigned the task of drawing up the manifesto of the new party to Peter Struve, the bright young man who had coined the phrase, "Let us go to the school of capitalism," which a few years earlier had aroused such furor among the Populists. Struve's statements were now more cautiously phrased. To appease the Economists, his manifesto opened with words of praise about the Petersburg strikes which "had forced the government to make significant concessions," but it proceeded to point out that this was only the first step in the struggle to satisfy the basic needs of the working class:

* The Petersburg Union was so seriously weakened by the inroads of Economism that it did not play a leading role, either in the convocation, or in the debates of the congress. This role was assumed by a number of new organizations which had risen partly through the stimulus of the Petersburg strikes: the Kiev, Moscow, and Ekaterinoslav *Soyuzi Borby za Osvobozhdenie Truda* (Unions of Struggle for the Emancipation of Labor), the Bund (the union of the Jewish Social Democratic groups founded in October 1897), and the editorial board of *Rabochaya Gazeta,* a new Social Democratic newspaper published illegally in Kiev.

And what doesn't the Russian working class need? It is completely deprived [of the rights] that its comrades abroad freely and peacefully utilize: participation in the administration of the state, freedom of the spoken and written word, freedom of meeting, [freedom] to organize collectively — in a word, all the tools and instruments with the aid of which the Western European and American proletariat improve their position and struggle for their final emancipation, against private property, for socialism. Complete freedom is needed by the Russian proletariat, just as clean air is needed for healthy respiration. It is the basic condition for the free and successful development of the struggle for specific improvements and for final emancipation.

This call to political action was followed by a description of the Russian bourgeoisie that was calculated to appeal to the partisans of *Rabochaya Mysl* (and about which Struve himself must have entertained serious reservations):

The further East [one looks] in Europe, the weaker, the more cowardly and abject the bourgeoisie appears in the political sphere, and the more do cultural and political tasks fall to the lot of the working class. On its strong shoulders the Russian working class carries the task of conquering political freedom. This is an indispensable first step in the realization of the great historical mission of the proletariat, in the establishment of the social order in which there will be no room for the exploitation of man by man.*

The triumph of the politiki proved extremely shortlived. A few weeks after coming into existence, the central organizations of the new all-Russian party were completely destroyed. The tsarist police captured the entire membership of the new Central Committee, as well as the leaders of the Bund and the editors of *Rabochaya Gazeta*, the Kiev newspaper that had been recognized by the Congress as the new party organ.

Five years were to pass before the party was reborn. The thin layer of politically minded members of the intelligentsia who had stood at the head of Social Democracy were now in foreign exile or in Siberia, and young intransigeant Economists had come in to fill their places. The Economists succeeded in getting Struve's manifesto rejected by the membership of the Petersburg Union, and by 1899 they managed to

* Struve subsequently commented about his draft of the Manifesto: "I did my best to avoid putting into it any of my personal views, which would have either seemed heretical, or been incomprehensible to an average Social Democrat. Therefore the Manifesto which, though written by me in its elementary and drastic statement of Marxism, did not in the least correspond to my personal and more complex views of that period, was fully approved both by the foreign group of 'Emancipation of Labor' and by Lenin. Only the 'Economists' did not like it, because of the stress it laid on the struggle for civic and political liberties — the point in the whole of that manifesto which was most in accord with my own ideas and feelings at that time" (Peter Struve, in *Slavonic and East European Review*, XIII, 75).

secure a majority in its leading center; they even gained a majority in the Union of Russian Social Democrats Abroad (*Soyuz Russkikh Sotsial Demokratov za Granitsei*), thereby forcing Plekhanov and Akselrod into renewed political isolation.

The news of this disastrous course of events did not reach Martov, who was serving his sentence in Turukhansk, an isolated settlement in Northern Siberia, until the end of 1899. When he heard it, he vehemently denounced the Economists and resolved to fight them inexorably. Yet the beliefs the heretics were so fervently defending constituted in a real sense a heritage from the pamphlet on agitation that Martov had been instrumental in presenting to the world. They reflected a side of his personality, an aspect of his vision of reality, which, however much he was now to deny, would one day bring him into irremediable conflict with Lenin, the very man with whom at this moment he was to side in the defense of orthodoxy.

Ob agitatsii had argued that the only path leading to the political mobilization of the working class was agitation among the workers, based on their *existing* petty demands and needs. Its conclusion had stated:

> The struggle incited by this agitation will teach the workers to defend their interests; it will raise their fortitude; it will give them a confidence in their forces, a consciousness of the indispensability of unity and confront them in the end with the more important questions which require resolution. Prepared in this way for a more serious struggle, the working class will proceed to the solution of its basic problems.

When F. I. Dan, Martov's most faithful lieutenant, drew up his political testament some fifty years later, he acknowledged frankly that *Ob agitatsii* had provided the theoretical foundation for the development of Economism, both in its moderate and extreme forms.[8] What he failed to point out was that this theoretical foundation rested on psychological assumptions which Martov was eventually to resurrect, and that these assumptions would constitute the core around which Menshevism was ultimately formed.

The assertion that before proceeding to political agitation the Social Democrats should pass through two phases of economic agitation — first against individual employers, and later against the capitalist class as a whole — constituted the essence of the "theory of stages" advanced by the moderate Economists grouped around *Rabochee Delo,* the organ of the Union of Russian Social Democrats Abroad. This "process" theory of tactics, as the Economists would call it, was based on a conviction, which the Mensheviks would themselves eventually voice in their struggle against Lenin's tactical and organizational schemes, that the tactics and organization of Social Democracy should develop gradually in the process of the movement's natural growth.

Second, Dan pointed out that the formula of *Ob agitatsii*

> created the impression that the working class could "ripen" to a capacity to absorb political agitation, without going out of the narrow sphere of its interrelations with the employers, without bringing into the range of its attention the problems of the general economic, social, and political development of the country. [It created the impression that the proletariat could develop this capacity even if] it isolate[d] its struggle from any contact, whether positive or negative, with the struggle of other social strata and even if it limited its political tasks to "a change in existing conditions for the benefit of the working class." [9]

The platform described by Dan in this passage was the one adopted by the extreme Economists represented on *Rabochaya Mysl.* Its planks were never endorsed by the Mensheviks, but the confidence they reflected in the free and unhampered development of the working-class movement, the trust they expressed in the workers' "spontaneous" attitudes and experience, were to become an integral aspect of the Menshevik world view. One of the basic issues that was eventually to distinguish the Mensheviks from Lenin's partisans was precisely the confidence that "spontaneity" was not necessarily at odds with "consciousness," the belief that a Social Democrat could afford to be a whole man, free to express himself fully without the restraint of rigid ideological or organizational bonds.

As the end of the century approached, the spread of Economism was fanned by a breeze blowing from the very citadel of orthodoxy, German Social Democracy. Since 1897 and 1898, a brilliant and articulate leader of the German party, Edward Bernstein, had been boldly attacking the intransigeant revolutionary spirit of Socialist doctrine. The labor theory of value, the iron law of wages, the class struggle — one by one, these sacred tenets of Social Democratic theory had been submitted to incisive and ruthless criticism, and in 1899 this criticism was collected in a powerful heretical statement, "The Premises of Socialism and the Tasks of Social Democracy." It wasn't true, Bernstein insisted (with the aid of an impressive barrage of statistics), that contemporary society was faced with an inevitable crash. It wasn't true that socialism could be attained only by revolution. The rise of a new form of economic organization, the stock company, proved that within the existing political and legal bounds society was gradually moving toward socialism.

The old formulas were outdated, and Social Democracy should revise its doctrine in accordance with contemporary realities, in accordance with the current activities of its mass movement. This segment of Bernstein's statement appeared to vindicate the program which the Russian Economists had been advancing for so many years: "The movement [was] everything, the final goal — nothing at all."

But the Bernsteinian heresy spurred the rise of yet another movement that would threaten the identity of Russian Social Democracy, and this time the threat originated not among unsophisticated factory agitators, not among *praktiki* carried away by the experience of the economic struggle, but in the group of "enlightened" young intellectuals who had led the political wing of Social Democracy. Involved were such glittering figures as Peter Struve, the precocious theoretician who had drawn up the manifesto of the aborted RSDRP; Tugan Baranovskii, who had led some of the most incisive attacks against Populism; Bulgakov and Berdyaev, who had been responsible for some of the early triumphs of Marxist social philosophy in the heyday of the early nineties.

Posing as constructive critics who aimed to bring Marxist theory up to date, the Russian Revisionists first directed their fire at individual dogmas of Social Democracy — the labor theory of value, the iron law of wages.[10] It was only a short while before their criticism was extended to the entire body of Marxist theory. In 1900 Struve and Bulgakov formulated a theory of social change diametrically opposed to the Marxist concept of revolution: they advanced the proposition that the transition from capitalism to socialism would take the form of a gradual socialization of capitalist society.*

Fundamental in the Marxist view of reality had been the idea that the pattern of history was being shaped by a developing conflict of social classes in the process of which the proletariat would eventually gain predominance. To be sure, differences of views existed among the leaders of Social Democracy as to the forces with which the proletariat would have to cope and the resources upon which it could depend in its struggle for supremacy. But even the Social Democrats who were most willing to entrust the fate of the working-class movement to the "spontaneous" development of its members, even those among them who chose to view this development as a continuous and harmonious pattern of growth, had identified the socialist cause with the cause of the proletariat, and the cause of the proletariat alone.

* See P. B. Struve, *Die Marxistische Theorie der sozialen Entwicklung* (1900). Bulgakov decided from an analysis of capitalist development in agriculture that: "The only conclusion which present scientific knowledge permits us to confirm is that present economic development is leading to the gradual elimination of the most difficult and severest forms of exploitation of man by man, although [this elimination is taking place] by various means: in industry [it is taking the form of] concentration of production and of social control over it; in agriculture, that of destruction of big enterprises and of their replacement by a strong peasantry. Both of these currents are uniting in one potent democratic stream — which, it can be stated with satisfaction, will bring about new social forms that will fulfill more satisfactorily demands for social equality." S. N. Bulgakov, *Kapitalizm v zemledelie* (Petersburg, 1900), p. 456.

In contrast with this view, the Revisionists were now making socialism an *immanent aspect* of social reality; they were tying its growth to the whole span of the development of society rather than to the triumph of any particular social force. Given this assumption, there was no reason to assign exclusive leadership over the progressive forces to the proletariat; there was no justification for the Social Democrats' insistence on the workers' independent political organization. Peter Struve stated that in his view

> the current historical task in Russia is not such that the "Hannibal's oath" of our time should be tied exclusively or even primarily to the fate and interests of a single social class, that other classes should be feeble, indifferent, or hostile to the content of this key task. The great contemporary task of reform is laid by the whole scope of living conditions in our country, and as such, it rules over the interests of all significant classes in Russia, being the condition for our further national development.[11]

The insistence that Social Democracy, as an independent entity, should rule over the chain of history had been founded on the claim that it was the sole embodiment of progressive values in the Russian land. To this claim the Revisionists now opposed the view that progress was an over-all pattern of social development drawn ultimately from the spiritual qualities of the individual human conscience.

From 1900 on, Struve was to direct his efforts toward the development of a liberal movement founded on the recognition of the absolute and universal value of the individual consciousness. His collaborator Bulgakov was to go one step further and insist that the liberal faith be given a religious foundation. Only through transcendental confirmation of a religious faith reflected in an equitable world order, he would insist, could the falsity of the Marxist claim of the class origin and material foundation of liberalism be demonstrated; only through religion could the insights of the individual consciousness be safely assigned absolute value.[12]

The organization of the liberal political movement for which Struve and his collaborators were calling did not immediately take place. In the meantime, the inroads of Revisionism in the Social Democratic movement had a temporary effect which the Revisionists had not expected and could not have approved. Struve had been affirming that much of the theoretical baggage of Marxism was outmoded and that it should be revised so as to reflect objective realities. But as the century drew to its close, objective reality still conformed on the whole to the image drawn by the Economists: the "possessing classes" had not yet emerged from their long political slumber; the rank-and-file members of the labor movement were still wholly preoccupied with the problems of the economic struggle. Consequently, as late as 1899, the Economists were able to use segments of the Revisionist doctrine to justify their own apolitical stand.

In 1899 the most extreme of the statements that had yet been made of the Economist position in Russian Social Democracy was published abroad and circulated in anti-orthodox Russian Social Democratic circles. This manifesto, which was to become known as the "Credo," had been drawn up by E. D. Kuskova, one of the new leaders of the Union of Russian Social Democrats Abroad. The opening statement of the "Credo" reflected the intermixture of Revisionist and Economist views that was taking place in this period of political quietism. It openly expressed sympathy for Bernsteinian Revisionism, which it described as a revolution in the practical activity of German Social Democracy as well as in the theoretical foundations on which this practice was based:

> This change will proceed not only in the direction of a more energetic conduct of the economic struggle but also and more basically toward a change in the relations with other opposition parties. Impatient Marxism, negative Marxism, primitive Marxism (which entertains too schematic an impression of the class division of society) will be replaced by democratic Marxism, and the social position of the party in contemporary society will radically change.

Having rested its case against the "sectarian traditions" of Social Democracy on the new and "enlightened" Revisionist doctrines, the "Credo" proceeded to present a twisted interpretation of these doctrines, carved in accordance with the Economists' theory of "spontaneous" development:

> *The basic law that can be derived from the study of the labor movement is that it follows the path of least resistance.* In the West, this path led to political activity, but [it does not do so] in Russia . . . While in the West the weak forces of the workers were strengthened and consolidated after being drawn into political activity, in our country, on the contrary, these forces stand before a wall of political oppression . . . They lack any practicable means for a struggle against it, yet they are systematically stifled and incapable of growing any sprouts [under its rule].

Only one practical solution existed for the Russian Marxists, the "Credo" concluded: first, to encourage the economic struggle of the proletariat, which, however arduous it might be, was an integral part of the workers' own lives and thus the only foundation upon which the labor movement could develop an organization in accord with Russian realities; second, to give up once and for all their unfounded prejudices against other opposition groups and to participate in liberal political activities. While political exclusivism was somewhat justified in the politically conscious societies of Western Europe, the "Credo" asserted, it made absolutely no sense in Russia, "where only participation in the life advanced by Russian reality, however un-Marxian it might be, [would] shake the Russian citizen out of his political lethargy." [13]

The demands of the rank-and-file Economists for a single-minded concentration on the struggle against the employers had been founded originally on a deep-seated hostility toward the possessing classes. In the peculiar intelligentsia brew contained in the "Credo," this hostility was now absent, and the Economist program was combined with the Revisionist demand for class collaboration and liberal leadership in the political struggle. In these otherwise dissimilar points of view, the authors of the Credo had "discovered" a basic common element — a willingness to trust in the process of life, a faith in the capacity of the individual personality for "spontaneous" development in the existing environment. It was because of this faith that Kuskova and her allies were now demanding the loosening of the exclusive and restrictive bonds of organization that had previously been considered as a necessary mold for the future development of Social Democracy.

It was inevitable that Economism would become a source of considerable concern for the leaders of Osvobozhdenie Truda, for ever since their conversion to Marxism, Plekhanov and Akselrod had been clamoring that Social Democracy should become an independent political force acting as the leader of all democratic elements in the struggle against absolutism. A detailed rationale for these theses had been presented in a pamphlet written by Akselrod at the end of the year 1897.

Social Democracy and the Russian labor movement, Akselrod stated, were now faced with two equally possible paths of political development. The first perspective had been drawn by the Economists:

> The labor movement does not extend beyond the narrow channel of purely economic clashes with the employers, and in itself is on the whole deprived of political character, so that in the struggle for political freedom the leading ranks of the proletariat follow the revolutionary circles and factions of the so-called intelligentsia.

The second perspective, favored by the leaders of Osvobozhdenie Truda, visualized that:

> Social Democracy organizes the Russian proletariat into an independent political party, which struggles for freedom, partly side by side and in alliance with bourgeois revolutionary factions (insofar as these will be in existence) and partly by drawing to its ranks or by drawing along the most democratic [people-loving — *narodolyubivye*] and revolutionary elements of the intelligentsia.[14]

The two perspectives outlined by Akselrod admitted of one variable factor, the degree of political activity and organization which the bourgeoisie might demonstrate in the immediate future. But whatever the future would bring in this respect, Akselrod insisted, the adoption of the perspective drawn by the Economists would be equally disastrous. If the liberals proved to be weak and unorganized, a refusal by the Social Democrats to assume the leadership of the opposition would result in the inevitable failure of the struggle against absolutism. If, on the other hand, the liberals should demonstrate a high degree of political activity and organization, political passivity by Social Democracy would result in the transformation of the labor movement into a purely physical force, politically led and exploited by the liberal elements of the "possessing classes."

As the influence of Economism and Revisionism continued to spread, it became apparent to Akselrod and especially to Plekhanov that a "relentless" struggle would have to be opened against these dangerous heresies. In 1898, after the Economists gained control of the Union of Social Democrats Abroad, Plekhanov was already writing to his colleague: "I ask you once more: don't delay! Rout the enemy, for the time has come to rout him to the death. See to it that he doesn't anticipate us [i.e., resign before they throw you out, thus causing an organizational split]." [15] It was especially the inroads of Revisionism that worried and angered Plekhanov, for here was a doctrine which attacked on its own theoretical level the scheme he had erected to include the present and the future. He wrote to Akselrod in April 1899:

> The struggle against Bernsteinianism is the basic task of our movement. To the influence of our quasi-Marxists, we must oppose our influence as Marxist revolutionaries . . . If you [Akselrod and Zasulich] want to participate in the coming struggle, well and good. If not, I alone will follow the path which my duty as a revolutionist requires me to follow.[16]

For a few months, Akselrod's counsels of moderation held Plekhanov back. But after a moderate appeal published by Akselrod in August 1899 [17] failed to make the heretics see the light, an open break became inevitable. In March 1900 Plekhanov published a sharp polemical pamphlet addressed to the editors of the émigré organ of the Economists;[18] in April of the same year, the leaders of Osvobozhdenie Truda withdrew from the Union and, joined by a few faithful followers, founded the Revolutionary Group Social Democrat (*Revolyutsionnaya Gruppa Sotsial Demokrat*), for the announced purpose of defending orthodoxy.

How was the new group to proceed in its battle against Revisionism and Economism? What program of action was it to adopt to defend revolutionary Social Democracy? To draw up such a program required a concrete picture, which neither Akselrod nor Plekhanov possessed, of the social milieu in which the new heresies had arisen.

During the preceding five years, Plekhanov had been wholly concerned with the construction of the grandiose theoretical edifice within which he hoped to include all aspects of human development. Akselrod had been just as immersed — in his dream of how the working class would triumphantly grow to maturity and throw off the shackles of ignorance and oppression. So deeply had the two men been intent on the pursuit of these personal visions that they had lost the sense of the social scene in which Social Democracy was now operating; they could evaluate the new deviations only as failures of consciousness, instances of stupidity and ignorance, or — worse — as deliberate plots to enslave the proletariat to the ideological rule of the bourgeoisie. Plekhanov was writing to his colleague in March 1899:

> Thanks to you, I received Bernstein's pamphlet. So far, I have only read the philosophical section, and I am simply struck by its weakness! Weak, it is simply impossible to write worse. Concerning my philosophical article, he not only didn't answer anything, but merely threw abuse, badly and stupidly, and limited himself to that. Well, all right, we will deal with him and no good will come to this Sancho Pansa when I thrash him with his own polemical whip . . . Now, brother, we must fight to the death. I will say again the question is who will bury whom: Bernstein — Social Democracy, or Social Democracy — Bernstein? [19]

And in a declaration written under Plekhanov's direction by Koltsov in May 1900:

> The so-called "critique of Marxism" which represents a sorry reactionary attempt to weaken the struggle of the proletariat against the bourgeoisie in practice and to ease its "rapprochement" and reconciliation with it in theory, has become fashionable among our learned and half-learned, educated and half-educated petty bourgeoisie.[20]

Akselrod's comments about Economism were couched in as personal and irritated a vein. "Dirt, triviality, and stupidity," he wrote in 1899, in reference to an editorial statement in *Rabochee Delo*. "This is what this opus is filled with and what it gives out." [21] Even in his more sober statements, Akselrod was proving as incapable as Plekhanov of coolly examining the origins of the menace that was confronting them. In a sense, Economism constituted a rebirth of *buntarstvo*, of the desire to fuse with the unrestrained revolutionary impulses of the masses which had characterized the Populists of the seventies, Akselrod had noted as early as 1897.[22] Its refusal to "force anything" on the movement really constituted a tendency to *artificially* freeze Social Democracy at a primitive level of development, he added in his open letter to *Rabochee Delo*.[23] Plekhanov had reiterated this thesis when, a year later, he had criticized the editors of *Rabochee Delo* for their failure to allow for the development of consciousness by Social Democracy, for their insistence on looking "to the side of the working class rather than ahead of it."[24]

But why had this revival of "buntarstvo" suddenly occurred? What specific features in the development of social forces had — at this moment — given rise to it? To these questions Akselrod and Plekhanov were incapable of providing an answer: they had been far too possessed by their positive vision of the future to be attuned to the negative realities of the present. In the face of the current upheaval, their impulse was to resort to the accustomed ways of doctrinal squabbles — pamphlets pointing out the doctrinal errors of their opponents, accusations of evil motives, schisms, and excommunications.

History was never to show whether these weapons would have sufficed, for the task of presenting Social Democracy with a concrete program of action "focused at contemporary realities" was now shouldered by another historic figure, a still youthful *starik* of the Petersburg movement, Vladimir Ulyanov, a stocky, prematurely bald young man, who had already become well known in Social Democratic circles for his merciless, tough-minded defense of Orthodoxy.

When the Credo was published, Ulyanov was serving the end of his term of administrative exile in the village of Shushenskoe, a small Eastern Siberian settlement perched near the mouth of the Lena River. Since the outbreak of the storm, he had been fretting over his forced inactivity, desperately trying to piece together an image of the recent developments from the veiled comments in the letters from his friends. A copy of the Credo had been smuggled to the Siberian exiles in the summer of 1899. It enraged Ulyanov, who immediately drafted a protest, which was endorsed by other deportees and published by *Rabochee Delo* in December 1899. This resolution, which became known as "The Protest of the Seventeen," struck at the core of the Revisionist position. It vehemently denied that the Marxist program developed in Western Europe had been merely a reflection of "existing practice." "On the contrary, Marxism had appeared at a time when apolitical socialism (Owenism, Fourierism, pure socialism) dominated the scene."[25] Marxism had not followed the path of least resistance in Western Europe and should not follow it in Russia.

The "Protest" reëmphasized the fundamental principles that Plekhanov and Akselrod had been stressing during the entire decade. Social Democracy should become the independent movement of a class-conscious and organized working class. It should engage in both political and economic agitation; it should struggle against both political oppression and economic exploitation; it should organize for the overthrow of absolutism as well as for the eventual abolition of capitalism. Of these two tasks of Social Democracy, the most immediate, the most urgent, was the conquest of political freedom. To fulfill it, Social Democracy had to maintain its political independence and yet assume the leadership of all democratic elements: "Only an independent labor party can be a solid bulwark in the struggle against absolutism, and only in alliance with such a party, only in support of it, can all the remaining fighters for political freedom make themselves heard." [26]

The labor movement should not be permitted to follow the path of least resistance. Rather than limiting themselves to the passive expression of the workers' "spontaneous" economic demands, the Social Democrats were to train and organize them into a force capable of leading the struggle for the overthrow of absolutism, capable of achieving the political conditions required for the proletariat's full growth to political maturity. But how was this program to be achieved against the opposition of the Revisionists and Economists? How was Social Democracy to reorganize its broken ranks and successfully to resume its two-front struggle? A concrete answer to these questions presupposed a clear diagnosis of the ills from which the movement was suffering; it required a clear evaluation of the forces on which Social Democracy could count in the current struggle, as well as of the obstacles it was called upon to surmount.

During the remaining months of his exile, Ulyanov struggled with these questions, and his answers, his proposed prophylaxis, was the grand design out of which *Iskra* (The Spark) was born. From that moment on, the figure of Vladimir Ilyich Ulyanov would dominate the history of Russian Social Democracy.

AGAINST THE STREAM: THE YOUTH
OF VLADIMIR ULYANOV*

In Krupskaya's memoirs is recorded an account of Vladimir Ulyanov's first appearance in intelligentsia circles. It was at an Easter party in the spring of 1894, at the height of the intoxication with theory that marked the first steps of the Social Democratic movement in Russia.

As it always did on these occasions, the conversation had turned into a discussion of "social issues." One of the speakers was extolling the importance of the Committees for Illiteracy, the small group of well-meaning members of the intelligentsia who were "preparing the working class for the responsibilities of power," when suddenly a burst of dry laughter sounded in the room. The laughter came, Krupskaya later recalled, from a young stranger who had remained silent up to that moment. "Well," he said ironically, "if anyone wants to save the Fatherland with the Committees for Illiteracy, we won't stop him, I am sure." [1]

This was Krupskaya's introduction to V. I. Ulyanov. Later that evening, the self-assured young man escorted her home, and as they walked along the moonlit banks of the Neva, they talked animatedly — she about her devoted work for the Committees for Illiteracy — he, about his revolutionary dreams and hopes, about his past, and especially about his heroic brother Alexander, who, seven years before, had died on the gallows for his participation in a terrorist conspiracy.

Just as in the case of Plekhanov, it is difficult to find anything in the family origins or background of Alexander and Vladimir Ulyanov that

---

* I am heavily indebted for this analysis of Lenin's early revolutionary development to the accounts contained in Bertram D. Wolfe's *Three Who Made a Revolution* and in the unpublished manuscript on Lenin written by Valentinov (Mr. N. Volskii, who sometimes writes also under the pen name of E. Yurevskii). I particularly wish to express my gratitude to Mr. Volskii for so generously allowing me to use his manuscript, which constitutes an admirable collation of personal recollections, literary materials, and available primary sources on Lenin's early development.

forewarned that the two brothers would become revolutionaries. Their father, Ilya Nikolaevich Ulyanov, had followed with exceptional zeal and industriousness — but with absolute political rectitude — the usual career path of a successful civil servant in nineteenth-century Russia. After serving conscientiously as a teacher of science and mathematics in the Gymnasiums of Penza and Nizhni Novgorod, this man of modest plebian origin had been promoted in 1869 to the post of inspector of schools in the small Volga town of Simbirsk. And it was in Simbirsk, the birthplace of Karamzin and Goncharov, that on April 23, 1870, his second son, Vladimir, was born.

Simbirsk was then a dormant provincial town, a town of unpaved streets and modest homes, interspersed here and there by the more pretentious winter residences of the provincial gentry. Among the indolent citizenry of Simbirsk, the members of the Ulyanov family must indeed have stood out for the impressive solidity and respectability of their virtues. An earnest, plodding, good-hearted, but rather humorless man, Ilya Nikolaevich Ulyanov was busy from morning till night supervising his teaching staff, teaching them "better pedagogical methods," spurring on the improvement of school facilities and the construction of new buildings. In 1874 he was promoted again, this time to the position of director of schools for the entire province, and his new post kept him frequently away from his family, as it took him, winter or summer, on long and exhausting inspection tours. Now an Actual State Councilor, decorated with the Order of Stanislav, first class, His Excellency, Ilya Nikolaevich Ulyanov, had become an important and respected figure in the official circles of Simbirsk.

Were there any unorthodox or disturbing characteristics about this newly elevated member of the provincial gentry? To be sure, he displayed real passion in his educational work, believing fervently that all social ills, all human miseries, were the result of illiteracy and ignorance. For the sake of his work, he was willing to sacrifice his comforts — to spend his Sundays teaching his more backward or impoverished pupils, to ride through sleet or snow to inspect the construction of his precious *narodni shkoli* (popular elementary schools).* But for all this zeal about enlightenment, Ilya Ulyanov remained throughout his life a fervent opponent of terrorism, a faithful servant of absolutism, a man of deeply religious and conservative views, who attempted to serve the people's welfare within the bounds of the existing autocratic system.[2]

Vladimir's mother, Maria Aleksandrova Ulyanova, was as shining an

---

* In his seventeen years as an official in the Ministry of Education, I. N. Ulyanov was credited with doubling the number of pupils enrolled in the schools of Simbirsk province and with the construction of 450 new school buildings, an accomplishment that was described by a gentry admirer of his province as the expression of "a strength and vigor bordering on abnegation." ("Letter from a Reader," *Vestnik Evropy*, 1876, cited in Wolfe, p. 47.)

example of conventional virtues as was her tireless husband. The daughter of a doctor and landowner of Kazan province, she had received, like most women of the gentry of her day, the smatterings of a classical education. The only distinctive feature of this upbringing had been a certain moral intensity and religious seriousness, characteristic of the tradition in which her mother, a Volga German, had been herself brought up.

Much of this moral intensity and seriousness was reflected in the upbringing of the Ulyanov children. From the various biographical accounts, one pieces together the image of a conservative, disciplined, religious household in which, from 1879 on, all discussions on political and social problems were expressly forbidden — to safeguard the children from the revolutionary crazes of the age. Although unrestrained emotional demonstrations were frowned upon, warmth was not lacking in the Ulyanov home. Ilya Ulyanov and his wife were both disciplinarians, but for the upbringing of their children they relied on the force of persuasion and example rather than on punishment. In the evenings, the children would frequently gather around their mother, as she read to them from the great Russian classics, from the works of Pushkin, Gogol, Turgenev.

It was thus in a tightly knit, conservative, but by no means unhappy household that Alexander and Vladimir Ulyanov grew up. From early childhood, the two boys exhibited unusual intelligence and memory and an exceptional capacity for concentration and attention. These gifts served them well in the Simbirsk Gymnasium, from which they graduated, four years apart, with the gold medal, the mark of highest achievement. But temperamentally Alexander and his younger brother were as different as two brothers could be. The thin and gaunt-faced Sasha, as Alexander was called, was a quiet, even-tempered, reflective, somewhat melancholic child and adolescent — by all accounts a veritable Alyosha Karamazov — loved and even worshipped by all those around him. The reddish-haired and sturdy Volodya was, on the contrary, a loud and boisterous boy, always burning with energy, impatient, imperious, self-assured. Although choleric by disposition, he rapidly learned to control his temper; in class, he became a model of good behavior, a disciplined, quiet, and attentive pupil; but as soon as school was over, he would revert to his "natural" tempestuousness and irascibility, disturbing the homework of his more studious brother with his loud "noises and cries."[3]

As the boys grew older, these temperamental differences sharpened into differences of interests: Sasha became passionately involved in the study of zoology and chemistry, Volodya was attracted to history and literature; Sasha became seriously concerned with social and political problems and began to read the articles of Chernyshevskii and Dobrolyubov in his father's collection of old issues of *Sovremennik*, while

Volodya — exhibiting the indifference to social problems that reigned among so many young Russians in the middle 1880's — was content to lie on his cot and read over and over the novels of Turgenev. During the family's vacation on the summer estate of Kokushkino, Sasha would spend his time reading "serious works," gathering collections of minerals, or observing the behavior of frogs and worms as he drifted in the family rowboat down one of the lazy streams of the estate. Volodya would never open a book during these summer vacations; he preferred to spend his time lecturing his cousins on Turgenev or going swimming, horseback riding, hunting, or fishing — the summer occupations of a healthy growing boy.

By 1883, the year that Alexander graduated from the Gymnasium and entered the University of St. Petersburg, the two brothers had become estranged. It wasn't just that they were so different in temperament and interests; it wasn't just that when they roomed together during Sasha's rare visits home Volodya continued to lie on his cot reading Turgenev, while his brother assiduously sat at his desk studying weighty political and economic works. Sasha simply could not condone his brother's sarcasm, particularly when it was directed at his interest in political and social problems and at his scientific observations on the sex life of worms.[4] Vladimir Ulyanov's arrogance and sarcasm now pulled his brother away from him just as it would later alienate many of his comrades. Anna Ulyanova recalls that early in 1887, at a time when she and Sasha were both studying in St. Petersburg, she asked him for his opinion of their younger brother. "Sasha answered: 'He is no doubt very capable, but we will never become close friends, as a matter of fact, not at all.' 'Why,' I asked. Sasha didn't wish to explain." [5]

In the fall of 1883 Alexander Ulyanov matriculated at the faculty of physics and mathematics at the University of St. Petersburg, headed, by all expectations, for a distinguished scientific career. His first three years at the capital were indeed a period of brilliant and single-minded concentration on scientific study and research. In his courses he continued to excel other students; as early as 1884 he plunged into original research, and the next year he was awarded the gold medal of the University Council for a monumental treatise on the anatomy of worms.

During these first years, Alexander stood resolutely aside from student political activities, not due to any lack of interest in political and social problems, but because he believed that these problems could be solved only through deep and scientific study. But he was not permitted to maintain this self-imposed isolation. In 1886 a series of student demonstrations in which he had participated as a matter of duty led to the arrest and expulsion of a number of leading students from the university. Alexander was now besought by his university comrades to take a more

active part in political action. Guilty as he felt for his escape from the
fate of his fellow demonstrators — and anguished by his father's death,
which had occurred a few months earlier — Alexander was easily convinced that the scientific study of political problems was a luxury he
could no longer permit himself and that his duty was to act, to strike
now against the hated autocracy. But how were this handful of students
to fight? Their petitions to "society" had been ignored, their demonstrations forbidden. Terrorism seemed their only course, and they chose to
aim their first blow at the fountainhead of absolutism, Tsar Alexander
III.

During the first months of 1887, the youthful conspirators prepared
feverishly. Each one of them was assigned his task: Alexander, the brilliant student of chemistry and natural science, was picked to manufac-
ture the bomb that would be hurled at the autocrat of All the Russias.
But even while he was studying the composition of nitroglycerin and
preparing it in his homemade laboratory, he was pursuing his studies.
In the daytime, he continued to attend his classes and to work on his
master's dissertation on the organs of sight in worms. At night, he poured
over voluminous tomes on political and economic questions: the first volume of Marx's *Capital*, Plekhanov's *Nashi raznoglasiya* — for he did not
wish to die before having found some answer to the problems that had
troubled him.

It was not until March 1, the anniversary of the death of Alexander
II and the target date for the new attempt at assassination, that the
Okhrana caught up with the pitiful webs of the conspiracy. Alarmed by
an indiscreet message written by a member of the group — which they
had accidentally intercepted — the police arrested the young conspirator
on Nevskii Prospekt, and to their astonishment found him carrying a
crude nitroglycerin bomb, hidden in a hollow dictionary of medicine.
One after the other, the conspirators were placed under arrest and
quickly confessed to the details of their terrorist plot. Alexander's sister
Anna, who had innocently called at Alexander's home on that tragic
afternoon, was herself held by the police.

The startling news of the disaster that had befallen them reached the
Ulyanov family a few days later, and Maria Ulyanova rushed to Petersburg to petition the authorities for mercy. The grieving mother was permitted to see her son, but although he fell on his knees before her,
begging her to forgive him for the grief that he had caused her, Sasha
stubbornly refused to make any effort to alleviate his fate. At his trial, he
took upon himself full responsibility for the conspiracy. After being sentenced to the death penalty, he did not appeal to the Tsar for mercy,
explaining to his mother that, like a duelist who has already fired his
shot, he could not properly beg his opponent to spare him.[6]

On May 8, 1887, at three-thirty in the morning, the participants in the affair of March 1 were taken out of their cells for execution. They embraced one another, knelt before the cross, and refusing to have their eyes shielded, walked firmly to the hangman's noose. The third victim, Alexander Ulyanov, had allegedly spent the last few hours of his life reading his favorite poet, Heinrich Heine.[7]

It matters little for our purpose whether Alexander Ulyanov really resembled the idealized picture that his friends and family drew of him after his death. For it was with this ikonized image rather than with the real Sasha that Volodya now had to make his peace. Up to the moment of disaster, he had never paid Sasha much attention. Indeed, he had considered his brother a rather comical and pitiful figure, as he watched him bent over his microscope studying the reproduction of worms or sitting at his desk reading heavy tomes. But now Vladimir realized "how mistaken" he had been. He discovered that aside from his microscope, aside from his cherished worms and weighty books, Sasha had had heroic thoughts and strivings for which he had willingly given his life. As he later told his comrade Lalayants, all this came to Vladimir with the greatest surprise.[8] And this surprise — and the memory of his earlier contempt — now added to his emotional upheaval and to the burden of his guilt.

Vladimir had instinctively endorsed his brother's act, but he was also determined to discover the causes that had driven him to it. And so, during the months following the execution, he painstakingly quizzed those who had known Sasha during that last year in Petersburg about every detail of his life: about the actions he had performed, the words he had uttered, the books he had read. When, in the summer of 1887, the family left Simbirsk for Kokushkino never to return, Vladimir began to study systematically the works of Chernyshevskii and Dobrolyubov, which had been his brother's *livres de chevêt*. He read them in the old frayed issues of his father's collection of *Sovremennik*, the very issues that four or five years before Alexander himself had held, while Vladimir was thoughtlessly playing with his cousins.

Vladimir first elected to read the issues of *Sovremennik* that contained his brother's favorite work, Chernyshevskii's *Chto Delat'?* (What Is to Be Done?). And according to all accounts, the grandiloquent work of the "Realist" of the sixties, which he had once dismissed as a rather senseless love story, now "captivated" him as completely as it had his brother. After reading its first page, he did not leave the book out of his sight. Withdrawn from the family group, he read it for days on end, studying every page, every line, every word, with such intensity that many years later he would be able to recall the most minute and apparently insignificant details of the novel.[9] *Chto Delat'?* had made upon him the most overwhelming impression, "it had gripped deeply the whole of his being," he told his comrade Valentinov some fifteen years later, in the course of an argument about Chernyshevskii:

> When did you read *Chto Delat'?* It is useless to read it when one's mother's milk hasn't yet dried on one's lips. Chernyshevskii's novel is too complex, too full of ideas, for one to be able to understand and evaluate it correctly at an early age. I myself tried to read it at the age of fourteen, I believe. But this was a worthless superficial reading. After my brother's execution, however, knowing that Chernishevskii's novel had been one of his favorite works, I started to read it in earnest and spent on it, not days, but weeks on end. Only then did I understand its depth. It is the kind of book that influences you for your whole life. Mediocre works don't exercise such an influence.[10]

In the course of this conversation — which was held in a Geneva café in the early 1900's — Valentinov was amazed by Lenin's worshipping remarks about Chernyshevskii and by the violence with which he attacked his own (Valentinov's) "blind and monstrous" dismissal of "the greatest and most talented representative of socialism before Marx." By the time he sat down to write his biography of Lenin, however, Valentinov had arrived at the conclusion that Chernyshevskii, more than any other writer, more than Engels, more than Plekhanov or Marx himself, had influenced the decisive years of Lenin's revolutionary development.

Even a cursory examination of *Chto Delat'?* appears, to some extent, to bear him out. For it was from this novel that Lenin drew his vision of the Utopia that Russia would become after the advent of socialism — a land criss-crossed by irrigation canals which would create orchards, vineyards, gardens, and tropical plantations, where formerly deserted steppes had stood; a happy people, enjoying prosperity and leisure, thanks to the wealth of mechanical equipment that would service their factories and their fields. And from *Chto Delat'?* Lenin also drew the belief that the realization of this socialist Utopia would depend mainly upon the exertions of the men of the "new age" — the thin layer of " 'strong personalities' who [would] impose their character on the course of events" and give a definite direction to the "chaotic movement of the masses."

Lenin's study of Chernyshevskii did not end in that summer of 1887. In December of the same year, three months after matriculating at the law faculty of the University of Kazan, he was expelled for participating in a student demonstration and ordered to return to Kokushkino. It was a lonely winter that he spent in Kokushkino and just as lonely a spring. He passed his time reading from morning till night the books that were mailed to him from the Kazan library, the issues of the periodicals to which he subscribed, and the old magazines of the sixties that had accumulated in the family library. By the time he left Kokushkino, he later told his friend Vorovskii, he had read every single one of the articles and reviews that Chernyshevskii, Dobrolyubov, and Pisarev had published in *Sovremennik*, and had "read them more than once and to the last dot." [11]

In describing the influence that Chernyshevskii and Dobrolyubov exercised on Lenin, one must recognize from the start that there existed between him and his youthful forebears a number of remarkable temperamental affinities. When one considers the subsequent evolution of Lenin's thought, one is compelled to emphasize just as strenuously that the Realists of the sixties gave Lenin's world view a mold that was not completely discarded even after his conversion to Marxism.

It is of course true that some important features of Lenin's inheritance from Chernyshevskii and his collaborators could be easily combined with the tenets of the Marxist faith, since they involved the use of concepts — such as "the concreteness of truth," the "law of transformation" and the famed "dialectic" — that Marx just as much as Chernyshevskii had borrowed from Hegel. For this reason, Western commentators have generally played down the significance of Lenin's indebtedness to Chernyshevskii — failing to notice that in many instances, Lenin borrowed from his Russian predecessors not only the names of these Hegelian concepts but also the specific *interpretation of reality* that they had drawn from them. And it was this interpretation of reality that gave its unique twist to Lenin's Marxist world view.

Even more than Chernyshevskii, Lenin combined a demand for tough-minded realism with an imperious need to mold reality in accordance with his will. This demand for objectivity, Chernyshevskii — and Lenin — satisfied through their interpretation of Hegel's definition of objective reality and of objective truth. They drew from Hegel the idea that truth was always concrete, always dependent on conditions of time and place, and yet always expressed in accordance with logical laws and forms, which were not mere jackets of reality but actually reflections of it. In 1915, some twenty-five years after his reading of Chernyshevskii, Lenin would write in his *Commentaries on Hegel's Logic:* "Hegel really showed that logical forms and laws are not a simple jacket but a reflection of the real world. To be correct, he did not exactly point it out, but rather guessed it by a stroke of genius." [12]

What Chernyshevskii and Lenin sought and found in Hegel's dialectic was not an indication of the relativity of all particular phenomena, but a reliable method for approaching absolute truth, absolute reality — a method that would enable the individual to exercise his will in the process of reality. In his famous summary of Hegel's dialectical method, written in the sixties, Chernyshevskii had described it as "an indispensable safeguard against deviations from the truth [born out] of personal desires and inclinations."

Its essence is that the thinker must not be satisfied with any primitive conclusion, but must seek to find whether there are not in the object that he is thinking about, qualities and forces opposed to those displayed by that object at first sight . . . when this [dialectical] method was adopted, a thorough "all sided" research replaced the previous one-sided understanding of the object, and it established a live understanding of all the real.

Lenin and Chernyshevskii were voluntarists just as much as they were realists, and consequently they both drew from Hegel a belief that consciousness was not merely "a reflection of the essence of nature" but also a phenomenon "external" to it.* To make room for consciousness and will in the process of history, they utilized Hegel's law of "transformation of quantity into quality" — the idea that relative quantitative changes could lead to absolute qualitative transformations: they found in this concept a rationale for the breaks in continuity, the historical jumps — that is, the revolutions — that they sought to impose on the process of reality.

Given the similarities between Lenin and Chernyshevskii, significant differences can undeniably be found in the *form*, the cast in which their voluntarism was expressed. Lenin's sense of reality was considerably more deep-seated than Chernyshevskii's. Even as a youth, he had been aware of the need to discipline his will in certain settings or circumstances. As Lenin grew older — and wiser — this sense of reality matured into a realization that it was difficult, if not impossible, to apprehend absolute reality at a glance; that it was impossible to prescribe ahead of time a course that could be inexorably followed through all the shoals and reefs of the historical process. How, then, was the man of strong character to seek to impose his will upon the world, without falling into the void of unreality? Lenin found the answer to this question by giving to Hegel's dialectic a subtle interpretation — that was truly his own and not Chernyshevskii's or Marx's. The changing stuff of reality was the product of conflicts between forces and of the contradictions within them: "Something is alive," Lenin wrote on his comments on Hegel, "insofar as it contains contradictions . . . [insofar as it] seizes and preserves contradictions." [13]

Only by pitting the strength of progressive forces against that of backward ones, only by mastering the recalcitrant aspects of phenomena with the aid of their higher and more progressive forms, could the man of strong character discover the twisting boundaries of reality. Only by pressing against the world, could he hope to discover its limits and to

---

* Lenin wrote in his *Commentaries on Hegel's Logic* that "the consciousness of man does not merely reflect the objective world, but also creates it." In this study Lenin also quoted approvingly paragraph 225 of Hegel's *Encyclopedia*, "in which *cognition* (theoretical) and *will* (practical activity) are depicted as two ways, two methods, two means of destroying the one-sidedness of subjectivism and objectivism" (*Leninskii Sbornik*, no. 9, pp. 256, 255).

delineate his path. In 1915 Lenin jotted down, with the attached comment "very good," the following quotation from Hegel's *Logic:*

> In [the realization of] necessity begins the escape from the boundaries of the finite . . . it is said that reason has its boundaries: this statement expresses a lack of awareness that it is precisely through the definition of something like a limit, that escape from that limit is achieved. The nature of the finite is to excel itself, to negate its negation and to become infinite.[14]

To discover these changing limits of the world, Lenin would point out in his master treatise of revolution, his own *Chto Delat'?*, the revolutionist would need to exhibit a combination of persistence and adaptability, obstinacy and flexibility, unfaltering determination and cool-headed objectivity.

The aspects of Vladimir Ulyanov's affinity with Chernyshevskii and Dobrolyubov that I have so far discussed were masked for a long time under the veneer of Marxist ideology. But there were two specific features of his inheritance from the Realists that never escaped the notice of his Social Democratic collaborators. The first was a feeling of impatience, an emotional reluctance to wait for the propitious moment, which, in spite of all his tough-minded realism, Lenin never quite succeeded in conquering. This impatience was expressed throughout his revolutionary career in a preference for radical solutions to problems, and in a frequently irrepressible feeling of being "on the eve" of great events — in world history, in Russian affairs, or in the internal life of Social Democracy. A second and even more significant "heretical" feature of his affinity with the Russian Realists was a tendency to evaluate individuals and groups on a psychological and moral plane rather than on the basis of "objective" materialist criteria.

Just as Chernyshevskii and Dobrolyubov, Lenin would consider it his mission to fight against Oblomovism, to combat the somnolence, the apathy, the inclination to live by dreams rather than by action, which he ascribed to the Russian "national psychology." According to Valentinov, who cites as evidence a conversation between Lenin and Vorovskii, the young Vladimir Ulyanov first set this mission for himself after reading a critical article of Dobrolyubov's about Goncharov's celebrated character. Lenin had read Goncharov before seeing Dubrolyubov's article, went this reported conversation, but after seeing the article he reread the book with Dobrolyubov's commentary in mind, and looked at it from a new point of view.[15]

"Oblomovka [the name of Oblomov's estate] is our homeland," Dobrolyubov had stated in his article. "Who will free us from this stupefying quiet and inertia? Who can give us in understandable language the all-powerful word forward?" [16] Lenin was to repeat Dobrolyubov's characterization of Oblomovism with great frequency in the course of his revolutionary career, and with exactly the same intent. As late as 1922 he stated in a speech to an All-Russian Congress of Metallists:

> There was such a Russian type — Oblomov. He lay on his bed all the time and made up plans. Many years have passed. Russia has undergone three revolutions, and yet the Oblomovs remain . . . for Oblomov is not only a landowner or a peasant, he is also an *intelligent;* he is not only an *intelligent,* but a worker and a Communist as well. . . . The old Oblomov has remained [with us], and we must wash him, cleanse him, shake him and thrash him, in order to get some sense [out of him].[17]

Lenin's impatience with the Russian Oblomovs is all the more understandable, when we consider that he believed that they would have to be made to fight not merely "on the side of progressive and economic social formations, and in opposition to backward institutions and groups," but against the designs of evil men, against the plots of devils incarnate. And among these evil men, Lenin would group not only the partisans of absolutism, not only the reactionary sections of the petty bourgeoisie, but also and especially the liberal representatives of the class which, according to official Marxist doctrine, was the most progressive social group aside from the proletariat.* Lenin apparently developed this hatred for the liberals quite early — in response to the boycott to which the respectable elements of Simbirsk society had subjected his family, upon the arrest of Alexander. According to both Krupskaya and Valentinov, Lenin himself advanced this explanation. Valentinov reports that Lenin once stated: "From the age of 17, I began to despise the liberals . . . not a single liberal 'canaille' in Simbirsk came forward with the slightest word of sympathy for my mother after my brother's execution. In order not to run into her, they would cross to the other side of the street." [18]

Chernyshevskii had had this aversion for the liberals, and it was his "exposure of the liberals," his insistence on the moral duty of every right-thinking man to become a revolutionist, and his emphasis on the necessity for the revolutionist to discipline his mind and his feelings in fighting

---

* The Revisionist Peter Struve claimed to have perceived this heretical feature in Lenin's political outlook from his very first meetings with him, in the winter of 1894. He comments in his memoirs: "The doctrines of class warfare, relentless and thoroughgoing, aiming at the final destruction and extermination of the enemy, proved congenial to Lenin's emotional attitude to surrounding reality. He hated not only the existing autocracy (the Tsar) and the bureaucracy, not only the lawlessness and arbitrary rule of the police, but also their antipodes — the 'Liberals' and the 'bourgeoisie.' That hatred had something terrible and repulsive in it; for being rooted in the concrete, I should even say animal, emotions and repulsions, it was at the same time abstract and cold like Lenin's whole being" (Struve, in *Slavonic and East European Review,* XII, 593).

the liberals, that constituted, according to Lenin, Chernyshevskii's great services to the revolutionary cause, the services that made him the greatest revolutionary thinker before Marx. Valentinov quotes from this same reported statement of Lenin's:

> Chernyshevskii possessed an absolute revolutionary flair. One cannot point at a single revolutionist of his day who with such prescience and such flair understood and judged the cowardly, infamous, mercenary nature of every sort of liberalism . . .
>
> Chernyshevskii's great service was that he showed, not only that every right-thinking and really decent man must be a revolutionist, but also something more important: what sort of a person a revolutionist must be, what his rules must be, how he must proceed towards his goals . . . to achieve their realization.[19]

The "unorthodox" beliefs that we have just discussed, Lenin would continue to uphold articulately for a good two years after his conversion to Marxism. No significant or interesting details have been recorded of this "matriculation in Marxism," and we shall consequently skip rather lightly over it. We know that Lenin's conversion took place between 1892 and 1893, at a time when he was engaged in a rather dull law practice in the Volga town of Samara. (Thanks to the efforts of his mother, he had finally been permitted to take the examinations for the bar.) It was during these two years that he studied, in his usual thorough fashion, the second volume of Marx's *Capital*, Plekhanov's polemical writings of the eighties, as well as numerous other documents on the Russian and economic scene. It was also during this period that he frequented the old Narodovoltsi exiles who were permitted to live in Samara, and quizzed them, for days on end, about the conspiratorial techniques and system of organization of Narodnaya Volya — only to break completely with these aged and shattered figures, as soon as his Marxist views solidified. At the end of 1893, his initial indoctrination completed, Vladimir Ulyanov left Samara for Petersburg, impatient to make his mark as a revolutionist and as a Marxist.

The reader will recall that at the party where Krupskaya first encountered Vladimir Ulyanov, the latter had contemptuously dismissed the value of the Committees for Illiteracy that were then the fashion among the Social Democratic intelligentsia. Indeed, everything about the political temper of the age was repugnant to the twenty-four-year-old Ulyanov; the smirking self-satisfaction with which his fellow Marxists were watching the unfolding of the "inexorable laws" that they had discovered, the unqualified approval with which they were viewing the development of capitalism and the growth of the bourgeoisie, the easygoing and ineffectual pace with which they were proceeding in the organization of the proletariat. Yet Ulyanov was too recent and youthful a convert to feel in a position to attack head-on the established Marxist authorities in Petersburg. He elected, instead, to direct his first polemical blows at the representatives of the Narodnichestvo, whom he attacked for many of the sins that his own comrades were committing.

The temper of the Populists had subtly changed since the 1880's. Many of them now chose to ignore, rather than to deny, the continuing growth of capitalism, admitting thereby, in fact if not in theory, that the reforms that they were advocating could take place within the confines of the capitalist order. It was for this "pale liberal illusion" so unlike the "positive revolutionary faith" of their fathers, that Ulyanov attacked the contemporary Narodnichestvo.

The notion that, under the existing order, the peasant's lot could be improved by petty credit or administrative reforms was nothing but an idle dream, Ulyanov asserted in 1894, in a long polemical work entitled *Kto takoe "Druz'ya naroda"* (Who the "Friends of the People" Are). Russia was already a bourgeois society, well in the throes of capitalist development; and as capitalism grew, it would carry in its wake in Russia, as it had in all countries, misery and exploitation — of men, women, and children. Neither piecemeal economic reforms nor political freedoms would arrest this inexorable process, and the Populists' refusal to face the facts was a true reflection of their "philistinism," of their "plain lack of guts," of "their fear of officialdom and desire to depend upon it." The Populists' "nauseating" phrases about "progress" and "science," about "good will" and "struggle against injustice," were nothing more than "liberal dirt," "liberal empty chatter," "liberal cretinism," "liberal treacherousness."

If it was futile for them to pursue their dreams of reform, what were men of good will to do? To come over to the side of the proletariat, was Ulyanov's ready answer. This was what "reality demand[ed] of every man who refuse[d] to become the willing or unwilling henchman of the bourgeoisie."

These expressions of Ulyanov's hostility toward Russia's emerging bourgeois society could not have been left in so unqualified a form without denying the side of his personality that had been drawn to Marxism, without frustrating his need for realistic safeguards for action, as well as his insistence on the pragmatic exploitation of historical necessity. Ulyanov's Marxist "objectivity" did not stretch to the naïve belief of his young fellow-Marxists that the laws of history could do their work for them, but it did extend to a determination to utilize these laws to the advantage of Social Democracy:

> The idea of historical necessity in no way undermines the role of the individual in history. All history is made up of the reactions of individuals who are undoubtedly active figures. The real question that arises in judging the social activity of an individual is: what

guarantee is there that this activity will not remain an act isolated in a welter of contrary acts? [20]

Acting like a good Marxist, Ulyanov proceeded to find such "guarantees" in the abhorrent economic and social developments that were now unfolding. With all its evils, Russian capitalism was, in the last analysis, a progressive phenomenon since it carried contradictions that would lead to the socialist revolution; political freedom could not improve the situation of the proletariat, but it could measurably ease the conditions for its struggle against the bourgeoisie. From all this, Ulyanov drew what seemed to him an inevitable practical conclusion: The Social Democrats could make use of the Populists and even enter into an alliance with them for a common struggle against absolutism, provided that the Populists ceased to "masquerade" as a socialist party. The proletariat should fight the petty bourgeoisie insofar as the latter attempted to hold back capitalist development, but it could support it wholeheartedly in its democratic struggle against every remnant of medievalism and serfdom.

This was all good Marxist doctrine. Yet a questioning mind might well have asked: why all this emphasis on the petty bourgeoisie rather than on the bourgeois capitalist class per se? Did not the petty bourgeois peasantry constitute a less progressive social formation than the bourgeois class? Lenin was not to answer these questions until almost ten years later, and his answers, as we shall see, would introduce his first major break with orthodox Marxism.

A few months after the completion of *Kto takoe "Druz'ya naroda"* Ulyanov found a more suitable opportunity to express his hostility toward bourgeois liberalism and toward the easy-going determinism of his fellow Social Democrats. The pretext was the publication of Struve's "Critical Remarks," an analysis of Russian capitalist development which contained the first seeds of the future Revisionist position. Not only was Struve's essay filled with references to the progressive character of capitalism — as was usual in this period — but it also suggested that the shift from capitalism to socialism might follow the pattern of a series of transformations rather than that of a sudden revolutionary overthrow. Upon reading Struve's essay, Ulyanov immediately undertook to write a review of it, which progressively swelled to the size of a small volume.[21] Ulyanov bitterly attacked Struve's unqualified regard for the capitalist bourgeoisie and his notion that socialism might be achieved without revolution. The struggle for reform, he insisted, was but a way to mobilize the forces of the proletariat for the final revolutionary overthrow. The bourgeoisie was now ruling "life in general, and liberal society in particular." It was consequently necessary for the proletariat to break completely with the liberal elements of society, and to organize into an independent revolutionary force.

Ulyanov read a section of his review to a small Marxist circle, which Struve himself attended, in the fall of 1894. A few days later he read the rest of his paper to Struve, to enable the latter to prepare a reply, which was to be published, along with Ulyanov's critique, in a symposium of Marxist essays. That reading, which lasted several evenings, took place at Struve's apartment, the latter subsequently recalled, "and it demanded not merely attentive, but even strenuous listening on my part, and was interrupted by conversations which often assumed the form of long and lively discussions."

As may be gauged from the original title, "The Reflection of Marxism in Bourgeois Literature" (Struve, after all, still considered himself a Social Democrat), Ulyanov's critique was apparently quite cutting. In a mocking and condescending tone, he described Struve's point of view as "narrow objectivism," opposing it to "Marxism" (or "Materialism") with its central concepts of class distinction and class warfare. If we are to trust his recollections thirty years later, Struve, then and there, took an instinctive dislike to his critic:

> The impression that Lenin at once made on me — and which re-mained with me all my life — was an unpleasant one. It was not his brusqueness that was unpleasant. There was more than an ordinary brusqueness, a kind of mockery, partly deliberate, partly irresistibly organic, breaking through from the inmost depths of his being, in Lenin's way of dealing with those on whom he looked as his adver-saries. And in myself he sensed at once an adversary, even though then I stood still fairly near to him. In this he was guided not by reason, but by intuition, by what hunting people call "flair." [22]

By the time Ulyanov's article was submitted for publication, most of the critical shafts that he had originally aimed at Struve had been con-siderably blunted; "partly for censorship reasons," Ulyanov later ex-plained, "partly for the sake of the alliance with legal Marxism required for the common struggle against Populism." But the hostility toward liberalism that had pervaded the original draft of his review remained, in this final version, substantially unmodified. To be sure, his statements were now qualified by references to the progressive character of capital-ist development, but these pious gestures did not restrain Plekhanov from perceiving and gently criticizing the "primitivism" of Ulyanov's Marxist views, when the young man visited him and Akselrod during a short trip abroad in the spring of 1895:

> You are forgetting [Plekhanov reportedly told him] that our most important immediate goal is the overthrow of Tsarism. In moving toward this goal, the working class has to seek the aid of allies, and these allies — to a greater or lesser extent — can and must be found among the liberals. One cannot discard [the liberals] and slight them in the way you are doing. By your tactics, you are isolating the work-

ers from liberal democratic society and weakening, thereby, the general blow against absolutism.[23]

When Ulyanov called on Akselrod, the latter also remonstrated with him:

> You identify our attitude toward the liberals with the Socialists' attitude toward the liberals in the West. And I was just preparing for the symposium an article entitled "The Requirements of Russian Life," in which I was out to show that at this historical moment the immediate interests of the proletariat in Russia coincide with the main interests of the other progressive elements of society. For in our country the workers are confronted with the same urgent task as the other progressive elements of society: to attain conditions permitting the wide development of their free and independent activity — to speak specifically, the task of overthrowing absolutism. This task is dictated to all of us by Russian life . . .
>
> Ulyanov smilingly replied: "You know, Plekhanov made exactly the same comment about my article. He expressed his thought in the following metaphor: 'You turn your back to the Liberals,' he said, 'while we turn our faces to them.' "[24]

In assessing Ulyanov's political attitudes during this period, it is important to note that despite his hostility toward Russian liberalism, and toward Struve's optimistic image of its future role, despite the instinctive — and prophetic — sense of antagonism that pervaded the first meetings between the two men, Ulyanov considered it both proper and necessary to maintain with Struve, in this period and for five years thereafter, a rather intimate political collaboration. He would firmly maintain his belief in the usefulness of such a collaboration (against the increasingly vehement objections of some of his colleagues) as late as the fall of 1900, two whole years after Struve had broken with the basic tenets of the Marxist faith.*

To be sure, there were certain important points of agreement on which this collaboration was made to rest, points which loomed increasingly large as the end of the century approached: Both Struve and Ulyanov were quite certain of the inevitability, and indeed the desirability, of further capitalist development (even if they favored it for somewhat different reasons); both men were convinced that the elimination of absolutism was the most urgent task confronting Russia's "progressive classes"; both realized that in order to achieve this objective, the proletariat would need to be awakened and mobilized politically.[25]

---

* During the intervening period, Struve rendered much aid and assistance to Ulyanov: while Ulyanov was in Siberia, he sent him most of the research material that the latter used in writing his "Evolution of Capitalism in Russia"; he assisted Ulyanov in finding a publisher for this work, and himself published a number of his articles in the reviews that he edited; and he also secured for him the job of translating Sidney and Beatrice Webb's *Industrial Democracy*.

Yet, it is extremely revealing of these two personalities — and of the psychological climate in which they were operating during this period — that they were able to keep these points of agreement so clearly in mind, even as Struve drifted down the Revisionist path. However different the two men were in other respects, they had drawn a common lesson from their matriculation in Marxism: to govern their political instincts, and their passions, in accordance with a "conscious" world view and a realistic code of political action. Since rationality required that they join forces, at least until Russia's political awakening, they swallowed their feelings and remained dutiful, if wary, political allies.

After his return from his visit to Western Europe, Ulyanov's hostility toward the Russian liberals was somewhat toned down, and some writers have consequently deduced that the cause of this change — which lasted for a good six years — was the series of conversations that he had held in Switzerland with Plekhanov and Akselrod. Actually, some additional and more substantial reasons may be advanced for the independent-minded young man's sudden change of mood.

For one thing, Ulyanov was confronted, immediately upon his return to Russia, with a dramatic shift in the temper of the whole Marxist movement. The wave of industrial strikes that broke out in 1895 shook the Social Democratic intelligentsia out of its awed and passive contemplation of capitalist development, and drew it into the workers' economic struggle against their employers. The "spell" that the capitalist bourgeoise had exercised over the minds of the Social Democrats had evidently been removed.

Ulyanov's approval of the new program of economic struggle was nevertheless qualified by significant reservations. Naturally, he welcomed the turn that the younger members of the intelligentsia had taken from futile discussions to action in the real world. But even at this early stage, he detected and opposed the tendencies in the movement that were eventually to flower in Economism. He agreed that, in order to utilize the revolutionary potential uncovered in the recent strikes, the Social Democrats should reckon in their propaganda and agitation with the immediate needs and frustrations that had led to the outbreak of the strikes. But this did not mean that Social Democratic tactics should reflect passively the contemporary state of the workers' consciousness. Rather, these tactics should utilize each outbreak of dissatisfaction, each particular abuse by the employers or by the government, to widen the consciousness of the workers, to present them with a vision of society as a whole, and to point out to them the identity and the sources of strength of their present and future enemies, the antiquated absolutist power and the bourgeoisie.

The agitation that Ulyanov conducted among the workers of St.

Petersburg shortly before his arrest in 1895 reflected this position. It reflected his rejection of the so-called "theory of stages" held by many of his collaborators. Every speech, every leaflet that he drew up during this period, was founded on a conviction that the workers could not by themselves develop Social Democratic consciousness, and that the growth of this consciousness would depend on the active efforts of the socialist intelligentsia. And the program that he drew up for Social Democracy, shortly after his arrest, emphasized that the basic task of the future Social Democratic Party would be "to aid, by means of this struggle of the working class, the development of the class self-consciousness of the workers, to aid their organization, pointing out to them the tasks and goals of the struggle." [26]

In February 1897 Ulyanov was released from prison and sentenced to three years of administrative exile in Western Siberia. He spent those three years in the isolated village of Shushenskoe. On the Russian scene, these were years of continued growth for the Economist movement, of continuing political apathy on the part of bourgeois society. As the worried Ulyanov pieced this picture together from the meager news in the periodicals to which he subscribed and from the coded letters of his friends, his attention was naturally diverted from the "menace" of the largely nonexistent liberal movement to the danger represented by the political indifference of the Economists.

As Economism grew, Ulyanov's diagnosis of the current crisis became more and more explicit. He continued to admit that the struggle of the workers against the employers constituted, even at this early stage, a precious and needed source of revolutionary energy, which indubitably reflected the strivings of the workers toward socialism. But these strivings of the workers were as yet "spontaneous," unconscious in character, and they would not progress beyond this primitive state, unless the Social Democratic intelligentsia actively assumed the political leadership of the working-class movement. Was it possible to point to a single popular or class movement that had "assumed an organized form [and] founded political parties without conscious interference on the part of its intelligentsia representatives?" [27]

By now, Ulyanov had fully come around to Plekhanov's and Akselrod's view that Social Democracy should combine with other opposition elements for the struggle against absolutism. From the continuing political apathy of the possessing classes, he now inferred, just as they did, that it was possible and even imperative for Social Democracy to assume the leadership of all opposition elements (see above, pp. 90–91). But already some subtle differences existed between him and his future collaborators concerning the rationale and purpose of this working-class leadership.

In the eyes of Plekhanov and Akselrod, the need for Social Democratic leadership in the struggle for political freedom had arisen solely because of the political apathy and backwardness of the Russian bourgeoisie, because of the incapacity of the Russian representatives of this class to fulfill the responsibilities that had been those of their Western "confrères." Social Democracy would make up for this temporary lag in Russia's historical development, but this did not mean that it would be in a position to violate the laws and natural rhythm of this development, or to alter significantly the objective character of the coming revolution. "At the present level of Russia's development," wrote Akselrod in 1898, "the Russian proletariat cannot go farther than radical democratic liberalism in its direct practical strivings. At the present time, there cannot be any talk of conquest by the proletariat of political power for itself or [even] of reforms of bourgeois society under the Socialist banner." [28]

Akselrod's and Plekhanov's vision of Social Democracy as the carrier of the laws of history, as the midwife of Russia's historical development, required of its members a degree of restraint that was obviously impossible to achieve. The Social Democrats were to assume the leadership that the bourgeoisie could not as yet exercise. Yet as soon as the job of overthrowing absolutism was successfully completed, as soon as the bourgeoisie attained a sufficient degree of political maturity, the Social Democrats were to relinquish their leadership and to enter the ranks of the opposition. To understand how these two mature political thinkers arrived at so impractical a plan of action, we must recall the degree to which their vision of historical development, their image of the social forces operating in the world were frozen — in Plekhanov's case, by a belief in inexorable objective laws of history, in Akselrod's, by a concept of natural and harmonious growth. Social Democracy might be able to aid the operation of historical laws, it might be able to speed somewhat the natural rhythm of growth of social forces, but it certainly could not safely violate them.

Since history had singled out the Russian proletariat by assigning to it, at this early stage of its development, a degree of consciousness superior to that of any other social class,* its members could safely be expected to acquire the political maturity required to observe these rules. They could be expected to realize that the Russian industrial bourgeoisie, even though it was not yet aware of it, was now a revolutionary force and that "every step forward in its development, however careful and moderate, [would] bring it into conflict with the existing order." [29]

---

* Plekhanov had stated in 1891: "One of the new social classes in Russia — and the most revolutionary one — the proletariat — is already well conscious of its political tasks, insofar as its best representatives are concerned . . . [It] shows the most certain signs of political awakening. Politically, it has already outgrown the bourgeoisie. It has arrived earlier than the latter at the idea of political freedom" ("O zadachakh sotsialistov v borbe s golodom v Rossii," *Sochineniya*, III, 405–406).

They could be expected to understand that the proletariat was objectively unprepared to hold the reins of power with its own resources, and that any attempt to enlist for this purpose the aid of the peasantry could only end in disaster, since after the overthrow of absolutism the peasants would inevitably turn into a conservative and counterrevolutionary force.[30]

It was impossible for Ulyanov to accept a view of the world that imposed such rigid restraints on the initiative of the revolutionist. Concerned as he was with the effectiveness and ultimate success of his revolutionary activity, he too had to hold onto a belief in historical necessity, but this vision had to make infinitely more room for the role of the individual's will. Even at this moment, so soon after his conversion to Marxism, his world view was far more fluid — it emphasized "subjective factors" such as initiative, intentions, and will to a much greater extent — than orthodox Marxism allowed.

As early as 1897, he insisted that no one could predict the course or the political alignments that the various social classes would adopt in either the political or the economic struggle. In the struggle for political democracy, neither the bourgeoisie, nor the peasantry, nor even the intelligentsia could be considered as reliable revolutionary forces. "The hostility of these segments of the population against absolutism" was not "unconditional." Their "democratism" was "continuously looking backward."

> The bourgeoisie cannot but be conscious of the fact that absolutism is holding up [its] industrial and social development, but it fears a complete democratization of the social and political order and may at any time enter into an alliance with absolutism against the proletariat.
> The petty bourgeoisie is two-faced by its very nature. It is drawn to the proletariat and democracy on one side, and to the reactionary classes on the other . . .
> Educated people, in general the "intelligentsia," cannot but rise up against the harsh police oppression of absolutism, which stands in the way of thought and knowledge. But the material interests of this class draw it toward absolutism, toward the bourgeoisie. They cause it to be inconsistent, to make compromises, to sell out its spirit of opposition and revolutionary ardor in exchange for a government salary, or a share in profits and dividends.[31]

Only the proletariat could constitute "a determined foe of absolutism — incapable of concessions and compromises"; only the proletariat would be "capable of carrying the democratization of the political and social order to the end, because such a democratization would bring this order into the hands of the workers." The degree to which Russian society was to be democratized during the coming struggle would hinge largely on the efforts of the working class. If it exercised consistent and vigorous leadership, it would succeed in "pushing all the other opposition elements toward the left." It would "push the liberals toward the political radicals," and the radicals "toward an irrevocable break with the entire political and social order of contemporary society." [32] Even in the later struggle for socialism, the proletariat might be able to utilize other opposition elements and "thus" force the course of history.*

Nothing was fixed on the political map of the future. On the persistence with which the Social Democrats pursued their long-range program, on the political flexibility and finesse that they displayed in its tactical application, would depend the moment at which the liberals would bare their anti-democratic tendencies. On the Social Democrats' political acumen and initiative would hinge, as well, the political future of the "diffuse and fragmented" radical intelligentsia and petty bourgeoisie, which were now oscillating between the proletariat and the bourgeoisie. From this necessarily followed the character of the arrangements Social Democracy should make with other opposition elements. The Social Democrats should never consider these arrangements as anything but temporary and conditional alignments that might be upset overnight.[33] They should never regard them, as Akselrod had done, as alliances between political equals. Rather, at every possible moment in the zigzagging course of historical development, Social Democracy should strive to impose its will on its political "allies."

"In my opinion," commented Ulyanov in 1898 about Akselrod's description of the relationship between Social Democracy and other radical political forces, "the term 'utilization' is a more precise and suitable word than the phrase 'support and alliance.' The latter points to an equality with these allies, when (I am in full agreement with you on this) they must go to the tail [of the movement], even if they grit their teeth! They have not grown to the right to equality and they will never grow to it because of their cowardice, their diffusion, etc." [34]

The outburst of moral indignation against the non-Marxist radical elements contained in this letter expressed the fundamental assumption that would govern Ulyanov's revolutionary strategy and tactics in later years. He still paid lip service to the Marxist axiom that political behavior is largely dictated by objective factors such as socio-economic position. But hidden under this veneer lay an irrepressible conviction that the course an individual chose to follow in the process of history hinged

---

* As yet this heretical conviction was presented in very guarded terms: "In the economic struggle," wrote Ulyanov in 1897, the proletariat would "utilize only (and far from always) those elements of the petty bourgeoisie which are drawn toward it" ("Zadachi russkikh sotsial demokratov," *Sochineniya*, II).

ultimately on the degree of dedication, consistency, persistence, and re-sourcefulness that he managed to display in his struggle for the realiza-tion of an ideal. If a well-meaning individual succeeded in achieving these intellectual and spiritual qualities, he could not, at this stage of history, become anything but a Social Democrat.* If he failed to do so, history would condemn him to the position of a blind instrument. His fate would hinge on the will of more conscious actors, and depending on the degree of initiative and skill that Social Democracy manifested in the coming struggle, he would become its agent or the agent of its ene-mies.

To no man had the qualities of mind and spirit of the true revolution-ary been irrevocably assigned by "objective" factors. At no man had his-tory pointed its finger and dictated: you will be a true and consistent democrat; you will be a true and consistent socialist. As Ulyanov pon-dered over the significance of the Revisionist and Economist heresies, his conviction grew that even the proletariat, even the most learned Social Democrats, might deviate from the narrow and precipitous road to so-cialism onto the path that led to reaction. The flowering of these heresies clearly indicated that in its existing primitive and dispersed state, the labor movement itself threatened to become "the tail of the liberals," [35] and that even within the thin layer of the Social Democratic leadership were hidden "dressed up" liberals.[36]

Thus, the image of the political map that Ulyanov had drawn by the time of his return to political action was one of complex, confusing, and treacherous fluidity. Social Democracy was confronted with the cata-strophic perspective of dissociation from its "spontaneous" basis, the labor movement. Its existing primitive and fragmented state threatened to "drive the labor movement onto the wrong road, the road of narrow practicality," on which, "torn as it would be from theoretical enlighten-ment," it would constitute an easy prey for its disguised enemies.

It was at this difficult moment that the leaders of orthodoxy had to outline a path for Social Democracy. Theirs was a tremendous respon-sibility, for on their energy and judiciousness would depend, not only the position adopted by the masses that were now wavering between Social Democracy and reaction, but also the future course of the proletariat itself. They had to trace this path and induce Social Democracy to follow them on it, with the knowledge that their allies of today would be their enemies of tomorrow and that these enemies were hidden within their own ranks. They had to discover the tactics that would insure that the

* Ulyanov remarked in his 1897 outline of the tasks of Social Democracy: "We stated earlier that all socialists in Russia must become Social Democrats. — We now add: all true and consistent democrats in Russia must become Social Democrats" ("Zadachi russkikh sotsial demokratov," *Sochineniya*, II, 312).

conflict lurking (as we shall see) *even in the breast of the most faithful Social Democrats* — between the forces of consciousness and the disruptive stream of diffuse "spontaneous" impulses — would end in the triumph of Social Democratic consciousness.

It was against this background that the program of action with which Ulyanov returned to his comrades from his Siberian exile was forged.

PART TWO

The Iskra Period

7

"FROM A SPARK A FLAME SHALL BE
KINDLED": ISKRA AND THE STRUGGLE
FOR CONSCIOUSNESS

During the last few months of his Siberian exile, Ulyanov formulated the organizational plan that was to lead Social Democracy out of its current crisis. "Vladimir Ilyich began to spend sleepless nights; he became terribly thin," his wife Krupskaya later recalled of this period. "It was during these nights that he thought his plan out in every detail, discussed it with Krzhizhanovskii, with me, corresponded about it with Martov and Potresov, discussed with them the journey abroad." [1]

Actually, during these last months of the year 1899, Martov was still largely in the dark about his comrade's plans. All that he could infer from the cryptic notes that Ulyanov sent to his lonely Arctic outpost was that the latter contemplated some sort of journalistic enterprise in which he, Martov, and Potresov would combine forces with Plekhanov and Akselrod.[2] It was only after the completion of Martov's term, upon his arrival in Pskov in the winter of 1900 to meet with Potresov and Ulyanov, that the latter told him what he had in mind. His plan envisaged the creation of two organs, a bimonthly theoretical journal (the future *Zarya*) in which the issues of doctrine that were now dividing the leaders of Social Democracy would be thrashed out, and a more widely distributed biweekly newspaper (*Iskra*) that would undertake the organizational and ideological consolidation of the movement as a whole.

The contemporary crisis, explained Ulyanov, had been an inevitable result of the unusually rapid and uneven growth of Russian Social Democracy during the preceding decade. So rapid had been the spread of Marxist ideology among the intelligentsia, so "spontaneous" and hurried had been the growth of the working-class movement, that Social Democracy was now in a state of "fragmentation" and organizational anarchy. Isolated from one another, lacking the guidance of leading centers, its local circles were moving blindly and erratically — with no established ideological tradition, with no stable tactical or organizational rules to direct their course. Such a state of fragmentation and disorganization was inevitable at this stage of the development of the movement — yet it was now threatening to drive it onto the road to destruction, it was now promising to tear the bond between socialism and the "spontaneous" labor movement. The current vogue of Economism clearly evidenced that here was a real and present danger.

In the face of this catastrophic perspective, one major practical step was clearly indicated: the restoration of party unity, the formation and consolidation of a strong and nationwide party organization, capable of leading the workers' struggle under the banner of revolutionary socialism, capable of holding the members of the movement on a steady and consistent course through the treacherous cross-currents of practical politics.

But before this process of consolidation could usefully take place, insisted Ulyanov, "before uniting and in order to unite" the members of the movement had to "come to a decisive agreement about boundaries." [3] It was essential that the issues that were dividing and befuddling Social Democracy be brought to light and that the signposts on the path of its future development be firmly delineated. "There is no particular reason to fear a struggle," Ulyanov wrote to one of his followers in October 1900. "The struggle may break up a few individual friendships, but it will delineate relations precisely, determine which disagreements are basic and which secondary, distinguish the people who really are following another path. There cannot be any real critique without struggle, and without such a critique, a successful forward movement cannot be achieved." [4]

This would be the task of the new publications — to provide a platform for the debate of crucial issues, and yet to defend articulately a consistent point of view, to draw the outlines, the contours, of the political physiognomy of the party. During the necessary interval before the formal restoration of unity, it would also be the responsibility of these new organs to maintain contact among the various centers of party life — to insure that until the party again became one, its members should guide themselves by the permanent interests of Social Democracy rather than by local or momentary conditions. [5]

The implications of Ulyanov's program for the future of the party were not as yet sufficiently clearly drawn for Martov to take exception to them, and neither did Plekhanov nor Akselrod object when Potresov discussed it with them upon his arrival in Switzerland in the spring of 1900. When, in the summer of the same year, Ulyanov himself arrived in Switzerland to confer with the leaders of Osvobozhdenie Truda, he immediately came into serious conflict with Plekhanov. But in none of his clashes with his older colleague did the fundamental theoretical differences between them really come to light.*

This absence of overt theoretical conflicts seems all the more remarkable when we consider that faithful to his belief in the progressive character of historical necessity, Plekhanov made a series of significant changes in Ulyanov's draft of *Iskra*'s statement of policy. Absent in the final version of this statement was the emphasis laid in Ulyanov's first draft on the *inevitability* of the rise of Economism; missing was the claim that the fragmentation of Social Democracy threatened to destroy the tie between socialism and the labor movement. Ulyanov's "objective" analysis of the origins of Economism was transformed, in this final version, into a rather dogmatic condemnation of "tendencies" that were "hampering the proletariat from fulfilling the task of rallying under its banner all the democratic elements in the country for a decisive struggle against absolutism." [6]

During the first year of *Iskra*'s life, Ulyanov reiterated time and again the fundamental assumptions contained in his original draft of editorial policy. An article of his in *Iskra*'s first issue, the first one written under the pseudonym Lenin, reasserted the proposition that if the labor movement were torn from Social Democracy, it would inevitably degenerate and assume a bourgeois character:

> The task of Social Democracy is to instill Social Democratic ideas and political consciousness into the mass of the proletariat and to organize a revolutionary party unbreakably tied to the spontaneous labor movement . . . Not a single class in history has reached power without thrusting forward its political leaders, without advancing leading representatives capable of directing and organizing the movement. We must train people who will dedicate to the revolution not a free evening but the whole of their lives; we must prepare an organization so strong that we can enforce a firm division of labor in the various aspects of our work. [7]

In the fifth issue of *Iskra*, a statement entitled "Where to Begin" outlined the character of the organization of true and tested revolutionaries that Lenin contemplated and the dominant role that *Iskra*'s agents were

---

* The clashes that Lenin had with Plekhanov in August 1900 are described at length in a document entitled "Kak chut ne potukhla 'Iskra'" (How the "Spark" Was Nearly Extinguished), which Lenin wrote for the private enlightenment of his comrades in Russia. In this document and in his private correspondence during this period, Lenin's complaints and criticisms were directed solely at Plekhanov's authoritarian and suspicious nature, at his "insincerity," at his desire to dominate *Iskra*'s editorial board. Plekhanov's expressed objections to Lenin's draft of the statement of editorial policy were apparently confined to criticisms of his "coarse literary style" and "excessively tolerant" attitude toward the Economists and the Revisionists (*sic*). See "Kak chut ne potukhla 'Iskra'" in *Sochineniya*, IV, 309–324, and pages 139–141 below.

to play in its creation. The network of these agents would constitute the skeleton of the kind of organization required: "One sufficiently large-scale to embrace the whole country, sufficiently wide and many-sided to effect a strict division of labor, sufficiently tried and tempered to hold back from an open clash with the overwhelming forces of the enemy when they were concentrated at a single point, and yet capable of taking advantage of the clumsiness of the enemy and of attacking him when and where he least expected it." [8]

Given Lenin's distrust of the "spontaneous" labor movement, a discerning reader might well have wondered how long his organization of "true and tested revolutionaries" would need to maintain its tutelage over the working class. But no such query arose in Martov's, Plekhanov's, or Akselrod's minds during the first year of publication of *Iskra*. This was not an issue of political actuality as yet, and for the moment the thoughts of Lenin's collaborators were obsessed with but one problem, with but one danger, the rise of Economism, which, they all agreed, constituted a major threat to the existence of Russian Social Democracy.

Russia had not stood still since the days of the "Credo." Between 1899 and 1901 the political atmosphere had rapidly become charged: Russian society was finally coming of age. And the precipitant had not been the planned activity of the Social Democrats, but a "spontaneous" phenomenon, the student movement. In 1899, under the spur of a reactionary speech by the Rector of the University of St. Petersburg, a student strike had been organized in the capital. The strike had spread rapidly to other universities, until thirty thousand students from thirty different institutions of higher learning became involved. Although the students confined their demands to the restoration of the corporate autonomy of universities, the government responded with its usual brutality. Undaunted, the students struck again in 1900 and 1901. This time they demanded political freedom for all of society, and in Moscow, in Kharkov, in St. Petersburg, and in Kazan, their demonstrations were joined by both working class and bourgeois elements.

Once more the government was to resort to force, but this time its repressive measures would succeed only in spurring the long-awaited political organization of liberal society. Thus, the two years that followed the publication of the "Credo" ended with the first really tangible signs of the political awakening of the proletariat and liberal bourgeoisie.

In the face of this political ferment, the Revisionists moved with increasing assurance on the course that they had adopted in 1899. On one hand, they continued to lay the ideological groundwork for the development of a liberal movement, attacking in this connection the "exclusivism," the "dogmatism," that was blinding the Social Democrats to the necessity of uniting with other opposition elements in the struggle for political freedom. Yet, at the same time, they persisted in encouraging the political consolidation of Social Democracy — throwing their weight, at every available opportunity, with those very leaders (of its orthodox wing) who were attacking them for their heretical tendencies. There was really no inconsistency between these two facets of the Revisionists' policy: Struve and his confrères still lacked any substantial political following, and in the absence of such a following, the task of drawing the working class into the struggle against absolutism still seemed to them paramount. Since the leaders of Marxist orthodoxy were fully aware of the significance of the "political" struggle (in contrast to their Economist opponents), the Revisionists felt no hesitation about extending to them their political and financial support.

(Struve initiated negotiations for a collaboration with the *ortodoksy* in the course of his talks with Lenin and Martov, during their stay in Pskov in the winter of 1900, and he reopened the subject during his visits to Munich in December 1900 and February 1901. That these negotiations finally came to nought was not really Struve's fault: as we shall see, Plekhanov, and later Lenin, proved to be the chief stumbling blocks. By the beginning of 1902, Struve understandably lost interest as the Russian liberal movement finally came to life.)

While Russia's political awakening did not affect the platform of the Revisionists, it did impose a major tactical shift on the Economist movement, the second major opposition to Marxist orthodoxy. Ever since the middle nineties, the moderate Economists had predicated on two major propositions the emphasis they laid on economic agitation. They had insisted, in the first place, that Social Democracy would become a real working-class party only if its agitation and tactics were made to conform to the contemporary state of the workers' consciousness. They had affirmed, as well, that the development of the workers' consciousness would be a slow process, which would have to pass *gradually* through a number of stages. From an initial awareness of his immediate needs and interests, the consciousness of the individual proletarian would slowly grow into a more encompassing realization of his solidarity with other members of the working class — until finally he became conscious of the political position and interests of the proletariat in Russian society as a whole.

Until the very eve of the outbreak of political activity in the working class, the moderate Economists held onto these fundamental tenets. As late as August 1900, one of their spokesmen was proclaiming in the pages of *Rabochee Delo*, their chief journal in the emigration:

> The masses are really enlightened only by the experience of their own struggle, which initially must necessarily be economic in character . . . the economic struggle constitutes the first form of the mass

movement, the beginning of the class awakening of the proletariat, the school of its political training . . .

Social Democracy succeeds [in remaining the class movement of the organized labor masses] only because it arouses the masses to political consciousness in the very process of their struggle and preserves the mass character of the movement throughout its gradual development . . . From this follows the well-known gradualness of our agitational activity. The latter constitutes a pedagogical method for the purpose of attracting the masses to the movement and developing their class consciousness.[9]

This was the position of the Economists when in 1901 political demonstrations broke out all over Russia. The groundlessness of their basic assumption was now exposed overnight. Many workers joined the students' demonstrations; suddenly, without a background in the economic struggle, without the benefit of careful indoctrination, they marched through the streets of Kharkov and St. Petersburg, calling for political freedom. In the face of this new situation, the Economists' line shifted with dramatic suddenness. Overnight, the pages of *Rabochee Delo* and *Rabochaya Mysl* * became filled with calls for an intensification of the political struggle. In March 1901, barely a month after the first political demonstration, the editors of *Rabochee Delo* were unabashedly urging all Social Democrats to activate the workers' assault on the fortress of absolutism. Wholeheartedly endorsing the terroristic act of the student Karpovich, these editors insisted that "in the bitter struggle" that was opening against tsarism the workers should meet "terror with terror, violence with violence."

How was this drastic veer in tactics to be accounted for? Some of the more moderate leaders of Economism were willing to acknowledge the past errors that had made the sudden 180-degree turn necessary. Thus, in May 1901, Martynov frankly observed in the pages of *Rabochee Delo* that:

> The propaganda literature of the nineties had stressed particular economic events . . . under the erroneous view that such gradualism was required to change the workers' world view . . . [but] the rhythm of change of the workers' views does not follow that of the changes in the conditions of their lives . . . for the individual's world view changes with dramatic rapidity when the conflict between it and the conditions of his existence finally explodes.[10]

But if Martynov was willing to acknowledge the errors of the past, other leaders of the Economist faction were not as ready to admit to the same degree of fallibility. Some of them even quoted the sudden change

---

* Beginning with issue no. 11, *Rabochaya Mysl* appeared as the organ of the *Komitet Rabochei Organizatsii* (Committee of Labor Organizations) of the Petersburg Union.

of line as evidence of the essential correctness of their tactics, as proof of an adaptability to changing circumstances which they contrasted to the dogmatism of their Iskraist opponents. In the tenth issue of *Rabochee Delo,* Krichevskii wrote:

> The change of tactics of *Rabochee Delo* was a praiseworthy attempt to help orient the Social Democrats to the new situation that had arisen. Basing ourselves on the general Marxist view that *revolutions happen and are not made,* we attempted to act as every revolutionary should act at a moment which forewarns the coming of revolution . . . The task of a revolutionary Social Democrat is to hurry objective developments by his conscious work and not to depart from them or alter them through his subjective plans.[11]

It was on this issue of flexibility of tactics that the Economists now chose to fight the leaders of orthodoxy. "Correct tactics," asserted Krichevskii, "are the product of an interaction between the principles that point to the final goals of the movement and the concrete conditions in which the movement is operating. In other words, the activity of the party must be determined by the permanent and abstract element of principles on one hand, the changing and concrete element of surrounding conditions on the other." The editors of *Iskra* had signally failed to see that their tactics should constitute the product of such a process of growth. Instead, they appeared to view tactics as "a prearranged and unchangeable plan of action." By "leaning toward such tactics," *Iskra* was "leaning in the same breath toward a conspiratorial view of the preparation of revolution." It was underestimating the significance of the "objective" or "spontaneous" element in historical development and "relegating the objective, spontaneous process to a secondary role" — to "the final act of revolutionary development." Concluded Krichevskii:

> In our view, a tactical task begins to exist only when it is thrust forward by the very course of the struggle. Up to that point, this task is a program, a theory, a historical preview, all that you wish, but not a task of the struggle — not a task for the realization of which the forces of the party and surrounding conditions have ripened . . . Regardless of the successes of social science, regardless of the growth of conscious fighters, the appearance on this earth of a new social order will be primarily the result of spontaneous outbreaks.[12]

With these arguments Krichevskii was attempting to turn the tables on his orthodox opponents. By defining the "objective" process as the concrete and fluid conditions in which the workers actually lived, by making the changing "spontaneous" urges of the workers an inherent element in this process, he could demonstrate, to his own satisfaction, that his was the objective, scientifically valid position and his opponents' the subjective, dogmatic point of view.

In the same issue of *Rabochee Delo* an article by Martynov drew the practical inferences that were to be made from Krichevskii's view of historical development. Now that the proletariat had grown into a political force, engaged in a deepening struggle with absolutism, insisted Martynov, the Social Democrats had to be made to realize that their agitation should become a series of calls to the masses for specific actions, for concrete interventions in social life. Socialist propaganda might continue to be phrased in general terms, and it might continue to be directed at the illumination in the minds of the workers of the entire existing order, but agitation now had to be focused on specific and tangible objectives, on immediate and practical goals.

Iskra was failing to observe this rule. It had a "tendency," Martynov observed, "to stress propaganda for brilliant and final ideas at the expense of the progressive course of the unadorned struggle." Its excessive reliance on the written word, its attempts to impose its narrow tactics on the form of the revolutionary struggle, showed that *Iskra* had more faith in "the revolutionary influence of dogma than in the revolutionary effect of life." [13]

Ever since the inception of Economism, Plekhanov had responded to its rise with the irritation of a defied schoolmaster. As early as 1898, he had called for a struggle against the new doctrine, for he had been prompt to distinguish in it assumptions that ran directly counter to his own vision of the Marxist world view.* The Economists had insisted that, in order to make good its claim to represent the interests of the proletariat, Social Democracy would need to adapt its program and its tactics to the pace of development of the workers' consciousness — a pace which they considered to be a "spontaneous" process, largely impervious to the influence of the Social Democrats. The Economist had committed an even greater heresy — *they had dared to identify this "spontaneous" element with the objective basis of social development*, and thus with Plekhanov's own goddess, History, whom no revolutionist could ignore without turning into a woolly-headed and ineffectual conspirator.

Plekhanov had dedicated his life to the demonstration of the rationality of history, to the delineation of the objective laws that governed all political, social, and economic developments. And he conceived it as his task and that of other Social Democrats to communicate this insight to

---

* Plekhanov consequently rejected the opinion held by some of his colleagues that the views advanced by the Economists had been justified at one time (back in the 1890's). In reference to a statement Martov made to this effect, Plekhanov commented in a letter to Lenin: "It comes out in his article that Economism is now bad because life has outgrown it, but that before this it was necessary and suitable. In my opinion, [Economism] was always a big mistake, which was noticed only at the present time" (letter from Geneva, November 1900, reproduced in *Leninskii Sbornik*, III, 93–94).

the group that history had selected as its "most advanced carrier," the proletariat, and to indoctrinate and organize this group for the role that history intended it to play. "The ideal of revolutionary Social Democracy *is* the reality of the future," he flatly asserted in answer to Struve's statement that the long range program of the Social Democrats had the quality of a religious dogma. "The entire course of contemporary social development *guarantees* its realization; and this is why our certainty about its future realization has, in our eyes, as little in common with 'religion' as does the conviction shared by the *kritiki* and ourselves that the sun will come out tomorrow." [14] So completely was Plekhanov possessed with this vision, so completely was he convinced that it constituted the "reality of the future," that he was totally unable to discern the dangers that the Economists saw looming in it. Consequently, most of his articles about Economism sounded as if they had been written by an exasperated teacher addressing pupils he considered to be unusually dense.

It was absurd for the Economists to insist, just because the workers were not as yet politically conscious, that the emphasis placed by the leaders of orthodoxy on the struggle against absolutism did not correspond to the *real interests* of the proletariat, Plekhanov asserted in the *Vademekum*, for the real interests of the workers were determined by the sum total of their political and socio-economic relations, and not by the current state of their consciousness. "The sum total of social relations determines what interests the workers can have, but it doesn't determine which of these interests they have already conceived . . . [which of these interests] have already entered their lives." In fact, the consciousness of the masses always lagged behind the objective conditions of their existence. "But the one conclusion that is logically to be drawn from this," argued Plekhanov, "is that, with all the means at its disposal, the 'revolutionary bacillum' (whether it originates among the intelligentsia or among the workers) should aid the consciousness of the workers to lag as little as possible behind the real relations of a given society." [15] The Social Democratic intelligentsia would act as the catalyst of history; it would "attempt to speed up the adjustment of the workers' consciousness to the conditions of their lives." *

The proponents of the new theory had committed one fundamental error, Plekhanov concluded. They had confused the identity of the Social Democratic Party with that of the working class as a whole. Social Democracy represented as yet only a section of the proletariat; it stood

* In another article written in this period, Plekhanov points out that the only tasks that appear real to the Economists are those of which the means for realization already exist. Social Democracy cannot bind itself by the shortsightedness of some of its potential followers, he observes, because as "the conscious expression of the unconscious tendencies of the development of contemporary society," it is responsible for the future just as much as for the present position of the working-class movement. See "G-n P. Struve," *Sochineniya*, XI, 263–266.

as yet only for the most advanced, the most determined, and the most forward-looking of its elements in all civilized countries. The duty of these more advanced and more farsighted elements was clearly to point out to the more "shortsighted" section of the working class the direction of their forward movement and, as much as possible, to speed this forward movement along.*

When in 1901 the Economists took up a new line calling for greater flexibility in the tactics of Social Democracy and demanding, now that the proletariat had entered political life, that tactics be adapted to the spontaneous outbreaks of the workers' "fermenting" revolutionary urges and impulses, Plekhanov once more dismissed the arguments of his recalcitrant pupils. It was silly, he claimed, for the Economists to argue that a rigid differentiation should be made between the tactics to be adopted "in the new revolutionary situation" and the principles, the program, advocated by the Social Democrats. The sharp distinction that the Economists were now making between propaganda as a process of enlightenment and agitation as a call to action "in real life" was nothing but absurd, since both propaganda and agitation necessarily had to be directed toward one common goal: the development of the self-consciousness of the proletariat. Only the further development of this consciousness would insure for the proletariat the leading role that had historically been assigned to it; only its further growth could increase the workers' capacity for action in both the current battle against absolutism and the later struggle for socialism. The contradictory tactics followed by the Economists — their defense of terrorism, their neglect of the political struggle at one moment and their insistence twenty-four hours later on the immediate storming of the fortress of absolutism — were calculated only to dim the self-consciousness of the proletariat. And since this was the case, their presence could no longer be tolerated within the ranks of Social Democracy.[16]

If Plekhanov was so concerned over the danger represented by the Economists as to demand their expulsion, it was not because he shared the fear of some of his colleagues that the Economists were setting the stage for the domination of the labor movement by the bourgeoisie. Plekhanov was far too certain about the future course of history and far too convinced of the superiority of the working class over the bourgeoisie to harbor any such anxiety. But from his vision of the proletariat

---

* See *Sochineniya*, XI, 265. In another article, Plekhanov applies this same argument specifically to the political struggle, "the best possible school for the training of the workers' consciousness." He ends with the following conclusion: "Just because the working class, taken as a whole, is not yet prepared to go over to the political struggle, it doesn't at all follow that the 'moment' for such a struggle has not yet arisen for the party encharged with the task of training this class politically . . . In every possible instance, we must give to the workers the greatest possible portion of the political understanding that we possess" (G. V. Plekhanov, "Esche raz sotsializm i politicheskaya borba," *Zarya*, no. 1, April 1901, pp. 81, 86).

as the carrier of historical development, he derived a fear of a rather different order about the Economists' "blows" against the political indoctrination and organization of the proletariat. Just because the Russian bourgeoisie was so weak and so retarded a social formation, the attacks of the Economists against the political indoctrination and organization of Social Democracy might indefinitely retard the overthrow of absolutism. For Social Democracy was called upon to lead and indoctrinate all the other opposition elements in the struggle against autocracy.*

Plekhanov's ultimate conclusion — that the differences between the Economists' point of view and his own were so fundamental that he and they could no longer remain in the same party — was undoubtedly justified. While the Economists could not help viewing the members of the working class as creatures of flesh and blood upon whose day-to-day impulses and feelings the future of Social Democracy would ultimately depend, Plekhanov regarded them merely as agents of the historical process. The "spontaneous" day-to-day feelings of the masses came to constitute for the Economists the essential element from which history was made, but they remained for Plekhanov just a pale shadow compared to the irrevocable laws — projecting into the future — of which the working class had to be made conscious. Thus it was that while the Economists ended by equating the objective process with the "spontaneous" factor in history, Plekhanov came to identify it with consciousness of the future, believing that on the triumph of this consciousness over "spontaneity" the ultimate triumph of the proletariat would be based.

At first sight, it appears astonishing that Akselrod should have joined wholeheartedly in Plekhanov's denunciation of the Economists, for in many ways his vision of life came far closer to theirs than it did to his colleague's. Like the Economists, Akselrod instinctively rejected the assumption that the process of history was just the reflection of reasonable and inexorable laws. In his eyes, as in theirs, history was made by the activities of man, and man determined to a large degree the condi-

* See the final draft of the declaration of *Iskra*'s editorial board. See also the following statement: "We, the Russian Social Democrats, must remember that the twentieth century lays before us a task which has already been resolved in the West . . . The destruction of absolutism is absolutely indispensable for the successful and correct development of our party. If between the Western European Socialists and their great goal stands the egoism of the possessing classes, between our newborn party and the Western European socialist family stand, like a Chinese wall, the absolutist tsar and his police state.

"But these are not walls that cannot be destroyed by human energy. The Russian Social Democratic Party will assume the initiative in the struggle against absolutism and deal it its death blow, leaning on the more or less energetic, the direct or indirect support of the elements oppressed by the indeflectible edifice of absolute monarchy" ("Na poroge dvadtsatogo veka," *Sochineniya*, XIII, 65–66).

tions of his own existence. In 1901, for example, Akselrod wrote, in criticism of Berdyaev's theory of progress: "Marx's theory . . . states that the activity of humanity is conditioned by objective factors," [but it also affirms] "that historical goals are the results of a series of . . . conditions created by humanity and fulfilled by it as well." [17]

This belief that the future would ultimately be decided by human initiative had led Akselrod to the conclusion that the fate of Social Democracy would hinge, in the last analysis, on the *samodeyatelnost,* on the free and independent activity, of the proletariat. He was also willing to admit that the form that this activity would take and the role that would be played by other historical factors could not be forecast specifically. No one was in a position to predict the specific form and timing that the determining factors of the future would assume. No one, therefore, stood in a position to control them. The condition of uncertainty pertained even to the timing of the coming revolution:

> We are dropping from view the fact that the final blow against the enemy regime will be dealt mostly by forces and events outside of the control of the acting parties [wrote Akselrod in 1897]. The core of the extreme opposition parties' historical mission has been and will continue to be not only the weakening of the enemy's forces, but also the development of social forces capable of utilizing the first serious confusions in the ranks of the enemy army to disorganize it and to seize its positions.[18]

But from the relative obscurity of the historical process Akselrod drew practical inferences radically different from those of the Economists. That the pattern of the future was not laid out clearly made it, in his view, all the more imperative for the Social Democrats to concentrate every effort on the development of the consciousness of the proletariat and on its further organization. The working class would have to be prepared to exploit any of the fortuitous events that might shake the edifice of absolutism.

> In order to utilize the critical moments in the life of the absolutist government, the struggle of the revolutionary elements against absolutism must constitute a process of winning over social forces capable of defending a democratic constitution consciously and energetically. The preparation of such forces will be made possible only by energetic, tireless propaganda and organizational activity among the workers.[19]

Enormous responsibilities lay on the shoulders of the proletariat: to act as a gigantic lever raising all opposition forces in the battle against absolutism, to organize at the same time for the eventual struggle for socialism. In view of these responsibilities, in view of the uncertainty of the future, how could the leaders of Social Democracy possibly refrain from presenting the proletariat with those features of its program that could be drawn from the objective conditions surrounding its development? Such an outline was needed critically; it was needed "as a banner and path-tracing star for the more conscious, the more advanced segments of the proletariat, in their efforts to lift the backward working masses to a consciousness of their general class interests and to an understanding of the basic conditions surrounding their emancipation." [20]

During the crucial years that preceded the 1903 Congress, Akselrod was to remain deaf to the Economists' argument that the attempt to impose on the party of the proletariat the rigid halter of a program and tactics for which it was not yet psychologically prepared could result only in the development of a party dictatorship that would stifle the workers' initiative and *samodeyatelnost*. Akselrod was still blind to this possibility; when it finally materialized in 1903, he reacted with unfeigned astonishment. That he proved so much less far-sighted in this respect than his Economist opponents was due, perhaps, to a difference in background. Undoubtedly it was easier for self-conscious members of the intelligentsia painfully aware of their dissociation from the masses, to perceive the evils that might arise from an externally imposed indoctrination of the proletariat into the revolutionary faith than it was for this self-styled child of the oppressed masses, to whom this indoctrination had meant spiritual maturity and freedom.

At any rate, Akselrod did not rebel against Lenin's plan of ideological tutelage over the proletariat until Lenin attempted to perpetuate it through the organizational bonds of the party. Until 1903 Akselrod continued, blindly and unjustifiably, to attribute the Economist "tendency to hold Russian Social Democracy up at a primitive level of development" [21] to a hidden and dark desire to "emancipate the conscience of the intelligentsia from the 'flaw' of socialist doctrine." [22]

If the editors of *Rabochee Delo* had been asked to point out the member of *Iskra*'s editorial board whom they were most likely to shake with their arguments, probably they would have chosen Martov. For had not Martov been responsible for the publication of *Ob agitatsii*, the pamphlet the Economists had brandished as their platform since the birth of the movement? And before his deportation to Siberia, had not Martov consistently given voice to an earnest concern for the growth of the proletariat into a force capable of free and independent activity?

But now Martov was to show that he had become an opponent of the Economists as obdurate and irreconcilable as any of his *Iskra* colleagues. Like Plekhanov and Akselrod and Lenin, he was to remain unmoved by their criticism, unresponsive to their conciliatory gestures. What had caused this newly aroused antagonism — bordering on animosity — for men who, even if in error, were his former disciples? It was not that, overnight, Martov had laid aside his concern for the growth of a real working-class party or that, as the Economists finally affirmed, he had become converted to a conspiratorial concept of revolution. Even at the height of the struggle against Economism, we find him stating in the fourth issue of *Iskra* that "the moment of decisive attack on absolutism will be determined by a whole series of conditions, of which those having the most decisive significance do not depend on the will of any organized forces." And his repeated attacks, during the first two years of the publication of *Iskra,* against the advocates of political terrorism are founded on the thesis that terrorism distracts the Social Democrats from the pursuit of their one main task — the organization of the proletariat into a conscious force, capable of free and independent initiative, capable of striking with a united will.[23]

What the leaders of Economism probably failed to realize was that even in the earliest phases of his development, Martov's concern for the free and unhampered development of the workers' psychological resources had been balanced by an "awareness" of the existence in the outside world of forces against which the workers and their friends would need to steel themselves. Given this background, the simultaneous rise of Economism and Revisionism and the coincidence of these heresies with the political awakening of the bourgeoisie, could not fail to implant in his mind the suspicion that the Economists, just as the Revisionists, had become agents of a perfidious bourgeois enemy, intent on the spiritual enslavement of the working class.

Thus, when during their conference in Pskov the members of the new *troika* (Lenin, Martov, and Potresov) had been besieged with offers of collaboration and support by delegates of the Economist-dominated Union of Social Democrats Aboard (*Soyuz Sotsial Demo-kratov Zagranitsei*) and by the leaders of Revisionism, Struve and Tugan Baranovskii, it was Martov who, of the three collaborators, had greeted these offers with the greatest wariness and skepticism; it was Martov who had been most ready to attribute them to sheer political chicanery.*

* In his recollections of these discussions with the Economists and Revisionists, Martov had this to say in an account published twenty years later: "At this time, two representatives of the Soyuz Zagranitsei, P. Teplov and Ts. Kopelzon, arrived in Russia to contact the local committees for the purpose of calling a second party congress . . . They invited our troika to become the editors of the official party organ that would be restored . . . The representatives of the Soyuz asserted that the Soyuz did not stand for Revisionism, for the denial of political tasks, or for the organizational fragmentation of the party, and they attributed the split with Osvo-bozhdenie Truda to the authoritarian tendencies of Plekhanov and Akselrod . . .

"I attributed this step of the Soyuz to political chicanery, resulting from the change in the general situation: the new economic crisis, its accompaniment by the stormy strikes of 1899, which showed that the workers would easily go over to the political struggle; the general awakening of public opinion expressed by the student strikes, which indicated that the political isolation of the workers on the arena of

As Struve and his collaborators moved with increasing success toward the consolidation of a liberal movement, Martov's conviction of the interrelated character and deadliness of the Revisionists' and Economists' attacks on orthodoxy rapidly solidified. He wrote in December 1901:

> The struggle between the "critics" and "orthodox" Marxists is really the first chapter of a struggle for political hegemony between the proletariat and bourgeois democracy. In the uprising of the bourgeois intelligentsia against proletarian hegemony, we see, hidden under an ideological mask, the class struggle of the advanced section of bourgeois society against the revolutionary proletariat . . .
>
> The Economists are attempting to turn the proletariat into an instrument of the bourgeoisie. By restricting it to the immediate economic struggle, they are preventing it from developing its own political program, from becoming an independent political force, and consequently from entering into conflicts with the liberals.[24]

This bourgeois plot to prevent the proletariat from growing into an independent political force was a matter of serious concern for Social Democracy, Martov believed, for, if given half a chance, the bourgeoisie would be wily and selfish enough to conclude a deal with reaction at the expense of the people. In the face of the heretics' threat to stifle the growing consciousness of the proletariat, the defenders of orthodoxy had every right to pull the unconscious masses onto the correct path to political adulthood. In the face of "the treachery and violence of the reactionaries," it was their duty to temporarily "organize the movement from the top down so as to insure the careful selection and training of its members." [25]

Thus, it was with the conviction that the Economists were really

---

active struggle would soon cease . . . For these reasons, the clever leaders of the *Soyuz* had turned to the left, and their invitation to our troika was designed to tear the latter away from Osvobozhdenie Truda . . .

"But in relating to me their conversation with Kopelzon, neither Lenin nor Potresov were inclined to explain the acts of the Soyuz exclusively as a war ruse. On the contrary, they saw in it a recognition of our strength and a readiness to take it into account . . ."

And concerning his conversations with his two comrades before the conference with Struve and Tugan, Martov recalled: "Having acquainted myself with the views of my friends [both Lenin and Potresov considered an agreement with the Revisionists possible], I expressed my doubts as to the possibility of an agreement with the *kritiki*, if we were not to abandon our open and irrevocable struggle for orthodoxy . . ."

Lenin and Potresov "agreed to carry on our discussions with Struve and his colleagues on the basis of a clear, formulation of our own credo in reference to both the struggle against tsarism and the theoretical struggle against Revisionism and reformism (and Ulyanov was to prepare a document for this purpose, that he would read at the meeting). I predicted that, in that case, the agreement would be broken from the very beginning. 'We will see,' answered my comrades" (Y. O. Martov, "Pskov," *Leninskii Sbornik*, IV, 51–60).

agents of the bourgeoisie insidiously attempting to disarm the infant proletariat that Martov committed himself to Ulyanov's plan of surrounding Social Democracy with the iron ring of *Iskra's* faithful agents — until the day when it would rise as a united party, ready to strike with but a single will.

Of the editors of *Iskra*, Lenin alone showed himself sufficiently realistic to view Economism as something more than a subsidiary or tendential, if dangerous, phenomenon in the growth of Social Democracy. Plekhanov had been content to regard the new heresy as a mental aberration, as a fundamental misunderstanding of the role of "objective" factors in history. Akselrod had been quick to diagnose Economism as an effort to free the intelligentsia from its *dolg*, from its duty and debt to the proletariat, and he had considered this effort dangerous only because it might hinder the preparation of the working class for the struggle against absolutism. In this effort of the Economists, Martov, in turn, had discerned an elaborate plan of the bourgeoisie to enslave the proletariat.

From the very start, such ready-made explanations seemed unsatisfactory to Lenin. Just as much as any of his colleagues, he had been ready to condemn Economism as "a theoretical vulgarization of Marxism," as a "helplessness before contemporary criticism in the arena of principles." Just as much as any of them, he had been prompt to denounce it for "its attempt to reduce political agitation to trifles and to dissipate it in trifles," for its "complete instability of tactics," and for its "failure . . . to understand that the mass character of the movement increased, rather than reduced [the Social Democrats'] obligation to establish a centralized organization of revolutionaries, capable of preparing and leading the struggle . . ." [26] But unlike Martov, Plekhanov, and Akselrod, Lenin saw in the new heresy the expression of a significant and deep-seated *internal* crisis in the working-class movement.[*]

The Economists' "eclecticism and lack of principle in the theoretical sphere," their "diffuse," "fragmented," and "unstable" tactics, their opposition to any vigorous party leadership of the labor movement could not be summarily dismissed on the grounds of craftiness or of masked and evil intentions. They were the signs of a "passive servility," of a failure of nerve in the face of the inherent "spontaneous" character of the labor movement. The Social Democrats had to acknowledge the unpalatable fact that these objectionable features of Economism constituted, in a very real sense, basic tendencies of the working-class movement in and of itself.

[*] Lenin wrote to Martov's brother, S. O. Zederbaum, in July 1901: "Disorganization is far more dangerous than Economism, for the deepest basis of Economism in life lies, we believe, in disorganization, in primitivism" (*Sochineniya*, 3rd ed., XXVIII, 123).

To be sure, the "spontaneous" labor movement had developed in the working class some "embryonic" elements of consciousness. It had aroused in the workers "a sense of the necessity of collective resistance," and it had even lent some purpose and direction to this feeling of resistance. But the revolutionary energy that it had unleashed was being spent diffusely and "uneconomically," in sporadic clashes with individual employers or government representatives. These clashes constituted as yet nothing more than disconnected and uncontrolled outbursts of dissatisfaction, to which the workers were giving vent blindly and haphazardly, without insight, without the benefit of an image of the social order against which they were "spontaneously jostling."

So blindly and wastefully was the labor movement now expending its strength that it was proving incapable of keeping up the revolutionary initiative and enthusiasm of its members. To gain any degree of effectiveness and consistency, Lenin insisted, it would need to concentrate and focus the energy of the workers on the realization of significant practical goals: "The masses of the workers are [already] aroused to a high pitch of excitement by the outrages committed in Russian life," wrote Lenin in *Chto Delat'? (What Is to Be Done?)*, "but we are unable, if one may put it that way, to collect and concentrate all the drops and streamlets of popular excitement that are called forth by Russian conditions . . . into one single gigantic flood." [27]

Such a concentration of dissatisfaction would not be achieved until the labor movement acquired an established, panoramic vision of its position in society, and until, on the basis of this insight into its present and future, it arrived at a firm and stable set of tactics. Only if the workers could consistently hold before their eyes a picture of the relation between their contemporary tasks and the vaster and more long-range aspirations of their movement, only if they could thus maintain a sense of being part and parcel of a grandiose enterprise, would they be psychologically able to refrain from premature and wasteful attacks and to concentrate their energy on more useful, if less inspiring, tasks.[28] Furthermore, only an established program and tactics could insure the "critical" and "independent" attitude toward contemporary experience that was required of the working-class movement if it was to concentrate on its most important and timely objectives, if it was to isolate and grasp, in the whirling day-to-day world of politics, the successive links that would give it "command over the whole chain." *

---

* Lenin writes in *Chto Delat'?*: "A critical attitude is required toward this experience [of Social Democracy] and an ability to subject it to independent tests . . . The whole of political life is an endless chain consisting of an infinite number of links. The whole art of politics lies in finding the link that is least likely to be torn from our hands, [the link] that is most important at the given moment [because it] guarantees command of the whole chain, and once having found it, to cling to it as tightly as possible" (*Sochineniya*, V, 342, 369).

Social Democracy would need to cope with the fact that with its own resources, the proletariat was incapable of developing such a program and such tactics. "The history of all countries," Lenin asserted flatly, "shows that the working class by its own efforts is capable of developing only a trade union consciousness . . . [by its own efforts] the labor movement cannot develop a socialist ideology . . . The theory of socialism was developed by the [alienated] intelligentsia representatives of the propertied classes and could be brought to the workers only by them . . . only from outside the labor movement." [29]

Not only was the working class incapable of developing independently a socialist ideology but, unless the Social Democrats proved successful in their efforts to indoctrinate it into the socialist faith, it would inevitably fall under the spell of its enemies — it would inevitably be converted to the ideology of the bourgeoisie:

> Subservience to the spontaneous character of the labor movement, belittlement of the role of the conscious element, means, whether one likes it or not, the influence of bourgeois ideology among the workers . . . Since there cannot be any talk of an independent ideology being developed by the masses of the workers in the process of their development — the only [possible] alternatives are bourgeois or socialist ideology . . .
>
> Hence, to belittle socialist ideology in any way, to deviate from it in the slightest degree, means the strengthening of bourgeois ideology. Hence, our task — the task of Social Democracy — is to combat spontaneity, to divert the labor movement, with its spontaneous trade-union strivings, from under the wing of the bourgeoisie, and to bring it under the influence of Social Democracy.[30]

The working-class movement was thus threatening to fall under the spell of bourgeois ideology. Lenin agreed with Martov that this was a clear and present danger, not so much because of the evil designs of the bourgeoisie, but because the labor movement was totally dependent for the development of its political physiognomy on the aid of Social Democracy, at a moment when Social Democracy was itself in its period of infancy. Social Democracy was just in the process of formation; its "features" were only just "becoming outlined," while bourgeois ideology was far older, far more fully developed, and faced, under the existing regime, with infinitely greater opportunities for becoming widespread. "Yes, our movement is in its infancy," Lenin concluded, "and in order that it may grow more rapidly, it must become infused with intolerance against all those who retard its growth by their subservience to spontaneity." [31]

Up to this point, except for their underlying emphasis on the relative indeterminacy of the historical process, the *practical* implications of Lenin's argument conflicted in no serious way with Plekhanov's point of

The Ulyanov Family, 1878. Vladimir (Lenin) is seated
at the right, Alexander and Anna are standing in the
center and at the right. *Sovfoto.*

V. I. Ulyanov (Lenin), 1891. *Sovfoto.*

Leaders of the Petersburg Union of Struggle, 1897. Left to right: V. I. Starkov, G. M. Krzhizhanovskii, Lenin, A. L. Malchenko, Y. O. Martov, A. A. Vaneev. *Sovfoto.*

Y. O. Martov, 1921   P. B. Akselrod, 1921

G. V. Plekhanov

view. For one as for the other, the victory of the socialist movement would necessarily depend on the preponderance of "consciousness" over "spontaneity." But while Plekhanov considered that the development of consciousness would once and for all establish the supremacy of reason and eliminate the "spontaneous," elemental strivings of the masses from any significant place in history, Lenin refused to adopt so negative and contemptuous a view of the "spontaneous" factor, or so magical an image of the powers of "consciousness."

It had been, after all, the "spontaneous element" in the labor movement that had originally aroused the revolutionary instincts of the masses. It had been the "spontaneous" revolutionary strivings of the workers that had originally responded to the calls of the revolutionists.* Clearly, therefore, the "spontaneous element" was potentially a positive as well as a negative factor in history.

Naturally, the Social Democrats should work to convert this element into consciousness; they should dedicate themselves to the task of "bringing spontaneity to the level of their program." But this, Lenin realized, would be a long and arduous task. In the meantime, it was necessary and possible to guide the "spontaneous" strivings of the masses, to "bring them into close proximity to the party and thereby to fuse the elemental destructive force of the crowd with the conscious destructive force of the revolutionists." [32]

It was this assumption that the "spontaneous element" constituted an inherent feature of the working-class movement, with potentialities for good as well as for evil, with which Social Democracy would have to wrestle for a long, if not an indefinite, period that differentiated Lenin from any of his collaborators. It was this twofold assumption that led him to infer that a correct diagnosis of the future and an impeccable tactical plan were in themselves insufficient to secure the future of Social Democracy. The future would be secured only if these conscious elements were attached to the "spontaneous" movement — by unbreakable organizational bonds. Firm organizational bonds alone could insure that the working-class movement would consistently follow tactics based on "the conscious, active perception of objective conditions." [33] Only such bonds would make it possible for the Social Democrats to "utilize the flashes of political consciousness gleaming in the minds of the workers to raise them to the level of political consciousness." [34] Only they could prevent the unstable "spontaneous" feelings of the crowd from overwhelming the conscious forces of the movement and driving it into

* Lenin comments on the activities of revolutionary circles during the decade of the seventies: "Circles of heroes like those formed by Alexeev and Myshkin, Khalturin and Zheliabov, are able to fulfill political tasks . . . because their passionate preaching meets with response among the spontaneously awakened masses, because their seething energy rouses a corresponding and sustained energy in the revolutionary class" ("Chto delat'?" *Sochineniya*, V, 345).

premature attacks or premature retreats. "It is precisely because the crowd may overwhelm and crush the permanent troops," Lenin insisted, "that we must manage without fail to keep up with the spontaneous rise of the masses in our work to establish an extremely systematic organization among the permanent troops. The more we manage to establish such an organization, the more probable it is that the permanent troops will take their place at the head of the crowd and not be overwhelmed by it." [35]

Existing Social Democratic organizations had proved themselves completely inadequate for this task. The numerous local newspapers and circles which had mushroomed since the abortion of the central party organs had proved themselves in the majority of cases to be "unstable in their principles, lacking in political significance, and extremely costly in their expenditure of revolutionary effort." [36] The party was now in need of a very different kind of organization, one that would not only provide it with the guidance of a program but also keep this program before the working-class movement until it "acquired the firmness of a tradition." It needed an organization that would train its members to accomplish specific and, when necessary, minute functions and yet would imbue them "with the conviction of the necessity and importance of their work." [37]

Only an all-Russian newspaper of the type that *Iskra* was aspiring to become could successfully fulfill these two necessary functions. Only the publication of such a paper would provide the main line that was needed to guide the development of the party's "physiognomy." Only such a paper could "enforce a firm division of labor in the movement, and yet avoid its breakup into tiny fragments." [38]

> Pray tell me [Lenin rhetorically inquired], when a bricklayer lays bricks in various parts of an enormous structure, the like of which he has never seen, is it not a "paper line" that he uses to find the correct place to lay each brick and to indicate the ultimate goal of his work as a whole . . . that enables him to use every brick and every fragment of brick, so that joined with the bricks laid before and after it, it forms a complete and all-embracing line? And aren't we passing now through a period in our party life, in which we have bricks and bricklayers, but lack a guiding line visible to all?

Not only would the contemplated newspaper trace this complete and all-embracing line, the metaphor continued; not only would it constitute a collective propagandist and agitator, but it would also act as a collective organizer, in which respect it would be "comparable to the scaffolding erected around a building under construction, which marks the contours of the structure and facilitates communication among the builders, enabling them, thereby, to apportion the work and to view the joint results achieved by their organized labor." [39]

The grandiose role Lenin envisaged for *Iskra* was further spelled out in a detailed plan of organization, the main lines of which followed inevitably from his belief in the resilience of the "spontaneous element" and in the dangerous, and yet indispensable role that this element would play in the further development of the working-class movement. The network of organizations that he envisaged was to constitute a veritable spider web controlled from the center. The center was to be composed exclusively of "professional revolutionaries," of conscious Social Democrats wholly dedicated to the revolutionary group. These men would be entrusted with the task of guiding the movement on the narrow and precipitous path that alone would lead to the socialist era.

From this citadel of orthodoxy, the arms of the party's organizations were to be extended as far out as possible into the mass of the labor movement. Consequently, the party centers would not only watch over the development of local party newspapers and circles, but they would also have to encourage and control the development of the trade unions, the mass organizations of the working class. The trade unions would constitute instruments of control over the "spontaneous movement," and even more important, they would be the feeding grounds for the supply of new members and new leaders on which the party's future life would depend. Therefore, these mass organizations were to be as flexible in their membership criteria as the party centers were strict in theirs; they were to be as large as these centers were small; as public as the centers were secretive. "It would be far from our interest to demand that only Social Democrats be eligible for membership in the trade unions," Lenin explained. "The only effect of this would be to restrict our influence over the masses." [40]

While nonconscious elements were thus to be recruited into the trade unions, they were not to be permitted into the higher echelons of the movement. The Economists clamored that such a rule could result only in a dictatorship of the intelligentsia over the working class. Lenin answered that only by following this rule would the party be able to recruit the ablest members of the working class and train them into leaders. The Economists stated that Lenin's plan put everything upside down. They insisted that:

> Unlike conspiratorial organizations, Social Democracy can grow only from below, only from the unification of local organizations, for without firm, living, and wide links with the labor masses, it loses all significance. . .
> A newspaper cannot give rise to a party, but a party can give rise to a newspaper. [41]

But, unmoved by this criticism, Lenin reaffirmed the fundamental axioms of his credo:

I assert that no newspaper can be durable without a stable organization of leaders to maintain continuity . . . that the more widely the masses are drawn into the movement, the more necessary it is to have such an organization, and the more stable it must be (for it is easy for the demagogues to sidetrack the backward sections of the masses) . . .

[I assert] that this organization must be composed chiefly of persons engaged in revolution as a profession . . . [For in a country ruled by a despotic government] the more we restrict membership in this organization to [such] persons . . . the more difficult it will be to catch the organization, and the wider will be the circle of men and women from the working class and other segments of society who join the movement and perform active work for it . . .

Give us an organization of revolutionists and we will overturn the whole of Russia.[42]

Like Martov's *Ob agitatsii*, Lenin's *Chto Delat'?* was an attempted synthesis of some of the conflicting trends that had characterized the development of Social Democracy. Like Martov's early scheme, it made room for both "conscious" and "spontaneous" forces in the organization of the working-class movement. But while Martov's pamphlet had assumed that the workers "spontaneous" strivings could develop into socialist consciousness by an even and relatively rapid process of growth and had emphasized that the workers could become "conscious" on the basis of their *own* experience, even if this experience had to be interpreted for them by the Social Democrats, Lenin was now insisting that "spontaneity" would be a persistent element in the development of the working class for a long and perhaps indefinite period. *Ob agitatsii* had been predicated on the assumption that the development of the workers' self-consciousness was the one and only path to the overthrow of absolutism, and the scheme of organization that it had outlined was consequently intended for the purpose of aiding (and hastening) this process of growth, and for this purpose alone. Lenin's new organizational model was designed to secure the overthrow of absolutism by harnessing the persistent "spontaneous" forces in the working-class movement, by insuring that these forces would be guided — and economically utilized — by a "conscious" Social Democratic elite.

Well could the Economist Krichevskii observe that Lenin appeared to view *Iskra's* role as that of "a spirit hovering over formless chaos."[43] This was an insightful, indeed a prophetic, description of the respective roles that Lenin would assign to "consciousness" and "spontaneity" in the dynamics of revolutionary action. For implicit in the conception of "spontaneity" that Lenin had broadly sketched in *Chto Delat'?* was not merely a lack of faith in the capacity of the labor movement to grow to consciousness by its own resources, but also a basic distrust in the ability

of any man to outgrow his "spontaneous" elemental impulses, and to act
in accord with the dictates of his "consciousness" without the guidance,
and the restraint, of the party and its organizations.

The precarious relationship that Lenin ascribed to "conscious" and
"unconscious" elements in the human personality as well as in society
at large reflected a recognition of the centrality of human passions, and
a deepseated fear of their unrestrained expression. Lenin himself was
fearful of his emotions. The composure that he generally displayed at
the height of the controversies that plagued the history of Russian Social
Democracy was but a surface phenomenon: after the hectic sessions of
party congresses and conferences, he usually succumbed to severe de-
pressions and nervous disorders, and would go off, alone or with his wife,
on long hiking or biking expeditions to try to regain his mental and
physical equilibrium. Yet so great was his reticence to express his feelings, and so successful, on the whole, was his effort to control them,
that we have been left with few indications of the emotional surges that
seethed within him. One glimpse is provided us by an extremely detailed
account,[44] which is all the more illuminating because it was written by
Lenin himself (for the private enlightenment of his friends) of the
bitter clash that he had with Plekhanov, shortly after his arrival in
Switzerland in the spring of 1900.

Lenin and his friend Potresov had come to Zurich in May of that
year to discuss with Plekhanov, Akselrod, and Vera Zasulich the organization of the two publications (the future *Iskra* and *Zarya*) that
they were jointly planning to launch. On the day of their arrival, they
explored a number of tactical and organizational questions with the "old
ones," and were startled, according to Lenin's account, by the "dicta-
torial," "petty," "insincere" attitude that Plekhanov displayed about
every issue that came up for discussion. The following morning, Plekhanov dramatically announced that he "preferred" to withdraw from editorial responsibility, thereby frightening Lenin and Potresov into making
concessions that gave him two votes and, in effect, a decisive voice in
the new publications. When the newly constituted editorial board held
its first meeting a few hours later, Plekhanov apparently presided in an
even more autocratic fashion than usual, imposing his views at every
turn, brushing lightly over Lenin's and Potresov's objections — leaving
them with the feeling that they had been tricked into the concessions
they had made.

Lenin and Potresov were in a rage when they left Zurich that
evening, and as they walked to the railroad station, they vied with each
other in the violence of their outcries against Plekhanov. Their "idol had
collapsed," and they "recklessly trampled over it": Plekhanov had entertained unclean thoughts about them, he had shamefully treated them as
if they were nothing but self-seeking "careerists"; his threat to withdraw

from the editorial board had been "just a trick" — "a calculated chess move aimed at naïve pigeons." No, they could not, and would not, work with Plekhanov under such conditions; rather drop everything and go back to Russia than to be "pawns in the hands of such a man."

"Our state of mind that evening was rather hard to describe; it was so muddled, so downcast," Lenin subsequently wrote; but mostly he felt ashamed, terribly ashamed. Never before in his life had he felt such "veneration," such genuine admiration and respect for anyone, never had he comported himself toward anyone with such submissiveness, only to receive, in return, so rude a "kick in the teeth." And a "kick in the teeth" was precisely what he and Potresov had received: "Like children, we had been frightened into submission by the threat that the grownups would abandon us, and leave us all alone, and when we had cowered (what a disgrace!), we had been brushed aside with an incredible lack of ceremony." And all this had happened to him and Potresov, Lenin concluded, because they had been "enamored" of Plekhanov, and had behaved toward him like loving children:

> Had we not felt such love [for Plekhanov], had we behaved toward him in a more circumspect manner, we would not have experienced such a crushing comedown, such a spiritual cold shower . . . This was a most severe, an injuriously severe, injuriously harsh life lesson. Two young comrades "courted" an older comrade because of their great love for him, and, all of a sudden, he injects into this love an atmosphere of intrigue, and makes them feel — not like younger brothers — but like idiots who are being led around by the nose, like pawns that can be moved around with impunity, like ineffectual careerists who must be cowed and quashed. And the enamored youth receives a bitter lesson from the object of his love: to regard all persons without "sentimentality," to keep a stone in his sling . . . Blinded by love, we had actually behaved like slaves.[45]

Several facets of this account are of considerable psychological interest: the ease with which Lenin discerned in Plekhanov's behavior an elaborate and calculated "plot," the readiness with which he assumed that Plekhanov was bent on making him a "tool," a "slave" of his designs, the emotional pathos with which, even in the aftermath, he viewed the entire affair. But what most concerns us here is the moral that Lenin drew from the incident — that it had been his own reckless worship of Plekhanov that had precipitated the whole drama by confronting his colleague with an almost irresistible temptation, and that if only he, Lenin, had been a little more wary, a little more guarded with his feelings, this sorry affair might never have occurred. In this assumption was reflected the deepseated fear, which Lenin seems to have entertained all his life, that the free expression of his "spontaneous" impulses, and particularly the open display of his positive feelings, would leave him disarmed and vulnerable, open to annihilation or to enslavement at the hands of others. One is tempted to conclude that the iron grip that Lenin felt it necessary to assign to "consciousness" over "spontaneity" in his scheme of revolutionary action was, at least in part, a reflection of this fear of his own passions: "The enamored youth receives a bitter lesson from the object of his love — to regard all persons without 'sentimentality,' to keep a stone in his sling."

8

A PROGRAM FOR SOCIAL DEMOCRACY

In all his writings since *Iskra*'s first issue, Lenin had been insisting that the successful development by the proletariat of an "independent political physiognomy" would necessarily depend on the fulfillment of two conditions: the erection by Social Democracy of a stable program and tactics — the guiding line required by the working class in its growth to political maturity — and the creation of the tight network of organizations that would insure that the workers follow this "paper line" during their political infancy. In *Chto Delat'?* Lenin had elaborated a masterful plan of organization to satisfy the second of these conditions, but the fulfillment of the first, the erection of the program that would delineate the path to the future, he was compelled, however reluctantly, to leave in the hands of his older colleague, Plekhanov.

During the last six months of the year 1901, Plekhanov labored slowly and painstakingly to complete the draft of such a "definitive" program for Russian Social Democracy. For month after month, with rising impatience, Lenin waited for the completion of this draft. As the signs multiplied of the political awakening of Russian society and of the rise of political rivals for Social Democracy, his impatience grew unbounded. But Plekhanov was not to be hurried, for the program was to constitute, in his eyes, an exegesis of the process of history, a definitive commentary, which would "define the interests of the proletariat at every stage of its development, and provide the doctrinal foundation upon which the influence of the conscious members of the working class over its more backward elements" would be made to rest.[1] Ignoring Lenin's urgent queries, Plekhanov worked for six months over this ten-page document, carefully weighing every phrase, every word of his would-be doctrinal masterpiece. Finally, at the beginning of 1902, the draft was done, and Plekhanov proudly presented it for the inspection of his colleagues.

From his very first glance at the manuscript, Lenin found it objectionable and utterly unsuited for the purpose for which it had been written. Plekhanov had indeed written an exegesis, an explanation of the historical process, and this explanation seemed to Lenin infinitely too general, too vague, too abstract. He found nothing in this elegantly phrased document to distinguish it from the program of any other socialist party in Europe. He found no comments about and almost no references to the specific and unique political and economic conditions upon which he wanted to base the party's agitation against *Russian* capitalism.

In line after line, in sentence after sentence of Plekhanov's draft, Lenin's irritated pen found "vague and foggy generalizations" instead of the concrete and forceful phrases required of the program of a fighting party. Plekhanov had referred to "the decrease in the significance of small producers and to the rise of large-scale production under capitalism." He should have spoken instead of the "expropriation," of the "squeezing out" of small producers. He had referred to the "rise of dissatisfaction among hired laborers against capitalism," when he should have spoken of the "stirring of revolt among the workers against their exploiters." By the time he put down the last page of the manuscript, Lenin had come to the conclusion that Plekhanov's draft presented a picture of the historical process as some sort of "painless evolution," incorporating "no severe conflicts," "ending in nothing definite" — everything that this process was not.

Even more important, Plekhanov had slipped into some fundamental errors in his analysis of the actual and potential revolutionary forces in Russia. He had placed in the same category and thus, in effect, equated the rise of discontent, the stirrings of revolt aroused among the workers by capitalist exploitation, and the development of the workers' self-consciousness. This was a cardinal error, Lenin insisted, since the rise of discontent was a "spontaneous phenomenon," while the development of the workers' consciousness could be brought about "only by us," only through the active agency of Social Democracy. For the same reason it had been incorrect for Plekhanov to write that Social Democracy merely organized the struggle of the proletariat; he should have stated instead that Social Democracy actually *led* this struggle.[2]

In the second draft of Plekhanov's version of the program, Lenin discovered even more crucial errors of doctrine. This draft referred, in the same breath, to the stirrings of revolt among the workers and to the growth of dissatisfaction of the exploited masses (against capitalism). It stated that "international Social Democracy [stood] at the head of the liberation movement of the workers and exploited masses" and that the Social Democrats were organizing "the fighting forces" of this movement. These lines of Plekhanov's draft, Lenin strenuously complained, presented a totally false picture of the relationship between the proletariat and the petty bourgeoisie, i.e., the small producers. It was erroneous to juxtapose and "fuse" in such a manner the strivings of the proletariat and those of the petty bourgeoisie, for the strivings of the small producers were far from always progressive in character. Their dissatisfaction frequently gave rise to an "attempt to defend their exist-ence as small property owners and . . . to defend the foundations of the existing order and even to turn it back." In this process, the dis-satisfaction of the petty bourgeoisie was being exacerbated, to be sure, but this dissatisfaction was being frequently directed in opposition to rather than in favor of the proletariat. "In the affirmative we can and must refer only to the conservatism of the petty bourgeoisie," concluded Lenin's "Remarks on the Second Draft of Plekhanov's Project of Pro-gram," "and only in the conditional sense may we refer to its revolu-tionary character." [3] "It is true," he admitted in a later commentary, "that there exists in Russia a greater possibility for attracting small pro-ducers in our ranks than exists in the West. But this is only a possibility, not an actuality, and still we must begin by distinguishing the proletar-iat, as a class, from the rest of the population." [4]

Only by stressing the independent identity of the proletariat, by pointing at the gap that separated it from other social classes, could the program induce segments of these classes to support the working-class movement. For these segments would support the cause of the prole-tariat only as individual "elements," and not as "classes"; they would join the working-class movement "fully and unconditionally," only if they gave up their own "class point of view" and adopted the point of view of the proletariat. Thus, it was precisely in order to widen the following of the proletariat that the program should begin by distinguish-ing it from other social formations. Only by "isolating the proletariat before mentioning its role as a representative," by defining the class struggle as a "struggle between just two classes" — the proletariat and the bourgeoisie — could the program confront the small producers with their one tangible choice: to join the working-class movement or to become the slaves of the bourgeoisie. [5]

Upon reading Lenin's remark to the effect that the intensification of the struggle of small producers could be expressed in reactionary as well as revolutionary behavior, in anti-Semitism and Caesarism as well as in peasant unions against compulsory labor, Plekhanov commented in a letter to Vera Zasulich: "I believe that the more capitalism develops in advanced countries the more parts of the petty bourgeoisie and of the small peasantry will need to go over to the side of the proletariat. I very well understand how Engels laughed at the comrades who considered that the petty bourgeoisie [necessarily] had to be reactionary." [6]

In the perspective of their later history, the positions that Plekhanov and Lenin respectively assumed in this controversy over the Social Democratic program may appear, at first sight, astonishing. For it is Lenin, the subsequent advocate of the dictatorship of the workers and peasants, who is insisting on the reactionary character of the petty bourgeois peasantry. It is Plekhanov, who would later condemn Lenin's plan to mobilize the support of the peasantry for the "extension" of the democratic revolution as a program that could result only in "absurd and reactionary conclusions" — it is Plekhanov who is criticizing Lenin for his harshness toward the petty bourgeoisie.

Lenin's position must have seemed all the more puzzling at the time in view of the fact that he had been the member of *Iskra*'s editorial board who had evinced the greatest concern for the demands and needs of the peasantry. As early as February 1901 he had called for energetic agitation in the countryside based on the "evident local needs of the peasantry," and for more vigorous efforts on the part of the Social Democrats to widen the mental range of the peasants. Such agitation, he had stated, was an absolute necessity for the party, if it wished to stand at the head of the people in the struggle against absolutism.[7] And at this very moment, he was the author of the "generous" agrarian plank that was included in the *Iskra* project of program, a plank advocating the expropriation and return to the peasants of the *otrezki*, the segments of land that had been "taken away" from them after the Emancipation.

In his commentary on this section of the *Iskra* program, Lenin even added the note that when conditions ripened for the democratic revolution, Social Democracy would not fail to extend its agrarian program to a demand for the "nationalization of the land," a promise that brought him into conflict with every one of his colleagues, and especially with Plekhanov.* Yet even in this article, emphatic as it was on the legitimacy of the peasant's needs and on the possibility of mobilizing their support,

* Lenin remarked in his statement on nationalization of the land: "This demand (if one is to understand it in the bourgeois and not in the socialist sense) truly 'goes further' than the demand for the return of the *otrezki*. In principle, we fully support it, and at the proper revolutionary moment, we will not refrain, of course, from advancing it. But we are presenting our current program, not so much for the period of revolutionary uprising, as for the period of political slavery, for the period that precedes political freedom. And in such a period, the demand for the nationalization of the land expresses *far more weakly* the immediate tasks of the democratic movement in the struggle against feudalism" ("Agrarnaya programma sotsialdemokratii," written in February and March 1902, published in *Zarya*, no. 4, August 1902; in *Sochineniya*, VI, 120). Plekhanov sent Lenin the following comment about this section of his article: "The nationalization of land in a police state would signify a new and colossal strengthening of that state . . . [such nationalization] is permissible only as part and parcel of a demand for the nationalization of all the means of production." Even Martov, who had sided with Lenin during most of his controversy with Plekhanov, substantially took the latter's side on this specific point. The nationalization of the land, he wrote, was permissible only as "a direct prologue to the socialization of all the means of production." For further details on this controversy, see L. B. Kamenev's account in *Leninskii Sbornik*, III, 117ff.

Lenin reiterated that Social Democracy would not permit any concession of its point of view to that of the petty bourgeoisie and that it would demand, on the contrary, that the petty bourgeoisie abandon its class outlook and adopt that of the proletariat.

After reading the manuscript of Lenin's article on the agrarian program, Akselrod wrote to him in complete puzzlement:

> More than anyone else, Vladimir Ilyich, I objected to your fear of using kind words in reference to the half-enserfed peasantry, even though you recommended kind measures. I see some sort of mania in you on this point . . . In the program you oppose excessively dry formulas, deprived of every agitational element, but in a propaganda agitational pamphlet, you artificially confine your thoughts to bookish formulas of doctrine as soon as [the discussion] turns to the peasants.[8]

Akselrod's description of Lenin's attitude toward the peasantry was accurate as far as it went. Indeed, in a footnote to his commentaries on Plekhanov's second draft of the program, Lenin had stated in terms almost identical to Akselrod's formulation of his views: "The kinder we are to the small producer in the practical section of the program, the firmer we must be in the section [devoted] to the statement of [our] principles, not giving in one iota in our point of view." [9]

But was this attitude as inexplicable, as inconsistent with Lenin's system of views as Akselrod seemed to think? The discussion in preceding pages should enlighten us on this question. The chief obstacle to an understanding of this, as of other seemingly unintelligible aspects of Lenin's world view, is the fact that his Marxist scheme of social and economic classes constituted only an attempt, even if an earnest one, to find objective correlatives for a more basic subjective system of revolutionary values in which the intellectual consistency and willful persistence of the conscious makers of history was opposed to the wavering and half-hearted character of their unconscious agents.

In Lenin's eyes the petty bourgeoisie, in general, and the small peasant property owners, in particular, constituted a "spontaneous" unconscious element par excellence. To be sure, Lenin found an objective Marxist explanation for this phenomenon — the fact that unlike the proletariat and even the bourgeoisie, the petty bourgeois peasantry had a foot in the past as well as in the present. Born out of the "feudal" precapitalist society of estates, it had constituted since the birth of capitalism a class in the process of transformation, a class that was gradually becoming split into a small minority of wealthy property owners and a vast majority of landless agricultural laborers. But it was not on this vision of the future that Lenin's scheme of revolutionary action came to rest, but on the contemporary evidence that the vast majority of the peasants did not as yet belong to either one of these two categories.

Most of these peasants were still small property owners, and their views and strivings could indeed be described as "wavering," "half-hearted," and "contradictory" — the psychological features that characterized in Lenin's scheme the "unconscious" elements of society. Toward both the outdated "feudal society" and the rising capitalist order, the peasants' sympathies were singularly divided: The peasants yearned to throw off the last shackles of feudalism, and yet they were resisting the development of capitalist agriculture; many of them were striving to become bourgeois employers of hired labor, while others were merely attempting to hold back the tightening squeeze of capitalist exploitation.

In the wavering and conflicting strivings of the Russian peasantry, Lenin already discerned a great revolutionary opportunity for Social Democracy. What segments of this unconscious element were to be utilized by Social Democracy, and for precisely what purpose, he did not as yet really state — for his Marxist faith, his desire for objective correlatives for revolutionary action, still held far too tight a grip on his conscience. But his writings already clearly indicated that it was by recruiting the aid of the small and middle peasants that Social Democracy would maintain its leadership in the democratic revolution, and that Social Democracy would do so by turning these peasants against the bourgeoisie, against the very class that this revolution was theoretically to benefit most! "The Social Democrats will never take away the property of the small and middle peasant owners who do not hire workers," [10] Lenin wrote in 1903. "The bourgeoisie says to the middle (and even to the small) peasant: we will sell you cheap land, cheap plows, and you will sell us your souls, you will refrain from struggling against the rich . . . The Social Democratic worker says [to the peasants]: it is never fitting to sell your souls." [11]

The Social Democrats had to make every effort to win the small and middle peasants over to their side. But "going to the tail" of the peasant movement, scraping and bowing before every demand of the peasants, was not the way to achieve this goal. It was only by subordinating the agrarian platform to their over-all Social Democratic program, it was only by reconciling the demands of the peasants with their own "general aim of developing the class struggle in the countryside," it was only by insisting that the petty bourgeoisie abandon its class point of view and adopt that of the proletariat, that the Social Democrats would be able to wrest the leadership of the peasantry from the bourgeoisie and to maintain intact their own identity. "By setting these conditions we will develop the leading thread that a Social Democrat can hold onto, even if he is abandoned in a country hole, even if he is confronted by rather confused social relations," Lenin wrote; "and with the aid of this thread," his statement continued, "he will remain a Social Democrat in the solution of general democratic tasks." [12]

In Lenin's image of the petty bourgeois peasantry and in the tactics that he advocated toward this social formation, the two strands of his revolutionary world view were easily blended. In the "objective fact" that the peasantry was a class with a foot in the past as well as in the present, he found a justification, which could be reconciled with his objective Marxist scheme, for the demand that the peasantry be compelled to adopt the point of view of the proletariat. In the "wavering," "half-hearted," and "contradictory" strivings of this potential instrument of the proletariat, he found a basis for his transcendent belief that the world could and should always belong to actors endowed with "conscious" and dedicated wills.

The urgent tone that pervaded Lenin's demands that Social Democracy assume control over the peasantry and impose upon it its own class point of view was partly a response to a number of significant political changes that were now taking place on the Russian scene. The awakening of society that had followed the student strikes of 1899–1901 was marked by two major phenomena, a revival of the Narodnichestvo among the members of the intelligentsia and the political organization of a bourgeois liberal movement.

Beginning in 1899, the students' agitation had led to the rise of a number of heterogeneous Populist circles, ranging all the way from pro-Marxist to pro-liberal groups. The most important of these groups had united at the end of 1901, and a few months later, they organized a new Socialist Revolutionary Party, adopting as their official organ the journal *Revolyutsyonnaya Rossiya*.

While by the end of 1902 the SR Party had not come forward with a definite and consistent formulation of its program and tactics (for that matter, it was never to succeed in doing so), it was already giving voice to a series of rather clear-cut political assumptions. And in many respects, the assumptions of the SR's strikingly resembled the definition of political aims toward which Lenin himself was striving. Just as Lenin eventually would, the SR's were insisting that the coming revolution would not be purely bourgeois in character — that it would be "accompanied by great democratic and social reforms, which [would] lay the initial groundwork for future socialist construction." [13] Just as Lenin would, they were demanding that this revolution be conducted so as to thwart the schemes of the bourgeoisie, so as to make the bourgeoisie "tremble" at the decisive moment.[14] Just as Lenin, they were affirming that the desires of some socialists "to act only on the basis of complete certainty and with a guarantee of inescapable success [could lead only] to complete inertia." *

---

* *Revolyutsyonnaya Rossiya*, no. 15, January 1903. Compare this statement with Lenin's answer to Martynov's assertion that his agrarian program was an unrealiz-

But the SR's were pushing this emphasis on indeterminism and revolutionary voluntarism much too far. They were extending it to an insistence that the "individual energy and initiative" of the revolutionist remain "unaffected by calculations" of actual social trends.[15] This extreme voluntarism Lenin found abhorrent and dangerous, not only because it was beginning to contaminate many Social Democrats,* not only because it seemed to constitute nothing more substantial than the "revolutionary adventurism," the reckless outbursts of self-affirmation that periodically swept over all "spontaneous" unconscious movements, but also because it was combined with an image of the political map on which all the objective signposts for revolutionary action had been summarily swept away.

Indeed, the picture that the SR's were now drawing of the Russian political scene was "shamelessly" blurring, far more drastically than had Plekhanov's draft of the program, all the essential differences that separated the various political and social forces. The SR's were advancing a vision — all too tempting at this moment of political turmoil — of a consolidation of "the ideological forces of the intelligentsia and the mass strength of needy and oppressed people" [16] into a majestic revolutionary movement, led by the united ranks of the intelligentsia and encompassing all workers and all laboring peasants. Such a united movement, the SR's insisted, would sweep everything before it; it would not only create a democratic order, but it would also lay the foundations for the future socialist society.

All criticisms of the need for unity among progressive forces were false and bigoted, stated the SR's. No basic differences existed among the different groups of the intelligentsia; unity was possible even with the liberals, since the latter were going basically in the same direction as the revolutionaries, and only getting off at a different point. Some of the SR's even went so far as to make the heretical claim that the awakening democratic liberal movement was really not tied to the bourgeoisie at all — that it represented, rather, an older generation of the intelligentsia, the members of which were related to the revolutionaries as "fathers" to

---

able Utopia: "Our program must be realizable only in the wide philosophical sense of the word, in that not a single letter of it contradicts the whole of our socio-economic evolution. And as soon as we have correctly determined this direction (in general and in particular), we must — in the name of our revolutionary principles and of our revolutionary duty — *struggle with all our strength,* always and unceasingly, for our maximum demands. To attempt before the final outcome of the struggle to assert that we shall not attain the whole of the maximum is to stoop to opportunism . . . Is not the attempt to write off in advance the degree of success of our pushing [of the peasantry] philistine?" ("Agrarnaya programma," *Sochineniya,* VI, 101–102).

* The years 1901 and 1902 were marked by the formation of joint SD-SR committees in a number of Russian cities and by the conversion to terrorism of some émigré SD groups (e.g., the followers of the journal *Svoboda*).

"sons." "They do not state where they found [the presence of] the bourgeoisie," stated *Revolyutsyonnaya Rossiya* in reference to *Iskra's* criticisms of the liberal *Osvobozhdenie* movement: "In reality, *Osvobozhdenie* unites only the 'fathers' of the intelligentsia, while the 'sons' constitute confirmed fighters for the revolution . . . The 'fathers' are distinguished from us by the moderation of their tactics and demands, but this does not constitute an opposition in principle." *

Not only were the conflicts among the members of the intelligentsia inconsequential, but so were the differences between the proletariat and the laboring independent peasantry. Most of the Russian peasants were paupers, and therefore half-proletarians, the SR's claimed.[17] The majority of them owned their land on a communal basis, and even those of them who no longer did, still adhered to the view that the land belonged to no one.[18] The strivings of most peasants were consequently socialistic rather than petty bourgeois in character, and in no significant way different from those of the city proletariat. Commented the editors of *Revolyutsyonnaya Rossiya,* about the 1902 agrarian disorders in the Ukraine: "Yes, the contemporary peasant movement is an embryonic form of a more conscious and articulated future movement . . . we need only give a rational, scientific formulation to these principles [of the peasantry about collective ownership and equal utilization of land] in order to draw from them the pure idea of socialism." [19]

The new exponents of the Populist position were reversing the argument that had been used by their predecessors. The latter had affirmed that the workers were peasants in psychology, if not in practice. The SR's were now arguing that the peasants were, for all practical purposes, proletarians. In the light of these "socialist" strivings of the peasants, the SR's demanded that the city proletariat "fuse" with the peasantry in "one socialist camp." The workers were few in numbers and "on the basis of the [current] evolution of industry and agriculture, they [could] not expect a significant augmentation of their ranks." Alone, they would sooner or later be crushed, even in their struggle for a democratic revolution, but together with the peasants, nothing would stand up against them in their march toward socialism.[20] "What can the intelligentsia and the proletariat do without the peasantry, and, even more, in opposition to the peasantry?" rhetorically inquired *Revolyutsyonnaya Rossiya* in June 1902. "Nothing! What can the intelligentsia and the proletariat do together with the peasantry? Everything!" [21]

---

* N. Novobrantsev, "Osnovnye voprosy rev. programmy," *Revolyutsyonnaya Rossiya,* no. 32. Novobrantsev attempted to demonstrate this proposition by an ingenious and not wholly incorrect argument. The bourgeoisie was bound to the existing order by "a thousand ties," and it was, therefore, ridiculous to assume that it should work against its own interests by participating in a movement for political emancipation. It necessarily followed that the awakening liberal democratic movement was not bourgeois in origin or purpose, but rather an offshoot of the non-class intelligentsia, as the SR's maintained.

Plekhanov's first response to the appearance of the Socialist Revolutionary movement was far more sympathetic, infinitely more patient and understanding, than had been his reaction to the rise of Economism. Rather than point at the great differences that separated the SR's from the Social Democrats, he chose to emphasize the degree to which the SR program had been "influenced by the Social Democratic position" and the extent to which it differed from the platform of the old Narodnya Volya. An article on the new movement entitled "A New Wine in Old Containers," written in June 1901, ended with the following ringing conclusion: "The SR's represent flesh of the flesh — bones of the bones of the Social Democrats. This is why they should unite with them." [22]

After the formation of the SR Party and the crystallization of its views, Plekhanov was compelled to abandon this optimistic vision of the future of the new movement. Within a year, he was attacking the "unscientific character" of the SR's program and the "moral plane to which they invariably seem[ed] to restrict their evaluation of revolutionary forces." [23] But even these criticisms were marked by a sympathetic tone that stood in sharp contrast to the contempt and venom that Lenin was injecting at this moment into his attacks against the Socialist Revolutionary camp.

In two savage articles, written in the spring and winter of 1902, Lenin dismissed the rising SR movement as a spineless intelligentsia group who preached vacillating, contradictory, and fumistic doctrines, and yet were impertinent enough to attribute their "diffusion and lack of principles" to "broad-mindedness." [24] Yet in this "blind and vacillating group," Lenin saw a serious threat to the future of the revolutionary movement and to the independent identity of Social Democracy, for they were openly advocating political terrorism and other forms of revolutionary pyrotechnics at a moment when revolutionary leaders needed to concentrate every bit of their strength on the massive organization of their followers. The contemporary task facing the revolutionary movement was comparable to that of "burning down a virgin dark forest," Lenin metaphorically explained. Only a "general and concentrated fire" could effect a task of such magnitude, and to build such a fire the proper materials had to be systematically accumulated. Instead of working for this careful accumulation of revolutionary energy, the SR's were calling on the revolutionists to engage in "excitation," they were asking them "to send off rockets to knock down the highest tree" and thus to expend "all available materials, uneconomically and fruitlessly." [25]

But even more than the SR's "revolutionary adventurism," Lenin found dangerous their "complete failure to understand the revolutionary principle of the class struggle." The SR's refusal to depend on any single social class, their desire to lean equally on the intelligentsia, the proletariat, and the peasantry, was conducive only to the "enslavement of the proletariat by bourgeois democracy." [26] It was this tendency of the SR's to blur class distinctions that impelled Lenin, as early as June 1902, to call for an implacable war upon them. It was in the light of this emerging trend on the Russian political scene that he attacked so vehemently the conciliatory character of Plekhanov's draft of the program.

But in order to fully understand the timing — and the vehemence — of Lenin's attacks of Plekhanov's draft, and against the SR's and the petty bourgeoisie as a whole, it is necessary to place Lenin's outbursts against the background of the birth of the liberal movement, of the growth of Russian bourgeois democracy.

Ever since the 1880's, most of the Russian Marxists had been waiting, with mixed feelings in many cases, for the appearance of a bourgeois liberal movement, for the rise of the political formation that, their masters had confidently predicted, would inevitably accompany the further development of capitalism. In 1899, the potential leaders for such a movement had appeared in the persons of the Revisionist *kritiki* — Struve, Bulgakov, Tugan Baranovskii — and in the following months, most of these kritiki had indeed set on the course that Plekhanov and Akselrod had predicted they would follow: they had broken their remaining Marxist ties and proceeded to outline the political and philosophical foundations for a new liberal faith. But it was not until 1901 that the political climate ripened sufficiently for these "leaders" to gain substantial following. With the student strikes and the first political demonstrations, the opportunity finally came, and Struve and his disciples were quick to seize upon it.

In the spring of 1901, Struve caused to be published abroad a secret memorandum that Witte had drawn up for the attention of the tsar. Struve used this document, which had stated that institutions of local self-government such as the zemstva were irreconcilable with the remainder of the absolutist edifice, to stress the significance of the zemstva and to call for the formation of a moderate liberal party. In March 1902 a series of private zemstvo conferences agreed on the publication abroad of a moderate liberal organ, and three months later, thanks largely to Struve's efforts, the first issue of this organ, *Osvobozhdenie* (Emancipation), was published in Stuttgart. During its first year of publication, the journal followed a moderate and temporizing course. The keynote of its platform was sounded by an editorial in its first issue, which called for a political "reorganization of the state order" through the agency of the existing organs of self-government, the zemstva and city assemblies:

> It would be desirable to leave to existing organs of self-government the right to select deputies not only from . . . the ranks of the zemstvo and city electors, but also from the whole of Russian society.

Such a course is preferable to the jump into the unknown that all attempts at ad hoc elections would constitute, [since they would have to cope with] inevitable governmental pressures and unpredictable states of mind among social classes unaccustomed to political life.[27]

The moderate line that *Osvobozhdenie* adopted during the year 1902 was largely dictated by its desire to enlist the support of zemstvo circles: conservative tendencies predominated in them at this moment as a result of the government's promise to widen the scope of their economic activities — provided they refrained from political agitation. The platform of *Osvobozhdenie* subsequently would be democratized, as the center of gravity of the liberal movement shifted from the liberal gentry to the professional classes, but for the moment at least, the pronouncements of the liberal organ were calculated to feed Lenin's and Martov's suspicion that the liberals were "opportunistic politicians," bent on stealing the benefits of democracy away from the long-suffering masses.

Martov had been extremely doubtful of the possibility of collaborating with Struve and his colleagues, even during the period when the Revisionists still viewed themselves as a group operating within the fold of Social Democracy, and he had consistently voiced his skepticism to his comrades about their long negotiations with them.[28] Already in Pskov, he had detected in Struve's eyes the "derisive gleam" of a satanic plotter who would "attempt to ride on the workers' backs and, at a critical moment, to exploit the labor movement." And his worst suspicions seemed to him confirmed now that Struve was candidly stating in the pages of *Osvobozhdenie* that "a moderate party [would] win out from the intensifying struggle between the extreme elements of society . . . and revolutionary Social Democracy." How else was one to evaluate the motivations of a "liberal" leader who directed at the autocratic power the arguments that it was "in the government's own interest to have reforms from above rather than reforms from below," that it was "better to have peaceful change than revolutionary change." [29]

Thus the original course of *Osvobozhdenie* inevitably strengthened Martov's long-held suspicion that the Revisionists' attack against Marxist orthodoxy had marked the opening of "a struggle for political hegemony between the proletariat and bourgeois democracy," [30] in which the task of Social Democracy would be to organize the working class into a mature and independent political force, "confident of its capacity to overthrow bourgeois society." [31]

> The constitutionalists are attempting to organize the liberal bourgeoisie, not so much to struggle for the overthrow of absolutism, as to prepare for a struggle for the right to rule undividedly over Russia after the victory of the people over absolutism . . . The aim of *Osvobozhdenie* is to bring forward the opinion it is organizing with a demand for a constitution at the moment when the government,

under the threat of the revolutionary movement, will finally recognize the need for reform.*

If the course adopted by *Osvobozhdenie* further confirmed Martov's prejudices against liberalism, it did not in the least shake Plekhanov's conviction that the liberals were "intelligent" and "incorruptible" men[32] — though, to be sure, less intelligent and less incorruptible than their natural leaders and allies in the democratic revolution, the Social Democrats. Plekhanov never quite lost the conviction that, next to the proletariat, the bourgeoisie was the most advanced, the most progressive social class in Russia. And since it was so progressive a class, he naturally assumed that its members would be rational enough to perceive the reasonableness of his arguments.

It seemed evident to Plekhanov that the immediate task of the proletariat was the overthrow of absolutism, the conquest of political freedom, which would give the labor movement "the possibility to grow, develop, and organize for the socialist revolution." Since the overthrow of absolutism and the triumph of socialism would "necessarily" be separated by "a significant interval," and since the inauguration of political freedom would benefit the bourgeoisie far more than it would the proletariat, the Social Democrats could "rightfully point out that their interests coincide at the moment with those of the free-thinking elements of society." "The bourgeois elements must be made to understand this, and to a certain extent already do," Plekhanov wrote in December 1901. So orderly, so rational, so deterministic, was his scheme of things that even at this late date he could affirm with the utmost conviction: "if only we will be capable of making clear to them their immediate political task, our final goal [of socialist revolution] will not drive the advanced elements of society away from us." [33]

To be sure, Plekhanov's attitude toward the *leaders* of the liberal movement had wavered considerably during the preceding two years. In the fall of 1900 he had criticized violently the agreement that Lenin and Potresov had negotiated in Pskov with Struve and Tugan Baranovskii. In those days, his hostility toward Struve had been unbounded, and in his conversations and correspondence with his colleagues, he had refused to refer to him by any other name than Judas. However, it was not the Revisionists' liberal inclinations that Plekhanov then found intolerable,

---

* "Programma russkikh liberalov," *Iskra*, no. 23, August 1902. Quite inconsistently with this view, Martov from time to time would still express the hope of bringing a considerable body of liberal opinion under the wing of Social Democracy. In spite of his realization that the emerging liberal movement was following interests and aims quite different from those of Social Democracy, he hopefully stated, as late as July 1902, that a number of conversations that he had held with recent arrivals from Russia had convinced him that "a more and more suitable basis [was] being created for *Iskra* to occupy the position of a truly leading paper for both the party and the liberals" (letter to Lenin, dated Paris, July 24, 1902, in *Leninskii Sbornik*, IV, 133–134).

but rather their claim to stand for a legitimate interpretation of Socialism and to represent a legitimate group within the folds of Social Democracy. When, at the beginning of 1901, the Revisionists abandoned this claim to sanctity, Plekhanov became quite amenable to the idea of collaborating with them (as a "non-party democratic opposition group"), and he even agreed to their proposal to join with him and his colleagues in the publication of a political journal.[34] But now that Struve and Company had set out on an independent and "wavering" course, Plekhanov was no longer certain of his grounds. He recognized that "Berdyaev, Struve, and the others" were extremely nearsighted and opportunistic leaders, who had to be "discredited as much as possible in the eyes of readers in general and liberals in particular." Yet, this still did not mean that one should "scold the liberals in general," but rather that one should "appeal from bad liberals to good liberals." In this vein, Plekhanov wrote to Lenin, at a moment when the latter's hostility toward Struve had gotten the best of him:

> You speak as an enemy when one should speak (if at all possible) as a friend. . . . Mr. R. N. S. [Struve] must be disposed of, but in such a way that no liberal thinks that in exposing poor R. N. S., we are exposing him, the liberal, in general . . . You say: judge if my comments on R. N. S. are justified. This is difficult to do, for the very existence of R. N. S. on this earth constitutes the greatest injustice.[35]

Thus Struve's early opportunistic course did not really shake Plekhanov's conviction of the feasibility of collaboration with the liberals. "A struggle against all bourgeois parties is not compulsory at every moment," he wrote in 1902, in criticism of Lenin's revisions of his draft of the party program: "for example, the Belgian socialist proletariat is now marching with one section of the bourgeoisie against another." [36] And as late as 1903, he defended his earlier formulations about the "intelligence" and "integrity" of the liberals, conceding merely that they were revolutionary "only in part, only within a specific and narrow range," and that the party of the proletariat alone was "revolutionary in the fullest and deepest sense of the word." [37]

The moderate course of the new liberal movement perturbed Akselrod even less than it did Plekhanov. For Akselrod had been the one leader of Social Democracy whose perception of the actual contemporary characteristics of the Russian bourgeoisie and of the liberal movement had never been dimmed by their symbolic significance as the carriers of capitalist development. Akselrod had been the one Marxist to see that, however contrary to the dogma, Russian capitalism had been won over, at least temporarily, by the favors showered upon it by the tsarist regime. And, as early as 1898, he had pointed to this unique phenomenon as the cause of the weakness of Russian liberalism and as the objective foundation for the emergence of Social Democracy as the historically selected leader of the movement for political liberation in Russia.[38] Consequently, the moderate course of the emerging liberal movement awakened no fear in Akselrod's mind, and as late as 1901 he welcomed Struve's proposal of a Social Democratic–liberal coalition, provided that the liberals agreed to differentiate their program from that of the Social Democrats, and to recognize the hegemony of Social Democracy in the struggle against absolutism.*

Therefore, it was not the moderate course that the liberal movement followed in 1901–1902 that disappointed Akselrod, but rather the fact that the liberals had exercised so considerable a degree of initiative and activism that they had succeeded in usurping the legitimate place of Social Democracy as the "central and leading force in the first nation-wide clash with absolutism." A disappointing feature of these political demonstrations, he wrote in the spring of 1902, "was the fact that the leading ranks of the working class were not at the head of the movement." Social Democracy "has a justification for existence in absolutist Russia only insofar as it systematically directs all its efforts to secure for the proletariat the significance of a leading and fully independent political force in the struggle for freedom."[39]

The way to achieve this goal, he wrote to the Munich section of the editorial board (Lenin and Martov), was not by giving voice to the barbed strictures that Lenin was now aiming to direct at the zemstva and at the liberals, but by making continued and repeated efforts to win the liberals over to the side of Social Democracy:

> The distinctive feature of Struve is not that he is a partisan of legal development or that he is afraid of revolution, but rather that he, a liberal, a partisan of peaceful progress, is pointing out and emphasizing, first, that the legal and zemstvo opposition will be able to play a serious political role only thanks to the labor movement led by Social Democracy; and second, that the existence of an extreme revolutionary party benefits first and foremost the moderate parties . . . This is not a "slip" as our friend [Lenin] thinks, but a distinc-

* Akselrod wrote to Struve about this prospective alliance, early in 1901: "[It is necessary] to designate clearly and strengthen formally the demarcation line of principles that separates both sides [the liberals and the Social Democrats] as collectivities, independently of the personal views and sympathies of those of their members . . . who consider it useful to act together, even though their views are not completely in agreement. I consider such a formal differentiation an indispensable condition for a coalition between the two groups, one of which constitutes — and must constitute in the interest of the job — the representative of the democratic opposition, and the other, a specifically Social Democrat direction. I have stood and continue to stand [for the view] that on the basis of the historical position of our proletariat, Russian Social Democracy must acquire *hegemony* in the struggle against absolutism. From this point of view, it is very important that in entering a coalition such as you propose it [Social Democracy] safeguard itself from any misunderstandings as to its program and party autonomy."

tive, fully thought-out statement which is useful to the liberals as well as to us. We should grab at these remarks with both hands . . . in order to teach the liberals.[*]

The issues raised by the appearance of the liberal movement and by its elected course did not appear as simple to Lenin as they did to his colleagues. As we have seen, his attitude toward the liberals had been singularly divided ever since his conversion to Marxism. The liberals and their supporters, the members of the bourgeoisie, had always been the objects of his hatred, as the great future enemies of the working class. Yet, he had viewed them as a necessary evil, for as the carriers, as the political expressions of the irresistible tide of capitalism — the impersonal objective force that no revolutionary could arrest — their appearance was a prerequisite for the final struggle for socialism. The entrance of a liberal movement on the historical scene was thus a condition for successful revolutionary action. Only such a sign of the political maturation of the bourgeoisie would enable the socialists to begin their struggle for the seizure of power with the certainty that they were not overstepping the boundaries of objective reality. This had been Lenin's position in the 1890's, when he had attacked the Populists for their futile desire to arrest the growth of capitalism. But during the interval before the liberals finally appeared, he had gradually sunk into the comfortable notion that this bourgeois democratic movement might take the innocuous form of individual participation by the radical elements of society in a nation-wide movement led by Social Democracy — the form and manner most suitable to the interests of the proletariat.

Nothing about the behavior of the Revisionists during the last years of Lenin's Siberian exile, or in the course of his negotiations with them in the fall of 1900, had been calculated to dispel this view. During Lenin's exile, Struve had been very helpful to him, and he had displayed the same readiness to assist Lenin and his colleagues during their brief reunion in Pskov. Indeed it seemed only reasonable that Struve should assume so helpful — and subsidiary — a position, despite his basic political differences with the Orthodox. For did not the revolutionary Social Democrats constitute, together with their working-class following, the only force capable of leading the struggle to overthrow absolutism? And did not Struve's lack of any organized support by this time clearly indi-

[*] Letter dated July 19, 1901, in *Pisma P. B. Akselroda i Y. O. Martova*, p. 50. In another letter, Akselrod suggested in the same vein: "The basic issue concerning the zemstva is whether they constitute an element of political ferment . . . If they constitute or can constitute such an element, they are, in their historical tendency, irreconcilable with absolutism . . . How can . . . the Social Democrats utilize the continuous conflicts between the bureaucracy and the zemstva . . . this is the basic question confronting us" (letter of the same date, in *Leninskii Sbornik*, III, 209–211).

cate that the Revisionists could not realistically hope to play, by themselves, a significant political role?

It was not very long before Lenin was jolted out of his complacency.
When Struve and Tugan Baranovskii arrived in Munich in December
1900 to discuss the implementation of their earlier agreement to collaborate with the editors of *Iskra,* they indicated at the very first meeting that
they intended to maintain their political autonomy, in order to act as a
liaison between the revolutionary Social Democrats and the liberal elements in Russia.[40] This gesture of independence came to Lenin with
considerable surprise, and it momentarily released in him a flood of emotional indignation. Patiently, Struve attempted to explain that it was
against the Orthodox's own interests for him to become "a mere instrument" in the hands of the revolutionary Social Democrats, for if he did
so, "his influence among the liberals and democrats would dwindle, or
even be reduced to nothing." [41] But his argument was to no avail. That
night, or rather at four o'clock the next morning, Lenin wrote about his
session with the Revisionist leaders: "It was a historic meeting in my
life . . . summing up the results of a whole period of my existence . . .
and determining for a long time to come my conduct and path of life." [42]
By the time he sat down to write an account of what had transpired for
the benefit of Plekhanov and Akselrod, his fury had not yet abated:

> Bliznets [Struve's code name] revealed himself from a totally new
> side; he revealed himself to be a real politician, a politician in the
> worst sense of the word, a bargaining and insolent intriguer. He
> came, fully convinced of our own weakness . . . to present us with
> surrender terms; and he did this with exquisite form, without raising
> a single harsh word, yet revealing, nevertheless, the rude bargaining
> nature of a robust liberal that was hidden underneath the refined
> civilized exterior of the new-fashioned "critic." [43]

On this occasion, Lenin's colleagues finally succeeded in patching up
an agreement of sorts with the Revisionists, but a few months later pan-
demonium broke out once again, upon the publication of Struve's Foreword to Witte's memorandum, which advocated the formation of a
moderate zemstvo party that could exploit the conflict between the autocracy and the "extreme" parties. At once, Lenin took up his pen and
composed a diatribe against Struve and the zemstvo elements. The original draft of this document has unfortunately disappeared, but its violence and vindictiveness can be gauged by the comments that Plekhanov
and Akselrod sent Lenin upon reading it. Insistently, they demanded that
Lenin moderate the tone of this document, which was "calculated only
to alienate the liberals completely from Social Democracy." Isn't it too
early to speak to the liberals in such a tone, since we want to utilize
them?" Akselrod conciliatorily pointed out.[44] Plekhanov elaborated the
same point in as diplomatic a manner:

Your comments about R. N. S. are fully justified. But, here and there, they should be softened, and here is why: In your comments is detectable an exasperation that we understand only too well, but which may not be comprehensible to the reader. In my opinion, one must not speak in an indignant manner, but rather from the heights:

"It is too bad that the author did not understand such and such, but everyone knows that he is an intelligent man. It is likely, therefore, that he will move forward, and that in his next article the following contradictions will not be present (then, you name the contradictions) . . . But we repeat, he again falls into error, and we must reassuringly take him, the little one, on the knee, and then say that he's nevertheless not without a head on his shoulders."

You speak as an enemy when you should speak, if at all possible, as an ally.[45]

It took a while before Akselrod's and Plekhanov's moderating counsels sank in, and meanwhile Lenin deluged them with stormy complaints. "I don't know whether I will be able to write diplomatically about a gentleman who arouses in me such stormy feelings," he wrote to Akselrod on July 21, 1901. "If I wasn't so exasperated with the author," he wrote to Plekhanov four days later, "I wouldn't write in such a fashion. And since I am exasperated (which is perfectly understandable not only to us but to every Social Democratic reader of the Foreword), there is no point in my hiding it . . ." And in a note to Akselrod dated July 26: "In principle, I cannot give up my belief in our right (and duty) to attack R. N. S. for his political chicanery. He is . . . a political juggler . . . and in my criticism, I have pointed out all that the last few months have brought us, I have unburdened my soul, 'j'ai réglé mon compte' with this fellow . . ."[46]

When Lenin's rage finally cooled, and his urge to evaluate all political phenomena coolly and objectively once more took the upper hand, he still found it very difficult to evaluate accurately the shape that the nascent liberal movement was assuming. Was the moderate and compromising course adopted by the liberals indicative, as he had instinctively felt, of the skillfulness and ruse of a mature political movement finally coming into its own and unmasking its true diabolic nature? If this was the case, if the liberal representatives of capitalism had finally arrived on the scene as mature and full-grown enemies, it was clearly permissible and even imperative for the Social Democrats to unleash a potent offensive against them, and to wrest forcibly the leadership of all opposition elements away from them. But just suppose that Plekhanov was right, suppose that the moderation and hedging of the liberals was merely indicative of their youth, of the wavering and hesitation that characterized the first steps of any political group that was as yet unconscious of its own true interests and needs. If this was the case, the duty of the Social Democrats was to act as "big brothers" toward the liberals. It was to guide them in their first political steps, to patiently explain to them where their real interests lay.

Temporarily, Plekhanov's moderate counsel prevailed, and in the final draft of his 1901 address to the liberals, Lenin assumed the role of such a "big brother," earnestly explaining to them that no compromises were possible with a police power whose every concession was merely the expression of a calculated policy of "divide and rule." The zemstva constituted an illustration of this policy of conceding the unimportant in order to retain the important, of "giving with the left hand while taking away with the right," he asserted, and the slogan of "power to the zemstva" that Struve was now advancing could succeed, therefore, only in "aiding the government in its attempt to get away with loud promises and half-hearted concessions." [47]

But the half-willingness to make conciliatory gestures toward the liberals that Lenin exhibited in this article was due, not so much to any sudden disposition to accept the existence of a powerful independent and organized liberal movement, as to a reawakening of the wishful thought that such a movement would probably not appear. "If the liberals are capable of organizing an illegal party," wrote Lenin, tongue in cheek, in the same article,

> we will welcome this growth of political self-consciousness in the possessing classes, we will support their demands, we will try [to have] the activity of the liberals and of the Social Democrats supplement one another. If they [the liberals] are unable to do so [organize] we will not, *in this more likely eventuality*, wash our hands of the liberals, but rather attempt to strengthen our ties with individual figures, to acquaint them with our movement, and then, by exposing in the liberal press all the dirty deeds of the government and all the tricks of local authorities, to attract them to the support of the revolutionaries.[48]

Thus it still seemed likely to Lenin that the liberals were incapable of organizing a significant political force of their own, at least for the moment, and that they would consequently be compelled to act as supporters of Social Democracy. "Unwillingly," and "with the worst grace," they would "come to the aid," they would "grumble but start helping the one party capable of directing an awesome blow against absolutism." [49]

But the year 1901 ended with no sign that the liberals were heeding Lenin's advice and adopting the minor role that he had assigned to them. On the contrary, rumors were now spreading of the impending publication abroad of an illegal liberal organ designed to represent all moderate elements in Russian society (the journal *Osvobozhdenie*). Doubts about the correctness of Plekhanov's diagnosis consequently gripped Lenin anew. "The absolutist regime," he wrote in February 1902, "satisfies some of the interests of the bourgeoisie even though, in a wider sense, it frustrates bourgeois interests." What would be the product of "these contra-dictory interests," what would be the outcome of "this interaction of conservative and liberal views and tendencies at a given moment?" The answers to these questions could not be deduced from general proposi-tions; they would hinge on "all the particulars of the contemporary politi-cal and social situation."

But one fact could be predicted — it was that the potential allies of the proletariat in the struggle for political freedom would "attempt to drag back," would "angle for compromises." And the only way for Social Democracy to prevent this was to raise its own battle standard, to thrust forward its own distinct identity, to push its potential allies steadily for-ward by the pressure of its own program and demands. "We must not forget," concluded Lenin, "that in order to push somebody forward one must always keep one's hand on his shoulder. The party of the prole-tariat must be capable of catching every liberal, precisely at the moment when he is preparing to advance, and to keep him within range." *

It was due to these suspicions about the liberals' intentions and future political moves (as well as in the light of the emergence of the SR's) that Lenin attacked so vehemently the conciliatory features of Plekha-nov's draft of the program. It was because of these suspicions that he insisted so strenuously that the draft sharply distinguish the proletariat from other oppressed elements and that these elements be called upon to come over to the point of view of the working class. Only by exercis-ing such pressure could the Social Democrats insure that the democratic revolution would not be arrested in its tracks, only through such pressure could they confront the petty bourgeoisie with its one and only choice — that of following the footsteps of the proletariat or becoming the tools of the bourgeois class.

By the beginning of 1903, the growth of the *Osvobozhdenie* move-ment and the character of its program finally solidified Lenin's conviction that "bourgeois democracy" had graduated onto the political scene, and that it was indeed harboring the dark designs that he had originally

---

* "Politicheskaya agitatsiya i 'klassovaya tochka zreniya,'" *Iskra*, no. 16, Febru-ary 1, 1902; *Sochineniya*, V, 315–316. Struve would assert subsequently that Lenin's condescending, if not contemptuous, attitude toward the liberal leaders, an attitude which he discerned to a lesser degree in Plekhanov, was the chief catalyst in his break with the editors of *Iskra*. He states in his memoirs: "I must say frankly that the leading Orthodox Social Democrats (I mean Plekhanov and Lenin) did every-thing to accelerate and facilitate — psychologically, so to speak — my rupture with them. Not only did they not show the consideration which I could claim as a political and intellectual personality, but, what was a much greater blunder on their part — and this applies above all to Lenin — they failed to realize that what-ever my personal views may have been, they ought to have regarded me . . . as a genuine representative of the views of a social milieu which could neither be ignored nor rebuffed, which was entitled to keep its own character and could only then be a valuable ally in the struggle for the political transformation of the country. (Struve, in *Slavonic and East European Review*, XIII, 81).

imputed to it. It was against this background that he was now to advance his program of Social Democratic leadership for the democratic revolution. It was against this background that he was to formulate his 1905 platform of a democratic revolution achieved by the proletariat, with the aid of a petty bourgeois following — and against the opposition of the bourgeoisie.

In this remarkable formula, as in his over-all view of the bourgeoisie and peasantry, were reflected Lenin's peculiar blend of determinism and indeterminism, of Marxist "objectivity" and Populist voluntarism. Since history had so prescribed it, the coming revolution was to be a "democratic" — and not a socialist — revolution; but it was to be guided and shaped by the proletariat, with the aid of petty bourgeois elements that would have been compelled to give up their own outlook and to come over to the point of view of the working class. Although the outline of Lenin's dream was already apparent in his writings of 1902 and 1903, it was not until the very eve of the Revolution of 1905 that his collaborators came to realize that their "tough-minded" and "orthodox" colleague contemplated so "fantastic" a scheme.

PART THREE

The Birth of Bolshevism and Menshevism

UNIFICATION AND SCHISM:
THE STILLBIRTH OF THE RSDRP

In June 1902, bravely presenting to the world the appearance of a united team, the editors of *Iskra* published a draft of the Social Democratic Party program, endorsed by every member of the editorial board. On many points, this final draft constituted a compromise between the views that Plekhanov and Lenin had so violently debated, but to *Iskra*'s opponents the editors denied that there had ever appeared any major differences among them.*

Yet, a growing, if as yet unrecognized, rift between Lenin and his older colleagues had been set in motion by the debates over the party program. What seemed particularly disturbing to Lenin, as he reflected about this controversy, was the emotional sway that Plekhanov had maintained over Zasulich and Akselrod, a sway that had impelled them to support Plekhanov (so Lenin thought), even when they were in disagreement with him. It was then, Martov's sister asserts, that Lenin "arrived at the conviction that it was necessary to reorganize the *Iskra* editorial board [and] to separate the 'stariki' from [its] affairs." [1]

The summer of 1902 marked a turning point in the relations among *Iskra*'s editors in yet another respect. This was the moment when the headquarters of *Iskra* were moved to London from Stuttgart, where the journal had begun to receive the unwelcome attention of the police authorities. When Lenin had originally decided to print the journal in Germany — rather than in Switzerland, where Plekhanov and Akselrod were living — he had been able to convince his older colleagues that his decision was entirely motivated by a desire to keep the journal away from

*Plekhanov commented on the Economists' allegation that the "bad features" of the program were the reflection of Lenin's influence: "If the project of program proposed by us to Russian Social Democracy is inadequate, we — i.e., P. B. Akselrod, V. Zasulich, and I — are no less responsible than Lenin or any other member of the editorial board" ("Ortodoksalnoe bukvoedstvo," *Iskra*, no. 41, June 1903).

the eyes of the tsarist police. But now that the anonymity of the enterprise had evidently been broken, no such justification could be offered
for not transferring the journal to Switzerland, and the move to London
inevitably offended the sensibilities of Plekhanov and Akselrod.

Yet, the "stariki" gave no voice to their wounded pride, and Lenin,
in turn, did not specifically refer to his plans for the reorganization of the
editorial board. That the differences between Lenin and his older colleagues were as yet kept so completely muted was, once again, due to
the insistent pressures of political realities.

By the beginning of 1903, dangerous developments on the Russian
scene appeared to be substantiating, at least on the surface, the fears
that Lenin had been voicing ever since the foundation of *Iskra*. In 1901,
the Russian Ministry of Internal Affairs had started to organize government sponsored trade unions, designed to divert the workers' attention
from politics, "to protect them against the wiles of revolutionary agitators." In 1902, the *Zubatovshchina*, as this policy was called, was introduced on a large scale in Moscow, where a Soviet of Workers in
Mechanical Industries was organized and placed under police protection.
By the end of the year, this soviet had gained a substantial following
among the masses of uneducated workers, a triumph that was considerably facilitated by the success of the police in tracking down and breaking up the agitational circles of the Social Democrats.

Thus, the theses that Lenin had propounded in his *Chto Delat'?*
now seemed to him to be confirmed. It appeared that without consistent
and vigorous leadership by Social Democracy, the workers would indeed
be easily diverted from the path to socialist consciousness and that only
an army of professional revolutionaries under the direction of secret centers could provide the required leadership. Not only was Social Democracy now threatened with the loss of its potential mass following among
the workers, but it was also running into increasingly severe competition
in its efforts to enlist new recruits from the members of the intelligentsia.
For the "demagogical" program of the new SR Party, its defense of political terrorism, its demand for a union of all revolutionary forces, was
gripping the imagination of young students and the older intelligentsia
alike.

The threatening character of these new developments did not escape
Iskra's editors, and in their newspaper editorials, as well as in their personal messages, they called with rising impatience upon their Russian
followers to perform greater feats in their political propaganda and agitation.*

---

* Rather typical of the tone of the messages *Iskra*'s editors now sent to Russian
SD centers was this letter of Lenin's to one of his followers: "If you yourselves are
inactive, no recipes can help you. If you yourselves are not energetic and nimble, no
one can help you. You howl: 'Find us this and that; give us this and that'; this is
all senseless, because you yourselves must take and find . . .

But prodding *Iskra*'s followers was clearly not enough. A decisive step was needed to consolidate the position of Russian Social Democracy, and to *Iskra*'s editors it seemed that this step might well be the long-delayed formal reorganization of an All-Russian Social Democratic Party, the long-postponed restoration of the party centers, which would indicate clearly to the world that the RSDRP had come to life again as a united party — more potent and more effective than ever before. The conditions that Lenin had laid out in 1900 for such a unification had now been achieved. The ideological issues that had then divided Social Democracy had been thrashed out, and — aided by the political awakening of society, aided by the infamous example of the government-sponsored Zubatovshchina — *Iskra* had won a clear-cut victory (in party circles) over the exponents of the "spontaneous" economic struggle.

By 1902, the Iskraists had won over a clear majority of the strictly Russian committees (i.e., of the Russian Social Democratic centers outside of the Jewish Bund). By the end of that year, they had gained a majority in the Organizational Committee that had been set up to make the arrangements for the party congress.* Having won over a majority of the Russian committees, it did not matter if a substantial portion of the following, of the so-called "periphery," of these committees, were critical of *Iskra*'s single-minded concentration on the political struggle, since these "peripheries" would not control votes at the party congress. But one real threat remained — the threat that the Jewish Bund, insistent as it was on the autonomy of its organizations, might join hands with *Iskra*'s opponents among the Russian committees, and thus endanger *Iskra*'s hard-won majority.

Lenin refused to allow this perspective to unfold, and he worked out a scheme to eliminate it by having the question of the Bund's demand for control over all Jewish workers (regardless of locality) placed before all others in the Order of the Day at the congress. Since in all likelihood the Bund's demands would be categorically rejected, it was possible that at that early stage — before any other issues had come up for a vote — the Bund might withdraw from the congress rather than bow, and thereby insure an Iskraist majority. If, on the other hand, the Bund succeeded in "forcing" upon the congress some doubtful compromises, *Iskra*

"Every month we send hundreds and hundreds of leaflets to all parts of Russia, and we haven't had one simple communication about the distribution of these hundreds of pamphlets among the masses, about the impression they have made, or about discussions among the masses about these things" ("Some Thoughts about the Letter of 7-Ts-6F," *Sochineniya*, 2nd ed., XXVIII, 279–282).

* This Organizational Committee, the OK as it was called, was formed after a conference in Belostok in November 1902, in which all Social Democratic organizations, including the Bund, participated. In its efforts to gain control of the OK, *Iskra* was aided by favorable circumstances. Shortly after the Belostok Conference, the members of the original OK were arrested by the tsarist police, and *Iskra* succeeded in winning a majority of the membership elected to replace them.

could seize that opportunity to create a split (*raskol*), which it could justify as a "division on a basic, serious issue." [2]

Now that everything had been worked out to insure *Iskra's* control of the coming party congress, it remained for its editors to draw up the resolutions and the plans that would be submitted for their prospective majority to ratify: as *Iskra's* editors had finally agreed on a compromise draft of the program, their main remaining task was to decide on the rules that should govern the party's organizations. The nexus of party organizations that Lenin contemplated had already been outlined in *Chto Delat'?*, copies of which had been circulating in Russia ever since the Pskov Conference. He now elaborated on his plan in a twenty-page document, composed as an informal letter to a member of the Petersburg Committee.[3] In this, as in other letters to his Russian followers, Lenin made it clear that the rules of organization to be adopted should transform the Russian committees into obedient instruments — "fists" as he would say later — of the top leadership of the party.

The agents of Social Democracy were to be governed from two main centers. The first of these would be a central organ, or CO, a spiritual center safely located abroad "out of the reach of Russian gendarmes"; this center would control all important publications and provide the ideological *rukovodstvo*, the spiritual leadership, the "firmness and continuity," needed to guide the course of the party. Side by side with the CO, separated from it only by the artificial boundary of the autocracy, was to be a Central Committee, or CC, entrusted with the immediate and practical supervision of local party centers and with issuing on-the-spot "direct and concrete commands." "Complete solidarity and unity of purpose" was to be secured between the two centers by appointing to each of them individuals "in full agreement with one another," and by instituting regular meetings between them.

The local committees operating under the two party centers were not to be representative organs but military commands, submitting "in every important matter" to the will of the party leadership. Through their filial organizations, the factory and district subcommittees and the agitational groups subordinated to them, these local committees would extend their influence over the working class in every direction. But the relationships within this organizational pyramid were to be those of a conspiratorial army. The membership of the local committees would be kept small, and with the exception of *one* of their members appointed to direct the activities of each filial organization, it would be kept strictly secret from them. Even the factory and district subcommittees would communicate with their agitational groups solely through the channel of a one-man link. By the adoption of this method, Lenin believed, every local committee, every factory group and district subcommittee, would be transformed into a "fortress of Social Democracy," buttressed against the blows of the police state.

The main features of this plan were incorporated in a statement of the rules that should govern the party's organizations which Lenin proposed to submit for ratification to the delegates to the Second Congress. Well before the congress, he showed a draft of his proposal to Martov (he may also have shown it to his other colleagues on *Iskra*'s editorial board, but only Martov's comments and suggestions have been preserved). Martov's remarks were sparse and inarticulate; but however blurred, they pointed to two major ambiguities in Lenin's proposals.*

The first of the ambiguities in Lenin's draft involved his definition of party membership. Who within the mass embraced by Lenin's network of organizations was to be given the title — and the rights — of a party member? Was this prerogative to be restricted to the relatively small group of professional revolutionaries who would man the committees and subcommittees of the party, or was it to be extended to the working-class followers of these party organs? Lenin's original formulation on this point stated: "Everyone is considered a member of the party who accepts the party program and who supports the party by material means as well as by personal participation in one of the party organizations." [4]

This definition was ambiguous; it left unanswered the following major question: at what point in Lenin's design of the prehensive arms — "stretching in every direction" — of the party's influence, was the boundary between party and nonparty to be traced? Subjugated as he had been by Lenin's influence ever since joining the editorial board, Martov was not as yet capable of raising the issue point blank. Instead, he offered an alternative formulation. This formulation read, in its original version: "Everyone is considered to belong to the RSDRP who accepts its program and works to carry out its tasks in [real] life, under the control and leadership of the party organs." [5] Martov, too, had not met the question head on. But his formula, however imprecise, indicated that in a showdown he would favor a far more elastic definition of party membership, a much wider concept of the party as a whole, than did his erstwhile teacher and friend.

The second major issue left in doubt by Lenin's project was the relative authority to be exercised by the Central Organ and by the Central Committee. The division of functions that Lenin had traced between these two centers did not really settle the issue, for where was the "ideo-

---

* Unfortunately the original draft of Lenin's statement of the party rules has been lost. But from Martov's comments about this draft, as well as from Lenin's subsequent discussions, we can deduce some of the differences between the original text and the resolution on party rules that Lenin eventually submitted to the Second Congress.

logical leadership" of the CO to end and the "practical direction" of the CC to begin? Lenin's formula was vague on this point, although its phrasing clearly tended to enhance the CO's ideological leadership at the expense of the "immediate," "practical" supervisory functions of the CC (indeed, Lenin had consistently used the term "leadership" only with reference to the role of the CO).

Martov was obviously disturbed by this section of Lenin's draft. But again he failed to voice any substantive criticisms, and instead suggested certain changes in phraseology. Again, his alternative formulation did not meet the issue squarely. Yet subtly, very subtly indeed, it attempted to put the respective roles of the CO and CC back into balance. "On the CC lies the general leadership of all the practical activity of the party," ran this alternative formulation; "on the literary organs lies the ideological leadership of party life, of propaganda for the party program, and of scientific and journalistic development of the world view of Social Democracy." *

Of course, the respective powers of the Central Organ and Central Committee would not be decided in the last analysis by such nuances in the phrasing of the party rules. The issue would be settled largely by the character of the individuals who entered the two centers by their relative prestige, competence, and determination. But in this respect, the advantage would lie wholly on the side of the CO. Recruited as it would be from the members of the old *Iskra* editorial board, it would be far better known and enjoy infinitely greater authority and prestige than would the necessarily secret membership of the CC. Yet Martov's comments suggest that Lenin attempted to load the dice even further in favor of the CO. His first draft of the party rules seemingly proposed — probably on the pretext that "harmony" was imperative between the two centers — that, during the intervals between party congresses, the members of the Central Organ and Central Committee *jointly* appoint new members to their respective bodies. Since the membership of the CO was likely to remain stable while that of the CC would inevitably be riddled periodically by police arrests, this rule of "mutual coöptation" would have led within a few months to the complete ascendancy of the CO over the CC.

Only in this one instance did Martov actually come out in opposition to Lenin's views, and even then he angled for compromise: "During the interval between party congresses," he asserted, "coöptation in the CC and the CO should be on another basis than mutual coöptation. Each

---

* Quoted in "Shag vpered, dva shaga nazad," *Sochineniya*, VII, 228. Compare this with the formulation in the final draft of Lenin's statement of the rules (the version submitted to the Second Congress): "The CC unites and directs (*napravlaet*) all the practical activity of the party . . . The editorial board of the CO leads (*rukovodit*) the party ideologically" ("Proekt ustava RSDRP," *Sochineniya*, VI, 432–433).

college [should] coöpt its own members. The other college [should] be entitled to protest; then the matter would go to the Soviet [a council composed of representatives of the two centers]." [6] Martov's modification of his formula proved acceptable to Lenin and on the eve of the Second Congress he abandoned his plan for mutual coöptation (only to revive it after his split with the Mensheviks). All in all, the differences between Lenin and his closest collaborator still seemed inconsequential to them both as they awaited the gathering that was to bring together — actually for the first time — all the representatives of Russian Social Democracy.

On July 30, 1903, G. V. Plekhanov, who for two decades had waited for this day, formally opened the Second Congress of the RSDRP. During its first few sessions the congress acted exactly as Lenin had planned. With the aid of the Machiavellian tactics that he had patiently taught his Russian followers, the *Iskra* committees had gained a majority of the votes.* And carefully rehearsed at daily caucuses, this majority block easily steam-rollered through, during the first few sessions, many of the proposals Lenin had prepared in the preceding months.

Just as Lenin had insisted, the Order of the Day adopted by the congress placed the problem of the Bund at the head of its agenda, and the selection of the Central Organ — i.e., the foregone recognition of *Iskra* as the official party organ — ahead of the all-important discussion of party organization. Just as he had hoped, the congress rejected categorically the Bund demand for autonomy, thus paving the way for the walkout of Bund delegates. (Unfortunately for Lenin, however, the walkout took place after the discussions of party organization had already begun and after some of the crucial votes had been taken.) Even the *Iskra*-sponsored draft of the party program was pushed through rather rapidly, but not without arousing a vocal and eloquent opposition which must have shaken and divided, if only inwardly, the members of the "united" *Iskra* team. For the criticisms of the opposition revived the very issues that had been debated at one time or another by the members of the editorial board — issues they had buried safely in the hidden niches of their minds.

It must have been difficult for Plekhanov to dismiss with any light-heartedness Martynov's complaint that, of all the Social Democratic programs in existence, *Iskra's* was the only one that failed to state that "one of the results of the development of capitalist society" had been "the

* In the days before the congress, these tactics were aimed toward creating organizational splits in those of the Russian centers, such as the Petersburg Committee, where *Iskra* could not gain control. As a result, rival delegations were sent to the congress by a number of committees, and the votes of these committees, which otherwise would have been cast solidly against the *Iskra* bloc, were split. For illustrations of the pre-congress tactics of Lenin, see for example his two letters, dated July 1902, to I. I. Radchenko, in *Sochineniya*, VI, 155–164.

development of the class consciousness of the proletariat," which had laid "the foundations for its struggle against capitalist society." [7] It must have been just as difficult for him to rise in rebuttal when, a little later in the debate, the same Martynov stood up and argued in phrases strikingly reminiscent of Plekhanov's own past statements: "It is precisely due to our conviction that the development of the proletariat follows the spontaneous laws of nature toward the realization of our theoretical principles that we are able to stand firmly and unswervingly for these principles and reject all theoretical compromises based on transient practical considerations." [8] Although Plekhanov would have objected to the old Economists' use of the term "spontaneous," it had been an equally deterministic conviction in the inevitability of the triumph of socialism that had fortified his long and difficult defense of Marxist orthodoxy and that had motivated his recent conflict with Lenin over the party program.

It must have been disquieting for Akselrod to hear the opposition's argument that Lenin's formula opened the door for "a struggle between the leaders of Social Democracy and the masses of the working class, between the activities of the self-enclosed party and the wide struggle of the proletariat." [9] How could Akselrod have remained indifferent, he who at the age of sixteen had dedicated his life to the emancipation of the people, upon hearing old Akimov's vehement assertion that the proposed program placed the party and the proletariat opposite one another, as if the first was an "active collective figure" and the second but a "passive medium"? [10]

Both Akselrod and Martov must have been further alarmed to hear Plekhanov, their old comrade-in-arms, declare during the same debate that all democratic principles had to be subordinated to the one supreme goal of a successful revolution, which might require under certain conditions the suppression of any democratic rights, down to and including universal suffrage.[11] What had happened to the long-held assumption that the hour would strike for the socialist revolution only when the vast majority of the population had come over to the side of the proletariat? (The specific point under discussion was an opposition proposal to add the term "consciousness" to the list of characteristics that would develop in the proletariat as a result of the growth of capitalist contradictions.)[12]

After the defeat of the Economists' proposed amendment calling for this addition of consciousness to the list of the proletariat's attributes, the debate shifted at long last to a discussion of the agrarian platform Lenin had been responsible for including in the program. But here again, the queries of the opposition proved embarrassing for Lenin's collaborators. *Iskra's* proposal to turn the *otrezki* over to the peasants was neither fish nor fowl, its opponents pointed out. Miserly as it was in comparison with the SR's demagogical platform of nationalization of the land, it could not be justified on the basis of its appeal to the peasantry. Yet it was folly to defend it as an objectively justified measure, as one of the steps required to "cleanse capitalist society from the survivals of feudalism." As Lenin himself had pointed out, the strivings of the oppressed classes could not always be trusted to be revolutionary in character. What guarantee was there, therefore, that the peasant committees to which the *otrezki* were to be turned over would not be reactionary rather than revolutionary? What insurance existed that they would not utilize their power to turn the clock backward rather than forward? [13] Concluded Liber, *Iskra's* most eloquent opponent on this issue:

> I submit that one cannot simply extract the remnants of feudalism from the capitalist order — like a big tooth from the jaw — assuming that all the rest will remain unchanged. No! Everything is tied together by a thousand threads. Along with the survivals that truly constitute remnants of serfdom, there are pre-reform survivals which the capitalist order has succeeded in attracting to itself. By brushing against these survivals, you will be brushing against the capitalist order per se.[14]

Upon hearing this convincing statement of the Utopian character of *Iskra's* agrarian plank, Plekhanov, who all his life had prided himself on the absolutely scientific character of his revolutionary beliefs, must indeed have felt rather helpless. For the only convincing rebuttal to Liber's argument, the argument at which Lenin was hinting (that *Iskra's* entire agrarian program — the return of the *otrezki,* the creation of peasant committees to take them over — was aimed purely toward the creation of a revolutionary situation which Social Democracy would exploit for its own ends), smacked of the tactics of a conspiratory *coup de main* rather than of the objective program of a party anointed with history's grace! *

In spite of the telling criticisms of the opposition, *Iskra's* draft of the party's program was ratified without any major revisions. Thus, without any apparent hitch, more than half of *Iskra's* agenda had now been ratified by its obedient congressional majority. Lenin's cherished goal appeared close to realization. The RSDRP seemed well on its way to becoming a united and monolithic party.

At this moment of triumph for *Iskra's* partisans, the congress was compelled to interrupt its activities. Since the very first session, its debates had been watched closely by the secret agents of the autocracy and by the political police of the Belgian government. Impelled by the repeated protests of the Tsar's diplomatic representatives, the embarrassed Belgian authorities finally arrested a number of delegates to the

---

* Lenin stated in answer to Liber's question why unreliable peasant committees rather than the party itself should handle the return of the *otrezki:* "This measure must not be handled in a bureaucratic fashion . . . [It must be handled] by the oppressed classes themselves. And this already is the path of revolution" (*Vtoroi ocherednoi s"ezd RSDRP, Protokoly,* p. 222).

congress and expelled them from the country. Undaunted by this turn of events, the congress temporarily adjourned its sessions on August 5, 1903, and moved to reconvene in London within a week, in the freer atmosphere prevailing across the Channel.

In the curious setting of a London socialist church, the congress resumed its sessions on August 11, 1903, and, in accordance with its agenda, turned to a discussion of the rules that would govern the reunited and consolidated ranks of the Social Democratic Party. Some discussion had been held already on this question during the Brussels sessions, and in these early debates *Iskra's* opponents had found another opportunity to direct shrewd and telling criticisms at Lenin's plans. They had pointed at the ambiguity of Lenin's distinction between the "spiritual" functions of the CO and the practical functions of the CC — and had insisted that party unity could be achieved only through the agency of a single leading center.[15] When the *Iskra* bloc came up with the compromise proposal to set up a council, or Soviet, composed of representatives of the two centers, to reconcile all major differences between them, the opposition had objected that the greater stability and prestige of the CO would enable it to take over control of the Soviet, and therefore, to dominate the Central Committee.[16]

But the most vigorous criticism of *Iskra's* opponents had been reserved for the absolute power of control that Lenin's draft of the rules had assigned to the party's centers — control over the most minute of the activities of the local committees and over their *individual members.* "By completely destroying the competence of subordinate organizations," you are "removing the very possibility of [continued] existence," explained one of the opposition spokesmen.

> An organization cannot survive if it is given but one right — to submit resignedly to whatever is dictated from above. If the present project is adopted, *the center will be bewitched into a void* . . . It will have no periphery around it, only some sort of amorphous mass through which will move its executive agents. On such a basis, no organization can possibly stand.[17]

In this argument, as in their earlier criticisms of Lenin's views, his opponents were voicing the fear that the tight and restrictive organizational bonds that he aimed to impose on Social Democracy would weaken rather than strengthen the mass support upon which the party's future growth would depend. Having stifled the life of its primary organizations, the party, like *Iskra,* would be reduced to "a spirit hovering over a void." Separated from the working class by a wall of its own making, Lenin's conscious elite would be alienated from the real world.

Although upon leaving Brussels, *Iskra's* opponents had probably felt that in these as in previous debates they had largely wasted their efforts, their speeches actually achieved a purpose: they planted seeds of discord in the minds of Lenin's collaborators, and in the London sessions of the congress, this discord was to come to life.

The first indication of the impending storm was Martov's insistence on submitting for the delegates' consideration an alternative to Lenin's definition of party membership. As it had before the congress, Lenin's proposal restricted the prerogative of party membership to individuals who *personally participated* in one of the party's organizations. Martov now suggested that this definition be extended to include all persons who, besides accepting the program and paying their dues, supported the party by "regular *personal assistance under the direction* of one of the party organizations" (this formulation was copied from the statutes of the German Social Democratic Party).

To many delegates, the distinction between the two formulas must have seemed at first to be rather minor, but two long sessions of bitter debate rapidly dispelled this impression. Martov and Akselrod led the attack against Lenin's formula, advertising thereby that for the first time in the sessions of the congress the leadership of the *Iskra* bloc had split, and on a major issue at that. The arguments of Lenin's old collaborators were focused on one fundamental point. The RSDRP was intended to be a class party, a mass party of the proletariat. Under the existing conditions of political terror, there could be no doubt that this party stood in need of a conspiratorial network of organizations, but the network would make sense only if it "was surrounded by a wider party," only if it constituted "a fly-wheel bringing into movement the work of the party as a whole." "We constitute [only] the *conscious expression of an unconscious process*," Martov explained. "The more widely the title of party member is extended, the better. We can only rejoice if every striker, if every demonstrator, proclaims himself a party member when he answers for his deeds." [18]

To these arguments, Lenin's carefully rehearsed supporters had one stock answer, which they repeated time and time again. Martov's formula would make it impossible for the party to exercise any real control over its individual members. Yet these members necessarily would have to exercise some voice in the determination of policy — and whether it wanted to or not, the party would inevitably be responsible for their actions. Some powers of control had to be assigned to the party, therefore, and the only possible and only real form that such control could assume was the one suggested in Lenin's definition — the control exercised by an organization over its regular membership.[19]

To this, Martov and his new-found ally, the former Economist Martynov, answered that the kind of control that Lenin had in mind was neither necessary nor realizable. It was unnecessary, argued Martynov, because the RSDRP was not an organization of plotters leading unreliable democratic elements of varying and transient shades, but a mass party, leaning on the proletariat — a homogeneous social class "with a definite historical tendency." This party was not intended to "act on the back" of the proletariat; it was designed to "guide" it, to "help it to become conscious of its interests, and to fight for them expediently." [20] The restriction of party membership to the organizational hierarchy of the party could not possibly be maintained, Martov in turn pointed out, because life was "procreating and developing working-class organizations faster than the party's capacity to incorporate and consolidate them into its fighting organizations of professional revolutionaries." Although some working-class organizations might not be wholly reliable, they could not very well be left out of the party if Social Democracy was to achieve its expressed aim of including all the active and leading elements of the proletariat. "I feel," Martov rather confusedly added, "that if such organizations agree to adopt the party program and party control, we can bring them into the party without making them at the same time party organizations" (i.e., component parts of the party's official organizational hierarchy). Martov concluded:

> In our eyes, the labor party is not limited to an organization of professional revolutionaries. It consists of them plus the entire combination of the active, leading elements of the proletariat . . . Our formula, alone, expresses the *striving* that between the organization of professional revolutionaries and the masses exist a [whole] series of organizations.[21]

Up to this moment, Plekhanov had remained on the sidelines, his precise and logical mind impatiently weighing the elaborate and confused arguments that were being offered by both sides. But after hearing Martynov's and Martov's speeches, which seemed to deny the necessity for any organizational safeguards against the heretics that he had been compelled to combat for so many years, he jumped head-on into the controversy:

> I have been listening carefully to the arguments presented by both sides, and the more I listen, the more I am convinced that Lenin is right. To speak of party control over people who are not in a [party] organization is to play with words . . . I also fail to see why some think that Lenin's project would close the party's doors to a great many workers. Those workers who wish to enter the party will not fear to enter an organization; discipline is not difficult for them to take. Many of the intelligentsia will fear to enter, contaminated as they are with bourgeois individualism; but this is all to the good, since those bourgeois individuals usually constitute representatives of all sorts of opportunism. The opponents of opportunism should there-

fore vote for Lenin's project, which closes the door to its penetration into the party.[22]

But Plekhanov's dictum did not silence the opponents of Lenin's formula. Even young Trotsky rose to challenge the master, and drew the first blood in his brilliant oratorical career:

> I was very surprised when Plekhanov proposed to vote in favor of Lenin's formula as a correct instrument against opportunism . . . I didn't know that a legal invocation could be made against opportunism . . . I didn't know that the opportunists were constitutionally incapable of organization . . . What is the sense, I would say, of worrying about the legal position of individual members of the intelligentsia who accept the party program and who are, once in a while, of service to the party under the leadership of its organizations. Is it that a member of the Central Committee should be responsible for each and every one of these lonely Social Democrats? . . . I, for one, do not attach any mystical significance to the rules, but if the juridical formula is to correspond to the actual state of affairs, Lenin's formula should be rejected . . . It defeats its own purpose: it will make it far more difficult for workers to join the party than for the intelligentsia, since organizations of workers are subjected to more pressures and break down more easily — for instance, through strikes.
>
> Plekhanov hopes to use Lenin's formula as a throttling noose against those politically corrupt *intelligenty* who call themselves Social Democrats and organize youngsters, only to sell them to Struve. But what prevents such people from joining Lenin's loose organizations, or from founding such organizations? You say that the CC will not recognize them — but why? Evidently not because of the character of the organizations as such, but because of the character of the individuals who go into them. This means that the CC will treat individuals M.M. and N.N. as political individualities [and not as members of organizations]. As such, they are not dangerous; they can be subjected to a party boycott . . .[23]

Wearily, Lenin rose to answer the arguments of his former protégé. Trotsky had failed to see the fundamental difference between his formula and Martov's — the fact that Martov's "extended," while his "narrowed," the concept of party membership. And at this moment in party history — when, "its unity restored," Social Democracy was expecting to absorb a great many new, and in many instances unreliable, elements — the elasticity advocated by Martov would inevitably open the door wide to every element of division, wavering, and opportunism:

> Trotsky says: wouldn't it be terrible if hundreds of workers arrested during a strike turned out not to be party members. This would only show that our organization is good — that we are fulfilling our task of organizing a narrow circle of leaders in secret and

[yet] bringing a wider mass into movement . . . Trotsky forgets that the party must constitute only the *leading ranks* of the vast masses of the working class. Wholly or almost wholly, these masses, in turn, work under the leadership and control of party organizations, but generally they do not and should not come into the party . . .

Martov's formula ignores one of the chief evils in party life, the fact that under existing conditions, it is difficult if not impossible to distinguish in the party between babblers and actual workers. Nowhere is this confusion more prevalent or more harmful than it is in Russia. Yet Martov's formula legalizes this evil; it strives to make each and every one a party member.

We must not forget that every party member is responsible for the party and that the party is responsible for every party member . . . Our task is to place real control in the hands of the Central Committee, in order to preserve the firmness and maintain the purity of our party. We must strive to raise the title and the significance of party membership higher and higher. For this reason, I stand opposed to Martov's formula.[24]

Lenin had made his last appeal. The debates closed, and the congress now went through the lengthy motions of an open roll-call vote. The result: for Martov's formula — twenty-eight votes; for Lenin's — twenty-two. Lenin had suffered the first important defeat of his political career!

Of all the delegates at the congress, Lenin was probably the only one to grasp the full significance of the setback he had just received. Martov's formula had opened a breach through which "the mud" might trickle into the party. The only thing left to do was to attempt to "mend the vessel as hermetically as possible," to "bind the party with a second knot," [25] by packing its command centers, the CO and the CC, with determined and reliable leaders.

And so, foregoing sleep altogether, Lenin appealed individually to each member of the *Iskra* bloc, cajoling, arguing, threatening, using every weapon at his command to win a majority of them over to his side. As soon as he felt certain of this majority, he called a meeting of the *Iskra* caucus for the purpose of selecting the candidates for the Central Committee. The list that he presented for the approval of the caucus was indeed one of hardened Iskraists: out of a total of five candidates, he had picked three from the minority that followed him in the controversy over Paragraph One of the Rules (the definition of party membership), leaving one seat to his *Iskra* opponents and one to *Yuzhnii Rabochee*, *Iskra*'s principal Russian ally. But so well had Lenin done his work that, by a vote of nine to four with three abstentions, he won a majority of the *Iskra* caucus. Victory seemed within his grasp, and generously he sent a delegation to visit Martov and to make some compromise proposals. But his delegation was in for a surprise: Martov announced that, from this point on, he would no longer feel bound by the decisions of the caucus.[26]

This was indeed a "declaration of war" — and it seemed that for Lenin the war would be lost from the start, since the Martovites could look forward to the backing of the Bund and of *Rabochee Delo* in their fight against the *Iskra* majority. At this moment, fortune — or rather Lenin's foresight in his preparation of the congress' agenda — turned the wheels in his favor. As prescribed by the Order of the Day, the question of the Bund's constitution came up for a vote — and, in accordance with its earlier resolution, the congress denied to the Bund the exclusive right of representing the Jewish proletariat in the RSDRP. The Bund delegates walked out, and with them went four votes of the Martovite majority. Next on the agenda was the issue of the party's official representation abroad. Cleverly seizing on his new-found opportunity, Lenin moved for the dissolution of *Rabochee Delo* and for the recognition of *Iskra*'s organization, the League of Russian Social Democrats, as the exclusive representative of Social Democracy among the exiles. Even Martov had to vote for this resolution against *Iskra*'s traditional opponents, and after it was passed it was the turn of the Rabochedelists to bow out. The Martovites had lost two more votes, and from a minority (of six) Lenin's bloc was now converted into a majority of one. (On the basis of this slender majority, Lenin now adopted for his faction the title of *Bolsheviki* [Majorityites]. Through the subsequent years of intraparty squabbles, his partisans held onto this title jealously, although they were frequently reduced to a small minority of the party.)

Relentlessly driven by Lenin, his slender majority now moved to push through the congress the measures he had designed for the purpose of binding the party with a second knot. It defeated the opposition's attempt to curb the direct authority of the Central Committee by setting up intermediary links between it and the local party centers. By the passage of clever rules of election and coöptation, it secured for the Central Organ predominance in the Party Council; and for the Party Council, control over the Central Committee. Lenin now needed only one more success to insure his mastery over the Party — to win a secure majority on the Central Organ. To achieve this purpose, he proposed that the congress select as *Iskra*'s directorate (*Iskra* having been recognized already as the party's official organ) a new editorial board composed of three members, Martov, Plekhanov, and Lenin — for his side a majority of two to one!

After the reading of this proposal, complete bedlam broke loose among the delegates to the congress. To strike the names of Akselrod, Vera Zasulich, and Potresov from the roll of *Iskra*'s editors was a deadly insult to these hallowed names in Social Democracy. Rising pale and shaken from his seat, Martov announced that he would refuse to serve on the new editorial board without his old colleagues. What was now taking place, he indignantly claimed, was the last act in Lenin's struggle for influence over the CC. The majority of his fellow editors had indicated their opposition to the transformation of the CC into an instrument of the editorial board, and this was why it was now necessary to eliminate them:

> I had hoped that the congress would set an end to the state of siege within the party. In reality, this state of siege . . . is being prolonged and even aggravated! Only by confirming the old membership of the editorial board can we insure that the rights given by the rules to the CO will not be harmful to the party.[27]

Some of Lenin's followers attempted to deny this indictment. It was necessary, they argued, to elect a new editorial board because the old one was too large, too cumbersome — because a small, businesslike body was now needed to direct the expanded functions of the party organ efficiently. But Lenin met the challenge of Martov's accusation boldly and openly:

> Martov stated that this is an act in a struggle for influence over the CC in Russia. I will go further than Martov. Up till now, this struggle for influence constituted the entire activity of *Iskra* as a private group. We are now talking about more than that, about the organizational strengthening of this influence, not just about a struggle for it . . . What would have been the point of our work, of our struggle, if it had to be crowned by the continuation of the same old struggle for influence, and not by the acquisition and consolidation of [this] influence.
>
> Yes, comrade Martov is quite right: the step taken is undoubtedly a significant political step, attesting to the selection of one of the existing trends [to guide] the further work of our party. And I am not in the least intimidated by awesome phrases like "state of siege," "extraordinary laws against individual figures or groups," and so on. Toward wavering and tottering elements, we are not merely permitted, but compelled, to establish a state of siege. Our party rules and the centralist policy confirmed by the congress are nothing more nor less than a state of siege against the many contributors to political diffusion.[28]

The opposition's proposal to confirm the old editorial board was finally brought to a vote and automatically defeated. Lenin's proposal was passed, and when Martov repeated that he refused to serve without his old collaborates, the delegates instructed the other two editors (Lenin and Plekhanov) to coöpt a third editor, as soon as they found "a suitable person."

Thus on every issue since the debates on Paragraph One, Lenin had won a majority. But how shabby, how misleading his majority was: on this last vote, the elections to the *Iskra* editorial board, the score had been twenty-two votes for Lenin, two blank ballots, and twenty absten- tions (the Martovites had refused to vote) — this, when seven votes of Lenin's opposition had already been eliminated with the walkout of the Bundists and Rabochedelists.

The delegates to the congress had now driven themselves into a state of nervous exhaustion. They had no strength, no funds, no time left for further debates. Desultorily, after spending the evening hours of its last session in passing hasty and sometimes contradictory resolutions on the important issues that it had left untouched — such as the party's atti- tudes toward the liberals, toward the SR's, toward trade unions — the Second Congress adjourned on August 23, 1903. At one stroke, it had restored unity in the RSDRP, and hopelessly divided its ranks.

10

BOLSHEVISM AND MENSHEVISM: THE SEARCH FOR A DEFINITION

Lenin had won a victory; by all appearances, a decisive victory. Deserted by most of his colleagues, opposed by a majority of the delegates at the Second Congress, he had turned the tide and imposed his will on the representatives of Russian Social Democracy. Yet, even in the days immediately following the congress, his was not the elated mood of a conquering hero. The angry denunciations of Akselrod and Zasulich, Potresov and Trotsky, and especially Martov's continued refusal to serve on the new editorial board, could not lightly be dismissed. Martov had been more than just a collaborator; he had been a trusted friend, a most gifted disciple — whom the usually reticent Lenin had regarded with the indulgence and unreserved affection of an older brother.[*] Lenin's first instinct consequently was to make his peace. Through the intermediary of personal emissaries and in letters to Martov's friends, he made light of the differences that had arisen, apologized for the lapses in his own behavior, and appealed for a restoration of party unity. A note to Potresov, written but a few days after the congress had adjourned, was typical of these conciliatory, almost contrite gestures:

> And now I ask myself: why should we separate as enemies for the rest of our lives? I admit that I often acted and behaved with frightful irritation and rage. I am quite ready to acknowledge this fault of

---

[*] Lenin had consistently maintained this devotion for Martov during their collaboration, despite his frequent irritation at his friend's disorderly working habits. According to Martov's sister, who was with them during the Munich period, this affection had been fully reciprocated: "Never subsequently, perhaps, did [Martov] feel such an absolute solidarity in his ideas, in his understanding of tasks [as he did with Lenin and Potresov], and of course never again did he entertain such a flaming, I would say romantic, friendship with comrades . . . All of them were then passing through their 'rosy, dreamy youth' . . . Lenin had not yet lost his youthful romanticism, at least with respect to the few people who he considered 'his' — human relations were extremely valuable to him" (Lydia Dan, "Okolo redaktsii 'Iskry,' " p. 61).

mine to any comrade whatsoever . . . But when I consider without rage the results arrived at . . . I cannot see in the outcome anything, absolutely anything, harmful for the party or hurtful or insulting to the minority.[1]

But Martov was adamant. Not only did he continue to decline Lenin's offer of a place on the editorial board, but he now joined with the rest of the opposition in a complete boycott of the new Central Organ.* Already, the Martovites were searching for some doctrinal grounds upon which to base their opposition, and at first this search was difficult, not so much (as we have amply seen) because such differences were absent, but because they were still so subtle and had been buried and evaded for so long. On September 20, 1903, following a five-day conference of the Mensheviks (Minorityites), the first such formulation was published over the signatures of Martov and Trotsky. With a pomposity suggestive of Trotsky's early rhetorical style, this resolution announced:

> Considering that at the Second Congress of our party there evidently triumphed, in a number of questions, a tendency to change radically the former tactics of *Iskra* and to place the juridical strengthening of the power of the new editorial board over the ideological-training and the ideological-organizing role of the paper; considering that this tendency was expressed in the creation of a Soviet . . . which constitutes solely a transmission mechanism of the administrative power of the new editorial board of *Iskra* and an instrument of its tutelage over the Central Committee, which relegates the latter to the role of a simple servicing technical apparatus; considering that this sort of action must inevitably split the party into an arbitrarily selected, self-enclosed central organization on one hand, and a wide broken-down mass of Social Democratic workers on the other, compromising thereby the very concept of a single, centralized, and fighting party, we recognize that in the interest of the preservation and consolidation of unity in our party, we must wage an energetic and principled struggle against the tendency of deformed centralism characterized above, and prepare public opinion for a Third Congress.[2]

*Martov's anger against Lenin was heightened when he heard his former colleague claim that he had informed him even before the congress of his plans for the editorial board. Actually, Lenin had mentioned what he had in mind only in the vaguest and most general of terms, and Martov was largely justified in feeling that he had been left in the dark. "I think that in the friendship between Lenin and Martov, this was the first 'concealed thought,'" Martov's sister comments, "and for this reason it played a fateful role in the relations" between the two men.

At this time, Martov's revulsion was further aroused when he discovered that in the days immediately preceding the congress, Lenin's wife, Krupskaya, who had acted as secretary for the *Iskra* editorial board, had kept him in the dark about many of the instructions that Lenin had been sending, through her, to *Iskra*'s agents in Russia, as well as about some of the messages that she had been receiving from them. "It seemed to Martov that, "to put it crudely, [Krupskaya] had been engaged in double-bookkeeping," and had thus abused his confidence in her and in her husband. See Lydia Dan, "Okolo redaktsii 'Iskry,'" pp. 68–69.

The Martovites had found a doctrinal position of sorts. They could now consider themselves not just as a defeated electoral bloc, but as a fraction struggling against a "hypertrophied" and "mechanistic" centralist tendency, which was threatening to divide the party and to reduce the initiative and *samodeyatelnost* of its members. And with this new-found identity, they felt justified in raising their former conditions for peace. No longer would they be satisfied with the restoration of the old editorial board, a demand that Lenin was now inclined to accept.* As one of the two conflicting factions in the party, they now felt entitled to equal representation in both the Party Council and Central Committee.

The Mensheviks' resolution caught Lenin unprepared. Since the conclusion of the Second Congress, he too had considered — in his private notes and in his letters to his Russian followers — the meaning and the significance of the differences that had occurred. But although he had noted in these early commentaries the controversy over Paragraph One and had pointed with great satisfaction to the fact that his opponents, the "soft" Iskraists, the "Iskraists of the zigzagging line," had received the support of the "opportunists" of the Bund and *Rabochee Delo*, he had been quick to dismiss the current behavior of the Martovites as an expression of ire and wounded feelings over their defeat in the elections to the Central Organ. Thus, his first detailed account of the congress, an unpublished statement written for the private enlightenment of his friends and close followers, had ended with the conclusion:

> In examining the conduct of the Martovites after the congress — their refusal to collaborate [when the editorial board of the CO officially requested them to do so], their refusal to work for the CC, their propaganda boycott — I can only say that this is an insane attempt, unworthy of party members, to tear the party apart. And for what? *Only* due to dissatisfaction about the composition of the centers, *because objectively* we parted only on this; and subjective evaluations (such as insults, affronts, expulsions, removals, smears) are the product of wounded vanity and sickly fantasy. [Emphases in text.] [3]

But Lenin now had to shift his position. The Mensheviks had given him warning of their intention to wage a bitter factional struggle, a struggle for supremacy, in which issues as well as personalities would be

---

* As late as September 26, Martov had transmitted to Lenin, using Dan as an intermediary, the following statement of his conditions for peace: "The basis for an agreement is the restoration of the old editorial board. This agreement must include the fomulation of editorial rules that will specifically determine the instances in which the members of the editorial board vote in two groups with equal rights" (*Leninskii Sbornik*, VI, 262). By the end of September, according to Krupskaya's memoirs, Lenin agreed to Central Committeeman Glebov's suggestion that these conditions be accepted; "even to drag along in the old way was better than a split" (*Memories of Lenin*, I, 107).

involved; and it was time, therefore, for the Bolsheviks to mobilize their forces and to define the grounds on which they would elect to fight. "There is absolutely no hope left for peace," Lenin now wrote to his followers in the Russian local committees. "War is declared, and they are already preparing to fight in Russia. Get ready for a legal but relentless struggle. In all the committees without exception, we must absolutely occupy places with our own people." [4]

The war was on, and at the Congress of the League of Revolutionary Social Democrats Abroad, which opened at the beginning of October, Lenin made his first statement of the issues on which he would elect to wage it. The meetings of the League must have been an unbelievable sight. Lenin had suffered a serious injury on his way to the congress; his bicycle had run into a trolley, and in the collision one of his eyes had nearly been torn out. He appeared at the first session with his head swathed in bandages, and as he read off his prepared address, his frenzied opponents interrupted his statements by standing up and banging on the tops of their desks. Pale and shaking, Lenin went on with his speech. This time he chose to explain the continued conflict with the Martovites on the basis of the controversy over Paragraph One, but his analysis of this controversy was still a mere rehash of previous arguments: In his impatience to transform Social Democracy into a mass party, Martov had attempted to widen the party's boundaries to the point of complete diffusion and to take away from its centers any semblance of control over the membership. His formula had been based on a completely erroneous diagnosis of the contemporary situation; it had opened the doors to every babbler, to every intriguer, at a moment when the party was still riddled with such creatures. Martov had "accidentally fallen into the marsh," and all his gestures since the Second Congress — and the support that these gestures had received from *Iskra*'s long-standing opponents — clearly indicated that instead of attempting to extricate himself from the marsh, he was now sinking into it more and more deeply.[5]

Lenin's statement had followed well-trodden paths, and so did Martov's rebuttal:

> We proposed a formula that would take better into account the actual impossibility of establishing organizational ties between the committees, the basic party organizations, and all conscious Social Democrats, especially conscious workers . . . We pointed out that the growth of the Social Democratic movement is overrunning our organizational work [because police conditions are preventing the formation of stable labor circles attached to the committees] . . . In the event of the adoption of Lenin's formula, we would find dozens of actual leaders of the masses outside the party.

Toward the very end of his speech, Martov's arguments finally approached the root of the controversy, but his statement was still veiled in the obscurity of the half-understood. He stated:

> Of the two opposed organizational tendencies, one is expressed in the statement made by Lenin yesterday that *"the wider the movement the wider already the organization,"* and in the argument of his partisans at the congress that [our version] of Paragraph One brings opportunistic *intelligenty* into the party; the second is expressed in the effort not to permit the strongly conspiratorial and necessarily narrow organizations of professional revolutionaries to tear themselves away from the masses of active fighters, from the conscious workers acting under the leadership of our committees . . . In our eyes, an organization on the whole constitutes an autonomously formed and secure collectivity.[6]

An organization is an autonomously formed and secure collectivity — this statement in Martov's speech constituted a first, if confused, definition of the views that the Mensheviks would eventually oppose to Lenin's theory of organization. But it was to take many long months of debate — and Lenin's own polemical efforts — to bring these views fully to the light.

The League Congress closed its sessions with the complete rout of Lenin's partisans and with the prospect of an enduring schism in Social Democracy. At this crucial moment, Plekhanov decided to sue for peace, not because he had suddenly discovered differences between his views and Lenin's, but simply because it finally appeared to him that the issues at stake did not justify the harm that the controversy was causing the party. But Lenin would no longer hear of any compromise, and rather than agree to Plekhanov's proposal to coöpt the old members of the editorial board, he decided to withdraw from the Central Organ.

Lenin had now been deserted by every single one of his old *Iskra* colleagues; yet he was determined to keep on fighting for true "Iskraism." Having lost control of the Central Organ, he would now strive to use the Central Committee as his chief instrument in the struggle against the Martovites. Frantically he tried to rally his followers in the CC, pleading with them almost daily to hold fast, to struggle to the end. In a typical note, dated November 5, a week after Plekhanov's defection, Lenin wrote, "I already wrote yesterday about the scandal here [at the League Congress], and about the fact that Plekhanov was frightened, and entered into negotiations with them. My personal view is that any concessions would be humiliating and would discredit completely the present Central Committee. Everything is at stake, and if the CC is not ready for a decisive struggle, for a struggle to the end, it would be better to give everything up to them at once."[7] And on November eighth, three days later: "I have left the editorial board for good . . . I am now fighting for the CC which the Martovites also want to seize, brazened by Plekhanov's cowardly betrayal." [8]

Many members of the Central Committee were inclined to make peace. To them, as to Plekhanov, the issues involved seemed too minor to warrant a split in the party. But prodded by Lenin's cajolements — and by his warnings of prospective doom — they finally rallied to his side; and although they held back from the more extreme of the steps he advocated, they stood by him for eight long months.

It was now Plekhanov's turn to be startled. Haltingly, he attempted to explain — to himself and to his readers — the reasons for Lenin's obstinacy, and all that he could find to account for it, and for the continuation of the split, was the "formalistic," "schematic," quality of Lenin's mind, the "inflexibility" of his approach to political problems, and his incapacity to stand "on a political rather than juridical plane"! "Individuals who are capable of rising above formalism argue about substance" rather than about form, he lectured the man who was to prove one of Russia's most agile tacticians.

> To rise to a political plane, [one must] guide himself, not by the rules, or better, not only by the rules, but by the actual state of affairs, by the existing relationship of forces . . .
>
> We must preserve unity at all costs [concluded Plekhanov], especially since there are no longer any basic differences among us. So complete a unity of views now rules in our ranks that a split would have no serious foundation, and would seem comprehensible and forgivable only to silly people.[9]

While Plekhanov was sententiously proclaiming that no serious differences of views existed to justify the continuation of the conflict between the two factions, Akselrod and Martov were continuing their efforts to find such a doctrinal definition for the split. They sought to outline such a definition through a historical interpretation of the evolution of Russian Social Democracy: The "development of the class self-consciousness and political initiative (*samodeyatelnost*) of the laboring masses, their unification into an independent revolutionary force," these had been the major goals of Social Democracy the world over. In Russia, however, due to the undeveloped state of the proletariat, the Social Democrats had been compelled to use a devious route in their pursuit of this objective; in their efforts to awaken the proletariat to political life, they had been compelled to use an outside force, the radical intelligentsia. Thus, a basic contradiction had arisen — between the Social Democrats' subjective goal of furthering the political maturation and independence of the proletariat, and their objective method of subordinating it to the intelligentsia of other classes.

Lenin's program was calculated to perpetuate this contradiction. In his anxiety to ward off the penetration of unreliable elements into the party, he and his partisans seemed ready to sacrifice the party's main purpose, its very *"raison d'être"* — the development of the consciousness and *samodeyatelnost* of the working class. The organizational apparatus that he contemplated, with "its great specialization of functions" and its "multiplicity of isolated roles under the control of leading centers," might result at best in the short-lived mastery of a radical democratic elite over the laboring masses, but it would never lead to the political maturation of the proletariat as a class.[10]

Akselrod had never been a particularly sharp social theorist, but this last broadside at Lenin's views was not far off the mark. An intelligentsia leadership leaning on the proletariat, "utilizing the labor movement as a simple instrument . . . in the preparatory phase of the bourgeois revolution," a conspiratorial party securing for itself a position of leadership through the superior technical competence of its organizational apparatus — versus a truly working-class party, depending for its strength on the *individual* maturity and initiative of its members: this was not a bad statement of the perspectives opened by the current controversy on party organization, or at least of the Mensheviks' position in it.

Now that Akselrod had defined the issues, the editorials of the new *Iskra* started to pound them. "Our chief concern should be the development of the class self-consciousness of the proletariat," stated the editorial in *Iskra* No. 58. "The attempt to establish harmony in the organization of the party by enclosing it with rules and regulations . . . [would] weaken the party's influence over the masses and leave their revolutionary strength behind it," asserted Martov in *Iskra* No. 60. And an editorial in *Iskra* No. 62 repeated: "All attempts to undermine by formalistic games free collective initiative in our chief job, the revolutionary indoctrination of the laboring masses and the organization of their vanguard, are particularly harmful at the present critical moment," the eve of the overthrow of absolutism.

But while the new *Iskra* had finally arrived at a relatively clear statement of the Menshevik platform, it was still somewhat vague about the fundamental assumptions of its opponents. While the editors were now clear about the potential effects of Lenin's organizational platform, they continued to attribute its *motives* largely to a desire to protect the party by mechanical means against the penetration of intriguing opportunists. And since he had originally favored Lenin's formula for this very reason, Plekhanov, quite understandably, continued to be the chief culprit in this respect. As late as May 1904, he was calling on Lenin to listen to reason and censuring him for his blind organizational fanaticism. Comparing the controversy that Social Democracy was now going through to the philosophcial disputes of the 1830's, Plekhanov exclaimed:

While at that time, people quarreled over minor philosophical issues, they do so today over minor organizational points. Even then, the most natural impressions were deprived of their naturalness by being viewed through the prism of philosophy. Now the simplest question of revolutionary practice immediately assumes a ludicrous scholastic character, as one attempts to fit it right away into an organizational scheme.

Plekhanov went on to explain that the Economists had previously supported Revisionism through "a misunderstanding," and that they had seen their error and corrected it. It was slanderous, therefore, to keep on calling them Revisionists: "If we kept these people, who now agree with us on party principles, from becoming full-fledged members of the party, we would weaken our forces, [our capacity] to combat those who have struggled and continue to struggle against us, not due to any misunderstanding, but because of error-proof class instincts." [11]

It was now Lenin's turn to shed light on the running controversy — to explain that the Bolshevik platform was motivated by wider concerns than the fate of the Economists. And he proceeded to do so in a long polemical pamphlet, which he appropriately named "One Step Forward, Two Steps Backward" ("Shag vpered, dva shaga nazad"), a title borrowed from Martov's previous statement that the organizational scheme formulated during the *Iskra* period had become "inaccurate or, at best, one-sided," once the development of party life had taken but one step forward.[12] Like so many of Lenin's writings, "One Step Forward, Two Steps Backward" was an extremely long, repetitive, and discursive political statement, which must have overwhelmed many of his readers through the sheer mass and doggedness of its arguments. Yet, in spite of its lack of continuity and its blunt and inelegant style, this work provided a most impressive presentation of the political and psychological rationale for Lenin's vision of party organization.

Akselrod was now denouncing Lenin's views as "formalistic" perversions of the concept of the party that the old *Iskra* had upheld. The *Iskra* idea had stood for a particular party program and for specific party tactics, asserted Akselrod, not for any concrete organizational plan. This program and these tactics were far more important than any organization, for they embodied the "content, the developing practical work of the party in its ideological struggle," while the forms of party organization represented nothing more than "forms . . . enclosing this content — the process of the party's ideological struggle."

To these arguments, Lenin answered that from its very beginning *Iskra* had constituted an organizational cell as well as a literary organ. He pointed out that as early as its fourth issue, *Iskra* had proposed (in Lenin's article, "Where to Begin") a detailed and complete plan of organization, and that for three years it had fought systematically and undeviatingly for the fulfillment of this plan.[13] And this fundamental characteristic of *Iskra's* policy had been founded on the realization, at least by some of its editors, that a correct system of organization was as necessary a condition for the unity and effective functioning of the party as was a satisfactory program and tactics. The problem of party organization, the problem of developing "forms of a higher type" to enclose the party's ideological struggle, was now the central issue confronting Social Democracy. This truth had been demonstrated neatly at the Second Congress, where, after voting for the desired party program and tactics, the Bund had split with the majority of the delegates on the organizational question, and on that question alone.[14]

Social Democracy could no longer be satisfied with "the loose Oblomov gowns and slippers" of the circle period. It was in need of "forms of a higher type," of formal rules to govern its activities. To those who had grown accustomed to comfortable gowns and slippers, such formal rules might appear "narrow and straight-lined," "burdensome and slow," deterrents to the "free" process of the ideological struggle. But now that Social Democracy had come of age, now that it was a party and not a group of isolated circles, it could no longer rely exclusively on "personal friendships and trusts." It had to depend on "formally prescribed procedures," on formal, "bureaucratically worded" rules; it had to insure that the activities of every one of its members and the decisions of every one of its constituent groups would be accountable before the entire party.[15]

Akselrod was asserting that because Social Democracy was by definition a class party it should now strive to become a mass organization. This was an erroneous and dangerous conclusion:

> For what reasons, on the basis of what logic, can we draw the conclusion from the fact that we are a class party that a distinction between those who enter the party and those who adjoin it is unnecessary. Just the contrary is true: because of the existence of different degrees of consciousness and activism [among our supporters], it is indispensable to bring out these differences in their degree of proximity to the party.[16]

The rules governing the party's network of organizations should therefore explicitly distinguish among the organizations included within the party, the organizations adjoined to it, the organizations not adjoined to it but in fact acting under its leadership and control, and finally those unorganized elements of the working class which would submit to Social Democratic leadership only during particularly strong outbreaks of the class struggle.[17]

The Mensheviks were denying the need for such an articulate differentiation of ranks, because of their readiness to entrust the fate of Social Democracy to the "process of the ideological struggle," to the process of life itself. But it wasn't true that (as Martov had stated) "life was creating organizations faster than the Social Democrats were capable of including them in the party." It wasn't true that Social Democracy could be satisfied to act as the *virazhenie,* as the passive expression, of the development of the working class, or that the juridical rules of the party should correspond to the contemporary position of the proletariat. Actually, life was "creating far fewer organizations than were required by the labor movement," [18] and, therefore, it could not be entrusted with the fate of the working class or with the development of its class consciousness. This was the responsibility of Social Democracy; it was its responsibility, as the conscious and active expression (*soznatelnaya viraszitelnitsya*) of the development of the working-class movement, to "work out organizational relations" which would secure for the proletariat "a specified level of consciousness, and systematically raise this level." [19] To satisfy this purpose, the juridical definition of the party had to correspond to the direction rather than to the contemporary state of development of the working class;[20] the party, as such, had to constitute a vanguard, capable of "raising wider and wider segments of the laboring masses to its [own] advanced level." [21] Only such a picked vanguard could successfully lead the masses of uneducated workers under the conditions of "endless fragmentation, oppression, and mental torpor," to which they were being subjected by capitalism.[22] The "more carefully selected" this party, the less "wavering and instability" were permitted within its ranks, "the wider, the richer, and the more fruitful" would be its influence over the laboring masses.[23]

This was precisely the assumption that the Mensheviks were now questioning. To them it seemed that the precariousness of the Social Democrats' hold on the loyalty of the laboring masses — as evidenced by the recent successes of the government-sponsored Zubatovshchina — had been due largely to the party's failure to open its doors wide to the leadership that the working class *had itself created* and to make room for the individual initiative of these leaders. And this difference of views was the first expression of a fundamental conflict between the Bolshevik and the Menshevik concepts of the development of the individual's consciousness. While Akselrod and Martov were satisfied to view the rise of class consciousness and initiative among the workers as a function of largely uncontrollable forces such as "the class struggle," "life," or the "free process of ideological struggle," and were therefore concerned about the restrictions that a tight organizational system would impose on the development of these forces, Lenin could not really conceive of the successful and continued growth of the workers' consciousness and activism except through the intervention of the party's organizations.

Only a united, unwavering, and completely monolithic party — acting as the very embodiment, as the very objectification of socialist consciousness — would be capable of drawing the fragmented and dulled laboring masses onto the path to socialist consciousness and to a victorious revolution. Only formal, "bureaucratic" rules of organization could safeguard this party "from the shameful stagnation and waste of strength" [24] that had prevailed during the circle period of the history of Social Democracy. Only the tightly knit organizations defined by these rules could protect the party's individual members from the "willfulness and the caprices," [25] "the diffusion and the elusiveness," "the discrepancy between word and deed" [26] that had characterized the "circle spirit" and were still typical of contemporary opportunism.

The Mensheviks were now complaining that the Leninist scheme of organization would transform the party into "an immense factory with a director in the form of the CC at its head." In raising this complaint, they were merely giving one more indication of the "anarchistic, individualistic" character of their "bourgeois intellectual" mentality. "For wasn't it this bogey, the factory . . . that [had] brought together and disciplined the proletariat and placed it at the head of the toiling and exploited masses?" [27] In the same way, a factory-like system of organization would transform the party into an effective fighting force, capable of acting as the leader and educator of the proletariat, capable of preventing its members from slipping into the marsh of opportunism.

In this argument, the basic tenets of the Bolshevik philosophy of organization were once more expressed. No rank-and-file Social Democrat could develop and consistently maintain socialist consciousness and will *without participating in and identifying with a party organization;* the party alone could give to the personality of its individual members its consciousness and its form. At the Second Congress, Lenin's lieutenant, Pavlovich, had been the first to give articulate expression to this facet of the Bolshevik faith:

> Rules are written not for individuals but for collectives. I would go further: without the sanction of a party organization, these individuals can in no way be considered as representatives of the party . . . If we adopt Martov's formula, we will allow [into the party] an anarchistic mass without accountability. How can we reconcile the picture of our party, ramifying its branches all over Russia, with the existence [in it] of unaccountable active members who have joined the party in their own right? How can this anarchistic conception be reconciled with comrade Martov's own demand that our Party be the conscious expression of the process [of history].[28]

In "One Step Forward, Two Steps Backward," Lenin had finally brought forth a clear if somewhat discursive statement of the Bolshevik view of organization. Yet the two major attempts that were now made in the opposing camp to dissect — and tear down — this theory of organization, unveiled as many blindspots as they did insights into the rationale of the Bolshevik point of view.

The first of these attempts at a comprehensive analysis of Lenin's views was made by the old master of Socialist doctrine, G. V. Plekhanov. Properly enough, Plekhanov chose to direct the brunt of his criticism at Lenin's long-held and long-since-stated assumption that the working class was incapable by its own resources of developing a socialist consciousness, and that only with the aid of a revolutionary bacillum coming from the outside could it develop into a movement determined and able to overthrow the capitalist order. Lenin's belief that the contradictions of capitalism could by themselves drive the proletariat only to trade unionism — i.e., only to a struggle within the framework of capitalist relations — Plekhanov pointed out, was a flat contradiction of the teachings of Marx and Engels. It denied the fundamental proposition of historical materialism that the conditions of existence determine thought. It denied that economic necessity could carry the working-class movement to its logical end, the Socialist Revolution. The revolutionary bacillum of the intelligentsia had accelerated this movement, to be sure. It had brought "a clearer consciousness," a "more scientific" point of view to the proletariat, and thereby aided its preparation for the struggle against capitalism. But even without the intervention of this external factor, the working-class movement would have moved sooner or later in the direction of socialism. Lenin's denial of this proposition was a telling commentary on the "subjectivism" of his point of view, on his failure to understand the role of objective factors in history.

Even if it was a bit belated, there was nothing wrong, up to this point, with Plekhanov's critique of Lenin's evaluation of the "spontaneous labor movement." * But his article proceeded to attribute these Leninist views on organization wholly to a belief that the proletariat could constitute only a passive instrument in the hands of the intelligentsia. It was, of course, true that during his polemic with the Economists two years earlier, Lenin had asserted that in and by itself — without the intervention of the revolutionary bacillum of the intelligentsia — the working class would be incapable of progression beyond trade unionism. But to deduce from this that Lenin placed any greater trust in the capacities of the individual *intelligent* than he did in those of

* Plekhanov offered a revealing explanation of his failure to criticize Lenin's heretical tendencies up to this moment. It wasn't that he had ever agreed with Lenin's arguments, Plekhanov explained. But he had refrained from open criticism of them, owing to a conviction that Lenin was an "instinctive Marxist" — although not a conscious one — who would progress beyond his erroneous views: "I was convinced that our instinctive orthodox would become more and more conscious" ("The Working Class and the Social Democratic Intelligentsia," *Iskra*, nos. 70–71, July 25–August 1, 1904).

the worker was, by this time, completely unwarranted. After all, it was only a few weeks since Lenin had published a violent critique in "One Step Forward, Two Steps Backward" of the "anarchistic," "individualistic" tendencies of the intelligentsia, and attributed the Mensheviks' behavior to these bourgeois characteristics.

Another comprehensive analysis of Lenin's organizational views now came from the pen of a considerably younger and far more sensitive critic, Rosa Luxemburg, a vibrant and dynamic young woman whose fame was already spreading in Social Democratic circles throughout Central and Eastern Europe. Luxemburg's discussion was more perceptive and richer in its implications than Plekhanov's, but it, too, went partly off the mark. Quite correctly, she discerned two basic characteristics in Lenin's organizational plan. The first was its emphatic distinction between the leading ranks of the movement and the surrounding, though active elements, a differentiation that Lenin had designed to correspond to the differences in the levels of consciousness present in the Social Democratic movement. The second was an insistence on "firm discipline and continuous interference by the central [party] institutions in all the expressions of the life of local party organizations."

What specific social and psychological factors had given rise to this ultra-centralist point of view? This was Luxemburg's promising first question. In her answer, she outlined two such conditions in Russia's political development that had differentiated it from that of Western Europe. First, there was the fact that while the organization of the proletariat had resulted in the West from the unification and class rule of the bourgeoisie, in Russia — in the absence of such a class rule of the bourgeoisie — this task of unifying and organizing the proletariat had fallen wholly on the shoulders of Social Democracy. The Russian Social Democrats had been compelled to pull the working class directly out of a politically "atomized" and fragmented state, and since this had been their legitimate chief concern, it was almost inevitable that they should have become fascinated with centralist slogans.

The second factor involved in the Bolsheviks' current hypercentralist craze, Luxemburg asserted, revolved around the peculiar psychological position of the intelligentsia. Unlike their Western European *confrères,* who enjoyed the luxuries of a secure class position and of parliamentary forms of government — and who were therefore mentally predisposed to a "bourgeois individualistic cult of the self" — the Russian intelligentsia had lived isolated and *déclassés* in a hostile environment and were consequently inclined to "self-abasement and self-doubt." For them, the path of least resistance was not the individualism of the Western intellectual, but rather the hypercentralism now being advocated by Lenin and his camp.

This was indeed a shrewd observation, but Luxemburg promptly forgot its implications in the remainder of her article. Using the model of the neo-Jacobin philosophy of Blanqui, she proceeded to attribute the doctrinal assumptions of the French revolutionist to Lenin: Lenin contemplated the subordination of the working-class movement to the leadership of the intelligentsia; Lenin viewed the organization of the proletariat, the growth of its consciousness, and its final struggle for emancipation as moments mechanically differentiated in time, whereas Marx had shown conclusively that these constituted but different aspects of one and the same process; Lenin believed that the Social Democratic leadership could formulate ready-made, rigid tactics for all political situations, and it was for this reason that he now insisted that all Social Democratic fighters be mechanically subordinated to the party centers. Every single one of these allegations was partly or wholly unfounded. Luxemburg herself would eventually discover this — and thereupon move over to Lenin's side of the fence.

But one of her long list of accusations was completely justified (and was to prove a source of repeated conflicts between Lenin and herself in subsequent revolutionary situations). Luxemburg discerned in the Leninist credo an inherent lack of confidence in the capacity of *individual* members of the party or proletariat to observe discipline, to act with a united will, to depend on their own resources and on the experience of their own struggle. It was due to this distrust of the individual personality — and to a failure to perceive the "creative character" of the "burning historical process" — that Lenin was so insistent on externally imposed standards of behavior, on externally upheld "slave-like and mechanical" discipline. To this view, Luxemburg now opposed a belief in the capacity of the masses to develop consciousness, *self-discipline, self-centralism,* in the process of their own "spontaneous" struggle.[29] And this became a basic component of the Menshevik faith.

Every one of *Iskra*'s editors now took up Luxemburg's arguments. The old and self-effacing Vera Zasulich, who never before had demonstrated any particular dialectical skill, published an article in *Iskra* No. 70, which demonstrated in the most illuminating manner that Lenin was confusing the idea of the party completely with the concept of organization. The organization that his scheme had designed, Zasulich pointed out, was not at all an organization of people but an organization of functions — an organization of leadership and control — that was intended to extend only as far as did the area of effective control by the Central Committee. "What is a party after all?" Zasulich rhetorically inquired. "A real life party is born — even without any organization — when people who think and feel in the same way oppose themselves to people who think and feel differently." In the specific instance of Social Democracy, the party had to be defined therefore as "that section of the population which Social Democracy [had drawn] to participate in its theoretical and practical struggle." In Lenin's eyes, this was the definition of a movement, not the definition of a party. But was it not "the chief task of the organized ranks of a party to absorb as great a portion of the movement as possible?" Lenin had refused to accept this premise — feeling that it would make it impossible for the central party organs to wield effective control over their membership. But was such control so crucially needed in a real party? In a real party, "the workers [would] consider party affairs as their own, they [would] consider themselves responsible for them, not the CC, but to themselves." [30]

In the Mensheviks' critique of Lenin's organizational views, Akselrod, as well, was now coming to the heart of the matter. He pointed out the fact that Lenin conceived of organization and of the consistency of principles achieved by it as some sort of sudden phenomenon, "appearing, as had Minerva out of Jupiter's head, as a ready-made product, as the result of some potent injunction or of some magic act." [31] This was a penetrating diagnosis of the psychological attributes that Lenin had assigned to organization. It was not, as Luxemburg had stated, that Lenin's view mechanically differentiated in time between the urge to struggle, consciousness, and organization. Rather, Lenin was conceiving of entrance into an organization as the one form of commitment by an individual that could effectively break the cycle of self-willed outbursts and apathy, impulsive activity and passivity, that characterized, in his eyes, the *natural rhythm* of the "spontaneous" labor movement, as well as the psychology of the individual member of the intelligentsia. Since the party member's decision to enter an organization involved in a sense merely a momentary act, since his assumption of responsibility before his fellows — before the party's disciplinary rules and criteria of value — was, at least symbolically, the matter of just an instant, the birth of an organization and the consequent consolidation of the consciousness and will to struggle of its members might also be perceived as a sudden phenomenon, as the product of a magical act.

To this view, Akselrod opposed the Mensheviks' vision of "a living organization and group of real leaders [developing] *gradually* — from inside the party — on the basis of self-training and collective adjustment to conditions of time and place." The development of the class self-consciousness and autonomy (*samostoyatelnost*) of the proletariat was now the paramount task of Social Democracy; it could successfully be achieved only if the party widened its organizations and intensified its agitation among the laboring masses.

This was now a task of the greatest urgency. Upon its immediate fulfillment, Akselrod and Martov warned, upon the successful transformation of Social Democracy into a mass party, would depend the very survival of the Social Democratic movement. For the final over-throw of absolutism was rapidly approaching, and following its down-fall, Akselrod and Martov foresaw the beginning of an era of political freedom and of "open political struggle," in which the politically eman-cipated proletariat would suddenly be confronted with new opportunities and with new responsibilities. In that rapidly approaching era, Social Democracy could not expect to hold the proletariat in line by any bonds other than the loyalty, the consciousness, and the activism of its individ-ual members. "Now that the fall of tsarism is approaching," Martov proclaimed, "our task is to prepare for the entry of the Russian prole-tariat, as a conscious class, into the spheres of political life that the Russian bourgeoisie is attempting to seize in its monopolistic clutch." [32] And Akselrod added that if Social Democracy failed in this task, it would have to face nothing less than annihilation: "Either Social Democracy will now actually become a proletarian class party, or it will be forced to depart from the [historical] scene." [33]

Thus Akselrod and Martov had wisely tied the problem of the in-dividual's relationship to the party with the revolutionary perspectives that were now confronting Russian Social Democracy. Indeed, the two questions were inextricably linked; the position to be assigned to the individual party member would inevitably depend upon the role defined for the party in the impending revolution. The character of the coming revolution, the tactics to be utilized in it by Social Democracy, were the last crucial issues that had to be debated before the identity of the Bolsheviks and Mensheviks could fully be defined. This final link in their world view was forged only at the last possible instant, at a mo-ment when the edifice of absolutism was already shaking under the impact of the gathering revolutionary storm.

11

THE PARTY AND REVOLUTION

Thus there is something about the very nature of the proletariat of our country which gives it the capacity to win even when "objective causes" are not for it but against it.

M. N. Pokrovskii, *Istoriya Proletariata SSSR*

As the first decade of the new century approached its half-way point, the rumble of a great impending storm was at last beginning to sound throughout the vast expanses of the Russian land, and to all but the most skeptical, it seemed clear that great political and social changes were in the offing. Outcries of dissatisfaction, intimations of revolt, could now be heard from the most diverse sections of European Russia and from the most varied of its social groups — from the enslaved agricultural workers of Western Russia and from the independent peasant farmers of Georgia, from the moderate gentry in the zemstva and from the passionate Socialist Revolutionary students in the universities, from the uneducated and unskilled workers in the Zubatovshchina and from the Social Democratic "proletariat."

The Russian autocracy had been living on borrowed time. The attempt to superimpose upon the edifice of absolutism the appurtenances of a modern state had resulted in the development of insoluble contradictions in every sphere of Russian life. The industrial giants that Witte had constructed at so great a cost could not be supported by the pauperized and discontented peasantry, and the generous government policy of industrial subsidies and protective tariffs had alienated the autocracy's long-standing ally, the land-owning gentry, which through the agency of the zemstva was now raising increasingly heretical outcries.

Not only had the attempt to modernize the Russian state proved economically unsound, but it had also given birth to two new social groups — the professional classes and the industrial proletariat — for which no place could be found in the old caste society. And the various palliatives to which the government had sporadically resorted to allay the dissatisfactions of these two groups (the most recent of which had been the Zubatov policy of government-sponsored trade-unionism) had succeeded only in increasing the articulateness of both the workers and the intelligentsia.*

The autocracy was now confronted as well by a redoubtable set of political opponents: an increasingly articulate zemstvo group at the right, a more radical liberal movement under the leadership of Struve's *Osvobozhdenie* at the center, and the irreconcilable Social Democratic and Socialist Revolutionary parties at the left.

In February 1904 the tsarist government embarked on the always dangerous experiment of a foreign war, a conflict with Japan for supremacy in the Far East, which was designed by some of its advocates at least (especially by Vyacheslav Plehve, the over-imaginative Minister of the Interior) to divert the country's attention and to restore its loyalty to the autocracy. It seemed at first that Plehve might succeed in his purpose. The zemstvo opposition quieted down and the Osvobozhdenie movement veered somewhat toward the right in support of the "patriotic war." But the war soon took a disastrous turn. Not only did the country sink into a deep economic depression, but the armies of the Tsar which had been expected to "bury the Japanese enemy under their hats," suffered instead one defeat after another.

Once more the edifice of absolutism began to totter. On July 28, 1904, the hated Plehve was assassinated while on his way to the St. Petersburg railroad station. He was succeeded by a far more conciliating and moderate figure, Prince Svyatopolk Mirsky, who now did his best to quiet public opinion. But the voices of the opposition could no longer be silenced. The journal *Osvobozhdenie,* the organ of the liberal movement of the professional classes, veered once more toward the left, and its editors now called for the establishment of a "democratic constitutional regime," affirming that there existed "no intermediary point between absolutism and constitutionalism." In October 1904 representatives of the Osvobozhdenie movement, of the SR's, and of the Polish opposition (the Social Democrats boycotted this conference), met in Paris to coördinate their activities and to work out a common program of demands. This conference adopted a platform calling for the creation of a legislature elected by universal suffrage, and urged that a more repre-

* A forewarning of the disastrous prospects opened by the Zubatovshchina had already been sounded in 1903, when one of Zubatov's agents launched a strike in Odessa over which the authorities quickly lost control. Although the Zubatov experiment was thereupon abandoned in Central and Southern Russia, it was continued in St. Petersburg under the leadership of Father Gapon. Its final product was the Gapon-led demonstration of January 22, 1905, which marked the beginning of the 1905 Revolution.

sentative and public conference be called in Russia to discuss current political and economic issues. In spite of a specific prohibition by the government, such a conference was held under the auspices of the zemstva between November 19 and 22 and its majority ratified the Paris meeting's demand for the election of an assembly with legislative authority.

Upon the adjournment of the zemstvo conference, the long series of events began that culminated in the Revolution of 1905 — the formation of professional and peasant unions to support the zemstvo program, the banquet campaign in the course of which this program was endorsed by various professional groups, the Gapon demonstration of January 22, the various liberal congresses, the general strike of October 1905, the formation of the Petersburg Soviet of Workers' Deputies. But already — at this moment in November 1904 — it appeared highly probable that unless the government initiated major political concessions, the country would soon be thrown into revolution.

This, then was the revolutionary situation to which Akselrod and Martov were pointing, the situation which, in their view, required the immediate reconstruction of the RSDRP. Both Akselrod and Martov had recognized clearly that the question of the organization of the party should hinge in the last analysis on the nature of the tactics that Social Democracy would adopt in the rapidly worsening political crisis. An ultimate question thus had to be posed before the issues could be clearly laid before the party: what would be the nature and the dynamics of the coming revolution? What were the objectives and the political role that, at this crucial moment, Social Democracy should assign to itself?

What objective characteristics had history assigned to the impending revolution? The Mensheviks could give but one answer to this question, the answer that had become sanctified as Marxist dogma: the coming revolution would be a "bourgeois revolution," a revolution that would "establish the conditions for the free development of the bourgeois economic order," a revolution whose chief beneficiary would be the bourgeoisie since the latter would inherit the class rule of society.[1] But the workers, too, would draw considerable gains from this "bourgeois revolution" — provided that they extended it to the objective boundaries assigned to it by history. They could gain from it a wide-open "field," an almost limitless "expanse" (*prostor*) for their further development as a class-conscious party. They could gain from it "political freedom, popular sovereignty, political and civic equality" — all the conditions required for the successful development of the class struggle that would eventually end in their complete emancipation, in the triumph of socialism.[2]

But the Mensheviks insisted that all the political advantages the proletariat might gain during the months and years ahead could not blur the fact that the political order now impending was a bourgeois order, under which a "democratic" government would rule "for a substantially long" period of time.[3] Thus, to all the leaders of Menshevism, to Plekhanov as well as to Martov, to Potresov as well as to Akselrod, the broad perspectives of the immediate future appeared at this moment preordained. And it therefore seemed to them that the main task of Social Democracy was to see to it that the *objective boundaries* of these future perspectives be reached.

What tactics should Social Democracy adopt in order to fulfill this task, in order to gain for the proletariat the "maximum favorable conditions" for its subsequent development? It would seem that the Mensheviks' answer to this question should have hinged on their expectations concerning the intentions of the bourgeoisie, concerning the political course that would be adopted by the social class that represented, after all, the future rulers of the country. But, surprisingly perhaps, this diagnosis of the liberals' intentions and prospective behavior varied considerably from one Menshevik leader to another.

Potresov, for one, was perfectly satisfied (and quite legitimately, on the whole) that "present-day liberalism" — at least as represented by the Osvobozhdenie movement — was characterized by "a definite pull toward the idea of unlimited constitutional freedom." Unlike the more conservative zemstvo elements, he asserted, "bourgeois democracy" did not dread the perspective of unrestricted political liberty. It was "sufficiently learned and sufficiently sophisticated to know that popular dissatisfaction and agitation [constituted] a valuable weapon for the liberal movement" and that the bourgeois world was not threatened with any immediate "danger by the perspectives of the revolutionary ideology" of Social Democracy.[4]

Plekhanov did not share this unbounded admiration for "bourgeois democracy": although he had always emphasized the progressive character of the bourgeoisie, he invariably had been rather contemptuous of its concrete political manifestations. Nevertheless, he now agreed with Potresov that "society" — provided the Social Democrats did not frighten it with "tactless outbursts" or unnecessarily radical proclamations — could be relied upon to join in the struggle for political freedom.[5]

This definitely was not Martov's opinion. Unlike Plekhanov, he had always viewed the bourgeoisie with a jaundiced and suspicious eye, and he saw nothing in its current behavior to allay his suspicions. "Struve and the *Osvobozhdentsi*," he wrote in an *Iskra* editorial dated December 1, 1904, "do not want to carry the bourgeois revolution through to its logical end"; they do not want "to develop the revolutionary energy of the social forces that are supporting the political leadership of the 'liberal democratic' parties up to the limits set by history." Rather, they wish "to assign ahead of time a boundary to this development. They appeal, not to the implacable logic of historical development, but to political considerations." [6] The proletariat was the only organized political force that could not and would not indulge in "half compromises" or deals. It was the "prime mover," the "central figure" advanced by the bourgeois revolution — and upon its shoulders, and its shoulders alone, lay the responsibility of working out the program for this revolution and of pursuing it to its logical end.[7]

Yet in spite of these serious differences with his colleagues about the political reliability of the liberal movement, Martov agreed with their diagnosis of the specific political tactics that should be adopted by the Social Democrats. These tactics, which were worked out chiefly by Akselrod and Plekhanov, were designed to encourage and support the liberal movement and to radicalize its political program, and at the same time to keep completely intact the political independence of Social Democracy. In accordance with these tactics, the Mensheviks refused to participate in the Paris "Conference of Revolutionary and Opposition Elements" — "so as not to appear to fuse with other parties" [8] — and yet offered to support each and every one of these movements, under the condition that they agree to the Social Democrats' demand for universal suffrage and freedom of speech and assembly.

To implement this program concretely, the Mensheviks worked out in November 1904 a specific plan of agitation for the campaign that was then being conducted by the zemstva. This plan contemplated the organization of political demonstrations by working-class elements under Social Democratic leadership before every zemstvo assembly. The demonstrators would agitate for wider political demands by the zemstva "without attempting to frighten, terrorize or — even less — expose, those representatives of the possessing classes," who were "taking their first steps in political self-determination." [9] In this way, stated Akselrod, the proletariat would "indicate its readiness to support the bourgeois opposition in its struggle for freedom, and at the same time demand of this opposition support for its own strivings."

Even Martov seemed to think that the pursuit of such tactics by the "conscious" proletariat would be sufficient for it to gain its legitimate ends. In December 1904 he wrote in support of the *Iskra* plan: "The proletariat will prevent [any] halfway compromise through its pressure upon the bourgeois opposition, through the strength of its influence over the laboring masses, and thanks to its consolidated and independent political position." [10]

With his usual heavy-handed irony, Lenin might have had a field day, toying with the contradictions in his opponents' plan — with their image of a proletariat, acting as the "prime mover" in the coming revolution and yet carefully restraining itself to the role of a pressure group for fear of frightening the bourgeoisie. But the moment seemed too grave, and instead Lenin launched into an earnest and systematic demonstration of the need for Social Democracy to adapt its tactics to the new power position of the liberal bourgeoisie.

His discussion of the *Iskra* plan was the first really articulate statement of the double-edged attitude he had always entertained toward the bourgeoisie and toward liberalism. Before the birth of the liberal movement, Lenin asserted, it had been proper and indeed necessary for the Social Democrats to devote a portion of their efforts to the encouragement and support of liberal tendencies in society. Indeed it was largely thanks to these efforts of the Social Democrats — and to the "generous hospitality" they had given to future turncoat *kritiki* such as Struve and Bulgankov — that the liberal movement was ultimately born.

But as soon as this movement appeared on the scene, "as soon as the liberals came out with an independent organ and with a political program of their own, the tasks of the proletariat in its pressure on 'society' radically changed." No longer could "Social Democracy content itself with rousing the liberals, with stirring their opposition spirit. At the head of the corner, it [now] had to place the revolutionary critique of the half-heartedness that [was being] clearly exposed in the political position of liberalism." By its very nature bourgeois democracy was condemned to "halfheartedness" and "indecisiveness." These were endemic, unchangeable characteristics, born of its objective position midway between two struggling sides, the government and the revolutionary proletariat.[11]

From this picture, Lenin asserted, only one practical conclusion could be drawn, and yet Martov had failed to draw it. It would be quite futile for the Social Democrats to reduce the boldness of their own demands in the hope of raising the daring of the liberals. For the bourgeoisie could not be expected, under any condition, to struggle for the removal of the monarchy, of the standing army, or of the bureaucracy, since these were "the main supporting points of its own supremacy.[12] Instead of pursuing such a hopeless chimera, instead of devoting so much of its attention and energy to an ally which, it knew — on the basis of objective evidence — to be at best "problematic, unreliable, and halfhearted," Social Democracy should direct its efforts at the organization and leadership of a decisive and concentrated blow against absolutism.[13]

Lenin's description of this second and preferred alternative was as yet quite sketchy, and Plekhanov took advantage of this weak side of his article to expose some alleged contradictions between Lenin's current views and the position he had defended in *Chto Delat'?* In his earlier work, Plekhanov asserted, Lenin had been emphatic about the necessity of Social Democracy's aiding the development of a nation-wide opposition movement against absolutism. Yet now that such a movement had arisen in society, he expected the Social Democrats to turn their backs on it, and to refrain from subjecting it to their influence and to their agitation: "It seems that as soon as people among whom we have agitated for an all-around opposition begin [this opposition], it would be opportunism to agitate among them for more democratic demands." [14] The only justification that Lenin seemed to offer for this absurd position, Plekhanov continued, was the fact that the liberals were "halfhearted." But this characteristic of liberalism had long since been foreseen. The Social Democrats' duty to expose it in no way precluded the possibility or the desirability of continued agitation among bourgeois opposition elements. It meant merely that these two facets of the activity of Social Democracy — agitation and exposure — had to be judiciously combined, so as not to frighten the bourgeoisie and yet to press upon it the proletariat's political demands. If Lenin's tactics were adopted, the proletariat would have to carry the entire burden of a revolution of which the bourgeoisie was to be the chief beneficiary. "We — the 'opportunists' — would like to see the pressure of the coming proletarian struggle transferred, if only in part, from the shoulders of the proletariat to those of the bourgeoisie," Plekhanov observed. "They — the 'radicals' — would like to have the entire weight" of the revolution "pressing on the back of the proletariat." [15]

The "weak points" that Plekhanov had discovered in Lenin's tactical views were actually the products of his own misunderstandings. As usual, he had been all too eager to believe that his opponent shared the fundamental axioms that governed his own world view and to conclude that his errors were the results of inconsistent and incorrect deductions. Thus Lenin's demand that the proletariat take over responsibility for the bourgeois revolution could be considered absurd only if it was assumed that the outcome and the results of this revolution were largely predetermined, regardless of the course adopted by Social Democracy. For more than two decades, Plekhanov had taken this assumption for granted — but Lenin had never wholly shared it. He had maintained, on the contrary, that by taking over the leadership of the movement to overthrow absolutism — instead of acting as a mere "tail" in this movement — the proletariat would gain considerable, though unspecified, political advantages.

To be sure, he had never asserted — and for that matter, he never would assert — that these potential gains might include the establishment of a socialist society. This would have been too flagrant a violation of the Marxist credo which represented to Lenin the map of the real world, the source of all objective criteria for political action. No! The first Russian revolution would be "democratic" and not "socialistic" in character, but this did not preclude the fact that if the Social Democrats assumed the leadership of this revolution, they would be able to extend

its boundaries considerably and thereby to shorten — though not eliminate — the duration of the workers' struggle for socialism.

To this first misunderstanding was related another error in Plekhanov's diagnosis of Lenin's views. Plekhanov assumed that in his esti-
mate of the potential forces of the opposition, Lenin — like he himself —
was seriously considering only two political groupings, the proletariat
and the bourgeoisie, the two progressive classes selected by history for
a significant political role. Plekhanov consequently inferred that Lenin
deemed it possible for the proletariat to undertake the completion of
the bourgeois revolution single-handed (since he refused to consider
the bourgeoisie as a trustworthy political ally). Here was an even more
glaring error, for ever since 1902 — ever since the appearance of an
organized bourgeois political movement — Lenin had been stressing the
crucial significance for the proletariat of the vast masses of the petty
bourgeoisie — the poor and middle peasant classes — whose strivings,
at this very moment, he asserted to be "largely indistinguishable from
those of the masses of ignorant and forgotten working people." [16]

For almost three years, Lenin had been insisting that through vigorous revolutionary propaganda and agitation the proletariat would be able
to wrest the leadership of vast segments of these "diffuse" and "formless"
peasant masses away from its bourgeois rivals, and to impel them to
come over to its own class point of view. Here, in germ form, was the
concept of the democratic dictatorship of the proletariat and peasantry
that he eventually would substitute for the classical Marxist view of the
bourgeois revolution.

Plekhanov's only excuse for so completely misinterpreting Lenin's
tactical views was the bewildering rapidity with which the concrete
expressions of these views had evolved during the decade in which he
had known him. In the spring of 1895, when Plekhanov and Akselrod
first met him in Switzerland, Lenin was devoting himself almost entirely
to denunciations of the Populists' fumistic and hopeless vision of the
road to socialism. His chief concern during the two years following his
conversion to Marxism had been to define reliable signposts for the
guidance of the revolutionary movement in its long and difficult march
to socialism. The bulk of his writings during those years had consequently been devoted to demonstrations of the necessity and inevitability
of capitalist development — of the inexorable, if "unpalatable," fact
that bourgeois rule was a necessary preliminary condition for the eventual triumph of the proletariat. To be sure, one could also perceive in
his writings of this period a deep hostility toward the concrete political
manifestations of bourgeois ideology, but Akselrod and Plekhanov had
lightly attributed this "unbecoming tone" to the revolutionary ardor and
lack of theoretical equipment of the young convert.

Then, seven long years had elapsed, seven years during which the long-awaited appearance of the organized bourgeois political movement predicted by the Marxist faith had not taken place, in spite of the proddings of Social Democracy. And gradually Lenin had come to the belief that this bourgeois political movement might take the form of unorganized participation by the radical elements of society in a nation-wide movement led by Social Democracy.

But in 1901 and 1902, an organized bourgeois liberal movement had finally appeared, exhibiting from the outset a will and a program of its own. Lenin's attention had then turned to the vast formless masses of the petty bourgeoisie, whose significance he had perceived at the beginning of his revolutionary career. In these wavering masses of the middle and poor peasants, he found a revolutionary potential that could be utilized by Social Democracy to maintain its leadership in the "democratic" revolution. And, thus, he finally arrived at the view that the bourgeois revolution could be completed successfully by the proletariat — with the aid of the peasantry — and against the opposition of the capitalist bourgeoisie.

It was this concept of revolution that ultimately led to his split with his *Iskra* collaborators, for it had the inevitable effect of making his views on party organization even more rigid. Lenin had always felt that there lurked in the breast of every proletarian, and of almost every Social Democrat, an inexorable conflict between the powers of consciousness and the elemental forces of "spontaneous" strivings. This belief had led him to emphasize the need for the party's organizations to define the goals, the values, the criteria of action for which its members had to strive. Now that the party was assigned the task of compelling the peasantry to come over to its point of view and the responsibility of struggling against an awakened and organized capitalist bourgeoisie for leadership in the coming revolution, this duty of its organizations — to delineate a consistent course for their members and to make them hold onto it without a single let-up — had become incomparably more pressing and immeasurably more difficult to fulfill. For the masses of the petty bourgeoisie constituted an unconscious "spontaneous" element par excellence, and in its struggle to assume the leadership of this spontaneous element, in its efforts to impel it to come over to its class point of view, the proletariat would need to parry the wily and skillful blows of an awakened and organized capitalist bourgeoisie. Impelled by this vision, Lenin finally came around to the belief that the party had to be bound with a second knot — a knot that would assure to the central party organs the same degree of control over local organizations that the latter were to hold over their individual members. And it was on this issue that Martov and Akselrod, and ultimately Plekhanov, parted ways with him.

These three men had originally been attracted to Lenin by images of his personality that were as varied as the specific motives that now led each of them to leave his side. Plekhanov had been attracted by Lenin's tough-minded insistence on conscious realism and discipline in revolutionary action — an insistence in which he had been ready to see a reflection of his own demand that the revolutionist faithfully follow the objective course prescribed for him by history. Akselrod, who for so long had waited for the collapse of absolutism, for the hour that would usher in a new era of free and unhampered development of the proletariat's consciousness and *samodeyatelnost,* had been drawn by Lenin's apparent ability to organize and mobilize the forces that would bring this era to life. Martov had been even more powerfully attracted by Lenin's tactical agility and organizational capacities, for more than any of the other future leaders of Menshevism, he had been impressed with the hostility of the ruling forces of the world — and with the consequent necessity to organize the proletariat into an effective fighting force.

Yet, in spite of the power of Lenin's attraction, each of these future Menshevik leaders had eventually drawn away from him. To understand the timing of this final separation, one must recall that, by the end of 1903, absolutism already stood on the brink of extinction, the liberal bourgeoisie had finally awakened from its long slumber, and the rank and file of Social Democracy had become committed to political action. Consequently, Plekhanov no longer had any serious reason to be concerned over the preservation of orthodoxy in Social Democracy, or over the lag in the historical development of the Russian bourgeoisie; Akselrod no longer had much cause to worry over the task of organizing forces capable of overthrowing absolutism; and Martov could look forward confidently to a moment in the not-too-distant future when the power of the hostile forces reigning in the world would at least be significantly reduced.

Lenin's decision to narrow the boundaries of the party and to maintain, and even harden, the degree of control exercised by its leading centers thus came at a time when Akselrod and Martov, at least, were expecting the loosening rather than the tightening of the party's disciplinary bonds.

Much longer than his two colleagues, Plekhanov had remained blind to the rationale of Lenin's organizational scheme. At first, he had been content to view it as a guarantee against the penetration of heretics into the party, as an additional insurance that each party member would follow — with absolute rectitude — the path defined by the objective laws of history. When Lenin's plan threatened to split the party, Plekhanov withdrew his support, for it seemed to him that the issues involved were not worth the stake: the major heresies in Social Democracy had already been defeated, and the danger that they might take over control of the party considerably minimized.

When Lenin refused to give up his hard-won victory, Plekhanov was consequently considerably puzzled, and he reproved his younger colleague for his dogmatism and lack of political sense. It was with the greatest surprise that it eventually came to him that Lenin was actually a greater heretic than any of the men he had ever fought, and that his scheme of party organization was designed not to safeguard orthodoxy but to move against the stream, to violate the objective laws of history — as he, Plekhanov, had defined them. And so it was that the great advocate of "consciousness," George Valentinovich Plekhanov, was compelled to side with the champions of "spontaneity" in Russian Social Democracy.

CONCLUSION

The Revolution of 1905 brought to an end the chapter in the history of the Russian intelligentsia with which this volume has been concerned. For a short while the pressure of events was to push the followers of Bolshevism and Menshevism closer together, but once the revolutionary wave began to recede — with the aims of both Bolsheviks and Mensheviks only partially realized — the issues that had appeared to divide them on the eve of the revolution came once more to the fore. And not only were these issues to separate Bolsheviks from Mensheviks, but they eventually threatened to divide each of the two groups into small and quarrelsome factions.

Already at this moment — January 1905 — it seemed clear that the accumulated changes in Russian political life had seriously upset the various preconceptions upon which the political alignments within the movement had hitherto been based. That Plekhanov, the prophet of "consciousness" had been compelled to side against Lenin with Martynov, the erstwhile advocate of "spontaneity," and that he would repeatedly do so during the remainder of the decade, was in itself indicative of the degree to which the old intellectual slogans were becoming outworn now that the Social Democratic intelligentsia was beginning to take stock of the changes that had occurred in its position in the world.

For almost three decades, the members of the various factions of Social Democracy had been content to interpret the data of their life experience — and to define and phrase their varied and changing political stands — through the medium of the two conceptual and symbolic categories, "consciousness" and "spontaneity." The whole complex of psychological and social factors that had conditioned the development of the intelligentsia had been reflected in the meaning that had been assigned to these two categories. It had been their common quest for consciousness, for a reasonable and responsible world view in the face of an alien and indifferent society, that had originally brought the members of the intelligentsia together. The influence of the West had been the chief agent of their alienation; yet it had been through this agency, through the prism of the abstract categories of Western philosophical systems, that they had sought to find a meaningful identity, an intelligible pattern and order in the process of reality. This search for a "conscious" identity — through the relentless exercise of a rationality trained in the school of Western rationalism — had widened the chasm that separated the intelligentsia from the world about them. It had also impelled most of them to suppress or deny those aspects of their personality and experience that threatened in the least to upset the order in which they were confining their image of themselves and of the world. The very intensity of their efforts to find a "conscious" identity had periodically given rise in many members of the intelligentsia to an opposite striving, to an urge to break out of their isolation and to give free, "spontaneous," expression to their feelings — by "fusing" with an outside popular force which, however oppressed by the existing order, was assumed to have the power and the "inner freedom" that the *intelligent* himself lacked.

The concepts of consciousness and spontaneity reflected the conflict between these two modes of orientation. They reflected the split that many members of the intelligentsia were making between reason and feelings — between the exercise of a rationality that had become inextricably identified with the alienating influence of the West and the free expression of emotions that still bound most of them, however much they attempted to deny it, to the world from which they had sprung. The delineation of the two categories also indicated that as long as the members of the intelligentsia continued to feel so alienated, the very exercise of their rationality would constitute an affirmation of will, a defiance of the ruling order in their contemporary environment.

In the turbulent years that had followed the appearance of the terms "consciousness" and "spontaneity" in intelligentsia discussions, many and varied views had been advanced of the relation between them, many and varied systems had been subsumed under each of them, but in all these formulations certain unchanging denotations had remained attached to the two concepts. Whenever and wherever "consciousness" was discussed — whether in highly abstract and all-embracing theoretical constructions or in narrower formulations of revolutionary action — it had almost invariably stood for an affirmation of the *intelligent*'s distinctive identity in the face of the ruling forces in his contemporary Russian environment; it had stood for an effort on his part to interpret, organize, and thus, in a sense, control his experience by the delineation in the process of reality of a logic and a purpose different from the predominant patterns in the existing world. "Spontaneity" had stood for a refusal or a failure on his part to so mediate his responses to the world and to his own impulses, it had stood for a desire to give free rein to his own feelings and to the expression of "elemental" forces in the external world, which were assumed to be imbued with the power to create as well as the capacity to destroy. In the many interpretations that had been made of the two categories, varying degrees of determinacy had been attached to the concept of "consciousness," varying degrees of explosiveness and destructiveness had been attributed to "spontaneity"; but in all these interpretations the denotations that we have discussed had appeared.

It was through the medium of these two concepts that the members of the revolutionary intelligentsia had been converted to Marxism in the 1880's and 1890's and had assimilated its propositions. In order to understand the fascination that the Marxist world view had exercised on so many of the intelligentsia in this early period, we must recall the new and positive element that Marxism had introduced into the vision of their relation to the world. In the proletariat, Marxist ideology had confronted the members of the intelligentsia with the image of a new and rising social force, born, as they had been, in the image of the West and yet drawn from, and nurtured by, the very masses of the people. It had provided the intelligentsia with the vision of an inherent segment of social reality — with strivings potentially akin to their own outlook — through whose agency the real world would be transformed in accordance with their wish.

Marxism had been the first Western philosophical system to offer the promise of a reconciliation of the conflicting strivings that plagued the lives of the members of the intelligentsia; it had been the first theoretical scheme to suggest the realistic possibility of their holding onto their distinctive Westernized identity while being at one with their Russian environment. Quite understandably, therefore, the Marxist movement had attracted a wide range of converts: it had drawn into its ranks individuals who were struggling for "consciousness," individuals who were attracted to "spontaneity," as well as individuals who were groping for some sort of reconciliation between these two orientations; it had attracted men who were searching for a "rational" world view as well as men who were primarily looking for a program of action.

The range of outlooks that the Marxist scheme could satisfy had been further widened by the nature of the setting to which it was applied. To many Russian observers, and particularly to those who had been trained to look through Western eyes, the Russia of the 1890's had seemed a society out of joint; in some respects, it was growing, and growing rapidly; in others, it stood arrested in its development. Russian financial and industrial capitalism was already a dynamic force; but it had not yet swept away the "remnants of the feudal order." The Russian bourgeoisie and the industrial proletariat were rapidly growing in numbers and in economic significance; but they stood as yet politically inert in the face of the impassive autocratic edifice.

These objective features of the Russia of the 1890's had been considerably different from the Western setting for which the Marxist scheme had originally been designed, and neither Marx nor Engels had been willing to volunteer any specific answers as to how their Russian disciples were to proceed in these differing circumstances. Provisionally, the leaders of Russian Marxism had turned for guidance to the experience of the West. Russia would have to pass, in some fashion, through the path of development that had already been traversed by Western nations: it would need to undergo the "bourgeois" revolution that would "liberate" Russian capitalism "from its shackles" and that would create the political and economic conditions required for the rapid growth of the proletariat to political maturity. But this vague outline of Russia's prospects had left unanswered a number of fundamental questions, the answers to which would eventually determine the shape that the Marxist movement was to assume in Russia.

The first of these fundamental questions was how active and leading a role Social Democracy should assume in Russia's transformation. Were the Russian Marxists to depend primarily on the objective laws of history to bring Russian society up to the level of development currently enjoyed by Western nations, or were they to depend on their own active efforts to make up for Russia's historical lag or even to exploit it for the benefit of Social Democracy? Linked to this issue was another major question: Were the Social Democrats to maintain strict political independence in their dealings with other parties, and to dedicate a substantial portion of their current efforts to the development of the self-consciousness and class organization of the proletariat — at the possible cost of arousing in the workers an unbending antagonism toward their bourgeois exploiters — or should they concentrate wholly on drawing the proletariat into a nation-wide movement against absolutism? And, one last consideration, to what extent were the Social Democrats' answers to these questions to be determined by the requirements of their long-range program, as against the workers' current demands and needs, as against the contemporary state of the workers' own consciousness?

The first of these questions — the form that the intervention of Social Democracy should assume in the unfolding of the historical process — had been much debated among Western Marxists. But in the West, where the objective conditions for the realization of the Marxist prophecy were assumed to be largely present, the issue presented itself in a much more circumscribed form. The existence in the contemporary environment of objective corelatives for the Marxist scheme, the presence on the political scene of an awakened and organized proletariat and bourgeoisie, made it possible for the more deterministically oriented of the Western Marxists to favor rather passive political tactics, confident as they were of the inevitable realization of the Marxist prophecy. The existence of these conditions also meant — given the Marxist insistence that history was determined by the collective behavior of socio-economic classes — that definite curbs were imposed on those individuals who would otherwise have leaned toward more voluntaristic solutions.

In the Russia of the middle 1890's, neither of these conditions prevailed. Even the most deterministically oriented and theoretically inclined of the Russian Marxists could be reconciled to the necessity of active intervention by Social Democracy — if only to bring into existence the objective factors that would permit the rapid realization of the perspectives outlined in the Marxist scheme. Neither did Marxism impose any real restraints on the more voluntaristic and activist of its Russian adherents. To be sure, such restrictions were implicitly present in the vision of the bourgeois revolution that Russia would have to undergo, but this vision was as yet so distant and so blurred that its only real effect was to sustain the faithful in their conviction that the success of their intervention was guaranteed by history.

Consequently, there was nothing in the nature of political and social conditions in the Russia of the nineties, or in the interpretation of these conditions by the Russian Marxists, that was conducive to a differentiation of the two strands that had been combined in the intelligentsia's conception of "consciousness." On the contrary, everything in the existing world still tended to hold together those of the Social Democratic intelligentsia who were content to identify "consciousness" with a rational view of reality and those who sought in "consciousness" the justification for an affirmation of will.

Thus it was that even the most deterministic of the Russian Marxists, even Plekhanov, had been agreeable to the active supervisory role that Social Democracy would exercise in Russia's transformation; thus it was that most of them had been reconciled to the completely independent political role that Social Democracy would maintain as the sole responsible agent of the historical process and as the only champion of the real interests of the proletariat. Only the Revisionists had opposed the exclusivist features of the orthodox Marxist platform. Impressed by the socio-economic transformations that had already taken place, aware of the changes that had already occurred in their own position in Russian society, these youthful members of the intelligentsia already affirmed that progress was an immanent characteristic of the development of society as a whole, reflecting the growth of the individual conscience, and urged that the Social Democratic intelligentsia unite with all other progressive elements in carrying this development forward. But despite these reservations, even the Revisionists supported the political activities of Social Democracy as positive efforts toward Russia's awakening to political life.

The most vigorous objections to the supervisory role that the exponents of "consciousness" had assigned to Social Democracy during the "transition phase" in Russia's historical development had come from the

more extreme advocates of "spontaneity," the radical wing of the Economist movement. The one principle that the members of this group had
elected to emphasize in the body of Marxist teachings was that Social
Democracy should be a real working-class party rather than an organization of intelligentsia conspirators. To become such a party, the advocates
of "spontaneity" insisted, Social Democracy should always faithfully reflect — in its program as well as in its tactics — the current mentality
and strivings of its working-class following. This meant that, under existing conditions, the Social Democrats should confine themselves to the
leadership of the workers' struggle against their employers, since the vast
majority of the working class were as yet impelled solely by economic
grievances.

During the half decade that the Economists had waged their campaign, they had leveled a variety of charges against their opponents: the
advocates of the political struggle favored the intelligentsia's "tutelage"
of the working class; they were dogmatically projecting onto the workers
their own intelligentsia preoccupations and strivings; their tactical and
organizational plans reflected a conspiratorial rather than an objective
view of the dynamics of the historical process. But all these accusations
had reflected one fundamental concern: the future of Social Democracy
depended on the Social Democratic intelligentsia's ability to "fuse" with
the labor movement; yet, the current efforts of the *politiki* to impose
their identity on the labor movement threatened to alienate the intelligentsia from the proletariat, and thus to relegate them once again to the
position of "a spirit hovering over a void."

There was much in the arguments that the Economists had advanced
with which Lenin's collaborators could have agreed. Of course, Social
Democracy should become a true working-class party, reflecting the
needs of the proletariat. Of course, the program and tactics that it
adopted should be made to conform to the dictation of the objective
process and not to the whims of a few conspirators of the intelligentsia.
But it was the Economists who had misunderstood the character of the
historical process and the nature of the workers' needs — through their
blindness to the historical travails through which Russia was passing. As
long as the edifice of absolutism stood in the way of Russia's progressive
forces, as long as the "remnants of feudalism" hampered the forward
movement of Russia's historical development, the growth of the workers'
awareness of their *real* class interests and needs would be at best slow
and tortuous. Thus, even to Plekhanov, adverse as he was to revolutionary adventurism; even to Martov and Akselrod, concerned as they were
with the development of the workers' own independent initiative, it had
seemed imperative that Social Democracy should do everything in its
power to remove the obstructions that stood in the way of the workers'

recognition of their true identity — and of their determination of their own fate.

This common impatience for the gestation of the new era in Russia's development had irresistibly attracted Plekhanov, Martov, and Akselrod to Lenin's vision of a centralized and hard-hitting revolutionary party. All three had been equally convinced that Social Democracy should maintain strict political independence in the struggle against absolutism so as to remain impervious to the vacillations of its bourgeois allies. All three had agreed that the Social Democrats would successfully thwart the last desperate maneuvers of absolutism, and insure the full realization of the proletariat's legitimate political objectives, only if they acted with a united will.

But there had been an additional and more basic feature in Plekhanov's world view that had impelled him to sympathize with Lenin's conception of organization. Like Lenin, Plekhanov tended to view "consciousness" and "spontaneity" as two mutually exclusive categories. Like Lenin, he had found it difficult, in practice if not in theory, to conceive that individuals and social groups could gradually mature, gradually and naturally grow from "spontaneity" to "consciousness," through the accumulating weight of their own experience. Not that Plekhanov, like Lenin, conceived of "spontaneous" impulses as a potent and almost ineradicable life force that might be mastered and harnessed by the powers of "consciousness," but that could not be eliminated — at least in any foreseeable future — but rather that he viewed "consciousness" and "spontaneity" as two completely alternative states, with no gradation between them. In spite of all his dissertations on the process of history, Plekhanov always tended to view the concrete manifestations of this process as either fully conscious or fully unconscious; he almost never perceived them in the process of becoming. It is not surprising, therefore, that Plekhanov had found little to criticize in the scheme of party organization that Lenin advocated at the Second Congress. Since in his eyes, just as in Lenin's, the party was to stand for the manifestation of socialist consciousness, it should include only "conscious," responsible members in its organizations; there would be time for adjoining elements to enter the party *after* they had achieved socialist consciousness.

The absence of any conception of man's and society's capacity for gradual and harmonious growth had been characteristic of the orientation of most of the intelligentsia ever since the appearance of this group on the Russian scene. To their complete estrangement from their contemporary environment the intelligentsia had responded by identifying with an image of history that was completely at odds with the realities of the present. To most of them this vision had seemed the only purpose and justification of existence, and in their confrontation of the ever recurring clash between ideals and realities they always held onto the un-sullied image of the ideal: of the future they could demand nothing less than a world turned upside down; to the present they could respond with nothing more than heroic defiance.

A cult of heroism became prevalent among the members of the in-telligentsia: punishment at the hands of the authorities came to be viewed as the price of admission to the society of the elect, and death as the apotheosis of the *intelligent's* life. In this code of heroic martyr-dom, little value could be assigned to the humdrum of maturity and middle age. The student youth, many of whose members could, and did, live out the heroic code, laid an incontestible claim to the spiritual lead-ership of the intelligentsia — a claim that their elders could not dispute since their survival was in itself indicative of their inadequacy. The stu-dent youth became veritable objects of worship for the intelligentsia, creating in Russian society what a critic would eventually describe as a "spiritual pedocracy": "This is one of the chief reasons why, with such an abundance of heroes, we have so few orderly, stable, understanding people . . . In his world view, the *intelligent* remains all his life a stu-dent youth . . . and following the course that the older generation set for them, the heroic youths themselves gradually turn into Chekhovian and Gogolian types, ending up with wines and cards if not worse."[1] Aside from this worship of heroism and youth, we have already alluded to another, and more basic, reason for the intelligentsia's "arrested" de-velopment. Striving for "consciousness" had meant for most of them the suppression or denial or all the feelings and memories, of everything in their existence that bound them inextricably to the environment from which they were attempting to separate themselves. The pursuit of "spontaneity" to which some had turned had also involved the denial of much of their own selves; it had meant, at least ostensibly, the rejection of the rationality, of the very capacity for logical and systematic thought that had originally brought them at odds with their Russian environ-ment. So much suppression, so much denial had been involved in both orientations that the members of the intelligentsia had lacked the per-sonality resources on which to grow. "A split between the activity of con-sciousness and the [individual's] personal affective life was the general norm," observed the critic Gershenzon. "In truth," he concluded, "a his-torian would not be in error if he began to study Russian society along two different lines, existence and thought, for between them there was almost nothing in common."[2]

In the last decade of the century, the first tangible signs of a change in the intelligentsia's orientation appeared. By this time, they had con-siderably grown in numbers and in strength: they were no longer a small minority living in a vacuum, but an important social group exercising a variety of constructive roles. The members of the intelligentsia had become doctors and lawyers, engineers and teachers, agronomists and veterinarians, in a society which, however haltingly, was clearly moving toward the modern age. Within the ranks of Social Democracy, the youthful Revisionists and moderate Economists had been the first to draw the positive implications of the changes that were taking place in Russian society. Although they had stood for quite different immediate objectives, the two groups had expressed a newly gained confidence in the individual's capacity to grow and mature through his own resources. But the majority of the Social Democratic intelligentsia had been too imbued with the traditions of the past and too concerned with the arrested features in Russia's contemporary position to draw any immediate practical inferences from the positive elements to which the Revisionists and Economists were pointing.

It was not until the autocracy had begun to totter, and Russian society awakened from its long political slumber, that the majority of the intelligentsia realized that they no longer stood isolated, and that Russia had finally come of age. When they were jolted into this realization, Lenin's former collaborators and many of his followers were inevitably drawn to a vision of party tactics and party organization that would make more room for the initiative of the proletariat's growing forces and reflect more passively the dictation of the unshackled historical process. And it now became clear to them that Lenin's organization of professional revolutionaries had been designed not to redress the distortions in Russia's historical development, not to clear the way for the growth of Russia's "spontaneous" elements to consciousness and freedom, but rather to exploit the distortions in Russia's history and to subject its "spontaneous" forces to an indefinite tutelage.

The split between Lenin and his collaborators — the emergence of the Bolshevik and Menshevik factions — marked a major turning point not only in the history of Social Democracy, but in the development of the Russian intelligentsia as a whole. A large number of the intelligentsia now broke with the traditions of the past. No longer did these individuals feel that a chasm separated them from the world around them, and that the affirmation of their identity required the denial of everything that bound them to their contemporary environment. It now appeared to them that a new world was emerging, a world whose logic confirmed the whole range of their experience. The categories through which they had been accustomed to interpret reality had lost their original meaning, for they were entering an era in which "spontaneous" forces would easily grow to "consciousness," an era in which, finding themselves for the first time at one with reality, they would be free to recognize and express the part of themselves that was inextricably bound to their Russian environment, as well as the part that had previously brought them into conflict with it. Most of them only dimly perceived all this, yet they responded with a new immediacy to the richness and the variety — and the confusion — of the life around them, feeling themselves to be parts of Russia's present, not heralds of an uncertain future.

In the Menshevik camp, the spirit of the new age was to be reflected in an ever increasing pressure for the removal of the artificial barriers that separated Social Democracy from contemporary reality. Many Mensheviks were now to demand a more conciliatory attitude toward other opposition parties; they were now to call for the liquidation of the party's underground organizations and for the immediate creation of an open mass party. And in these gestures of emancipation, they turned for leadership not to Plekhanov, not to the prophet who in his lonely splendor had delineated for them the pattern of the future, but to Akselrod, the one leader of Social Democracy who had never felt alienated from the world about him, confident as he had always been of his dual identity as an emancipated *intelligent* and as a son of the Russian people.

Even Lenin's followers were not immune to the new spirit. But temporarily at least, the impact of the new spirit was only to solidify their revolutionary intransigeance, to redouble their faith in the imminence of the apocalypse. It was against Lenin's counsels of moderation that most of them would rebel, confident that the day of reckoning was fast approaching. In all the pronouncements of these critics from the left — in their discussions of tactics and organization just as in their obstruse philosophical writings — one major theme would now become dominant: reality was but a function of man's apprehension of it — no mechanical objective law, no uncontrollable noumenal universe stood in the revolutionary's path; nothing could prevent the "man of the new age" from deciding his fate and mastering the world.

However misguided, however unrealistic, the impatience of the Bolshevik left was in a sense justified, for Lenin was running a race against time: the realization of his plans now depended entirely on whether an opportunity would arise for the unleashing of Russia's "spontaneous" forces before these forces finally grew to maturity. Under the policies of more enlightened, if not more benevolent rulers, a new class of peasant proprietors was beginning to emerge, whose ambitious and hard-working members had a stake in the existing order. With the rise of this new social group, the revolutionary potential of the Russian peasantry — that "spontaneous element" upon which the Bolsheviks' hopes now rested so largely — was slowly but surely beginning to decline; this, at a time when the traditional carriers of "consciousness" — the members of the intelligentsia — were deserting in droves from their old revolutionary mission.

It seemed that a new society was being born, a society whose members would be confronted with new and different problems, and inspired by new and different hopes. At the beginning of his revolutionary career, Lenin had mercilessly attacked those of his contemporaries who still dreamed of an irretrievably lost past. Russia's progress now threatened to leave him the keeper of as hopeless and lonely a dream.

Notes

Bibliography

Index

NOTES

CHAPTER 1. The Background

1. Bertram D. Wolfe, *Three Who Made a Revolution* (New York, 1948), p. 33.

2. Ivan Turgenev, "Rudin, a Romance," *The Works of Ivan Turgenev* (New York, 1904), pp. 106, 108–109. Italics in this and in all other quotations are mine, unless otherwise noted.

3. M. Gershenzon, "Tvorcheskoe samosoznanie," in *Vekhi* (Moscow, 1909), p. 71.

4. See the discussion of this problem in Paul Milyukov, "Lyubov' u idealistov tridtsatykh godov," *Iz istorii russkoi intelligentsii* (St. Petersburg, 1903).

5. N. G. Chernyshevskii, *Chto delat'?*; see, for example, N. G. Tchernyshevsky, *Que Faire?* (Lodi, 1875), pp. 243–244.

6. S. Kravchinskii, *Podpol'naya rossiya* (London, 1893), p. 15.

7. This summary of Lavrov's views is drawn from the articles he wrote in the journal *Vpered* (published in Geneva between 1873 and 1877), and particularly from his statement in the fourth issue of this journal.

8. M. R. Popov, *Zapiski zemlevol'tsa* (Moscow, 1933), p. 60.

9. A. O. Lukachevich, "V narod," *Byloe*, March 1907, pp. 12ff.

10. Quoted in Feodor I. Dan, *Proiskhozhdenie bol'shevizma* (New York, 1946), p. 119.

11. Quoted in Dan, pp. 122–125.

12. P. N. Tkachev, *Zadachi revolyutsionnoi propagandy v Rossii* (Geneva, 1874), quoted in Dan, pp. 100–103.

13. P. N. Tkachev, "Nabat" (originally published in *Nabat*, no. 1, December 1875, Geneva), in P. N. Tkachev, *Izbrannye sochineniya na sotsial'no-politicheskie temy* (Moscow, 1932–33), III, 221.

14. Quoted in Dan, pp. 138–139.

15. Quoted by Vera Figner in "Zapechatlennyi trud," in *Polnoe sobranie sochinenii* (Moscow, 1928–29), I, 181–182.

16. B. Chicherin, "Zadachi novogo tsarstvovaniya," in *K. P. Pobedonostsev i ego korrespondenty: Pis'ma i zapiski*, I (Moscow, 1923).

17. G. V. Plekhanov, *Nashi raznoglasiya* (published originally in Geneva, 1885), in *Sochineniya* (Moscow, 1923–1927), II, 230.

18. "You do not consider that capitalism is opposed not only to the link that follows it but also to the link that precedes it in the chain of historical development . . . that it is struggling not only against the revolutionary attempts of the proletariat, but also against the reactionary strivings of the gentry and petty bourgeoisie" (*ibid.*, p. 341).

19. *Ibid.*, pp. 203–204.

20. G. V. Plekhanov, "Kak dobivat'sya konstitutsii," *Sotsial Demokrat,* I (Geneva, 1888); in *Sochineniya,* III, 16.

21. Plekhanov, "Sotsializm i politicheskaya bor'ba," in *Sochineniya,* II, 86.

22. See Plekhanov, "Nashi raznoglasiya," in *Sochineniya,* II, 104ff.

23. *Ibid.*

24. *Ibid.,* p. 348.

25. *Ibid.,* p. 271.

26. Tikhomirov, *Vestnik Narodnoi Voli,* no. 2, 1883. See also P. B. Akselrod, "Gruppa Osvobozhdenie Truda" (neopublikovannye glavy 2–go toma "Vospominanii"), *Letopis' Marksizma,* VI (1928).

27. N. K. Mikhailovskii, "Pis'ma postoronnego," *Otechestvennyie Zapiski,* April 1883.

28. V.V. (V. P. Vorontsov), *Sud'by kapitalizma v Rossii* (St. Petersburg, 1882), preface. See also Nikolai (N. F. Danielson), *Ocherki poreformennogo khoziaistva* (1893), the first section of which, entitled "Kapitalizatsia zemledel'cheskikh dokhodov," was published in the journal *Slovo* in 1880.

CHAPTER 2. The Marriage of Feeling and Reason

1. *Perezhitoe i peredumannoe,* pp. 73–74.

2. *Ibid.,* p. 75.

3. *Ibid.,* p. 112.

4. *Ibid.,* pp. 128–129.

5. *Ibid.,* p. 130.

6. *Ibid.,* p. 157.

7. Plekhanov, unlike Akselrod and Martov, never wrote an autobiography, and if he had, it would probably have reflected his usual reserve. Some memoir material concerned with his early revolutionary activities in St. Petersburg is contained in his "Russkii rabochii v revolyutsionnom dvizhenii," *Sochineniya,* III. His chief biographer, L. G. Deich, a member of Osvobozhdenie Truda, didn't meet him until the end of the 1870's. As for the recollections by Plekhanov's acquaintances, recorded by Soviet historians after his death, many are the stuff that legends are made of. See V. V. Pozdnyakova-Plekhanova, "Detstvo i otechestvo G. V. Plekhanova," *Gruppa Osvobozhdenie Truda,* no. 1, 1924; A. A. Frencher, "Na rodine G. V. Plekhanova," *Proletarskaya Revolyutsiya,* no. 8, 1922; N. Smirnov, "G. V. Plekhanov v Voronezhskoi Voennoi Gimnazii," *Katorga i Ssylka,* no. 61, 1929; also L. G. Deich, *G. V. Plekhanov, materialy dlya biografii* (Moscow, 1922).

8. G. V. Plekhanov, "Russkii rabochii . . ."

9. "Zakon ekonomicheskogo razvitiya obshchestva i zadachi sotsializma v Rossii," *Zemlya i Volya,* no. 3 (January 15, 1879). *Sochineniya,* I, 55–56.

10. *Ibid.,* p. 73.

11. *Ibid.,* p. 67.

12. *Ibid.,* p. 69.

13. *Ibid.,* p. 71.

14. Akselrod, *Perezhitoe i peredumannoe,* p. 198.

15. P. B. Akselrod, "Itogi Germanskoi Sotsial Demokratii," *Obshchina,* no. 5, 1878; quoted in *Perezhitoe i peredumannoe,* p. 276.

16. *Ibid.,* p. 282.

17. *Ibid.,* p. 275.

18. G. V. Plekhanov, "Pochemu i kak my razoshlis' s redaktsiei 'Vestnik Narodnoi Voli,' " *Iskra,* no. 54, 1903.

19. Deich, *G. V. Plekhanov*, p. 45.

20. Another source from which this account of the Voronezh Congress is drawn is L. G. Deich, "G. V. Plekhanov v 'Zemle i Vole,'" *Gruppa Osvobozhdenie Truda*, no. 3, 1925.

21. L. G. Deich, "Kak G. V. Plekhanov stal Marksistom," *Proletarskaya Revolyutsiya*, no. 7, 1922, p. 113; also Deich, *G. V. Plekhanov*, p. 48.

22. "Chernyi Peredel," in *Chernyi Peredel*, no. 1, January 15, 1880.

23. *Ibid.*

24. Akselrod, *Perezhitoe i peredumannoe*, p. 326.

25. *Ibid.*, pp. 333–334.

26. *Chernyi Peredel*, no. 1; *Sochineniya*, I, 119ff.

27. *Ibid.*, p. 356.

28. See *Perezhitoe i peredumannoe*, pp. 348ff.

29. R. Plekhanova, "Nasha zhizn' do emigratsii," *Gruppa Osvobozhdenie Truda*, no. 6, 1928, p. 94.

30. L. G. Deich, *G. V. Plekhanov*, p. 50.

31. *Chernyi Peredel*, no. 2; *Sochineniya*, I, 131.

32. For a circumstantial account of the break and for two conflicting interpretations by the same author, see L. G. Deich, in *Proletarskaya Revolutsiya*, no. 8, 1923, and his article written a year later, "Pervye shagi Gruppy 'Osvobozhdenie Truda,'" *Gruppa Osvobozhdenie Truda*, no. 1, 1924.

33. "Sotsializm i politicheskaya bor'ba," *Sochineniya*, II, 71.

34. *Novyi zashchitnik samoderzhaviya* (Geneva, 1889), in *Sochineniya*, III.

35. "Nashi raznoglasiya," *Sochineniya*, II, 271.

36. *Ibid.*, p. 113.

37. *Ibid.*, p. 337.

38. *Ibid.*, pp. 342, 272–273.

39. *Ibid.*, p. 350.

40. "Sovremennye zadachi russkikh rabochikh," *Sochineniya*, II, 367.

41. "Sotsializm i politicheskaya bor'ba," *Sochineniya*, II, 63.

42. "Sovremennye zadachi," *Sochineniya*, II, 367.

43. "Sotsializm i politicheskaya bor'ba," *Sochineniya*, II.

44. *Ibid.*, p. 84.

45. "Nashi raznoglasiya," *Sochineniya*, II, 271.

46. "Politicheskie zadachi russkikh sotsialistov," *Sochineniya*, III, 94.

47. "Sotsializm i politicheskaya bor'ba," *Sochineniya*, II, 58.

48. "Politicheskie zadachi russkikh sotsialistov," *Sochineniya*, III, 91.

49. "Kak dobivat'sya konstitutsiu," *Sotsial Demokrat*, I (Geneva, 1888); *Sochineniya*, III, 30.

50. "Novyi zashchitnik samoderzhaviya," *Sochineniya*, III, 56.

51. *Rabochee dvizhenie i Sotsial'naya Demokratiya* (Geneva, 1884), Introduction, p. i.

52. *Ibid.*, p. xiv.

53. *Otvet na zapros o zadachakh i tseliakh russkoi zagranichnoi literatury*, 1887, quoted in A. N. Potresov, *P. B. Akselrod, 45 let obshchestvennoi deyatelnosti* (St. Petersburg, 1914).

CHAPTER 3. The Rise of a New Faith

1. Partiya Narodnogo Prava, *Nasushchnyi vopros*, quoted in A. Potresov, "Evolyutsiya obshchestvenno-politicheskoi mysli v predrevolyutsionnuyu epokhu," *Obshchestvennoe dvizhenie v Rossii*, I, 554.

2. See Danilov, p. 454.

3. For a more detailed discussion of the temper of the Marxist movement in Russia during this period, see Peter Struve, "My Contacts and Conflicts with Lenin" (I), *Slavonic and East European Review*, XII, 573–578 (London, 1933–34).

4. V. Vorontsov, *Nashi napravleniya*, pp. 112ff.

5. Dan, *Proiskhozhdenie bol'shevizma*, p. 219.

6. *O zadachakh sotsialistov v bor'be s golodom v Rossii* (published in Switzerland in 1893 and circulated in Russia illegally), in *Sochineniya*, III, 357.

7. *K voprosu o razvitii monisticheskogo vzglyada na istoriyu* (1895), in *Sochineniya*, VII, 244–246.

8. *Kto takoe "Druz'ya naroda" i kak oni voyuyut protiv Sotsial Demokratov* (Otvet na stat'i "Russkogo Bogatstva" protiv Marksistov) (1894), in V. I. Lenin, *Sochineniya* (4th ed.; 35 vols.; Moscow, 1941–1951), II, 125. (All references made hereafter to Lenin's *Sochineniya* refer to the 4th edition unless otherwise specified).

9. Yu. Martov, *Zapiski sotsial demokrata*, *Letopis revolyutsii*, no. 4 (Petersburg, Berlin, Moscow, 1922), p. 236.

10. Nadezhda K. Krupakaya, *Memories of Lenin* (New York, 1930), I, 1.

11. "O zadachakh sotsialistov v bor'be a golodom v Rossii," *Sochineniya*, III, 390.

12. "The socialists take pride in the fact that if they call the workers to a struggle against economic slavery, the latter happens at the same time to be a struggle against the intellectual slavery, against the ignorance of the proletariat" (*ibid.*, p. 399).

13. See his 1893 pamphlet, *Zadachi rabochei intelligentsii*.

14. *Zapiski sotsial demokrata*, p. 149.

15. Cf. L. Martov, *Proletarskaya bor'ba v Rossii* (Petersburg, 1907).

16. See K. M. Takhtarev, *Ocherki Peterburgskogo rabochego dvizheniya 90–kh godov, po lichnym vospominaniyam* (Petersburg, 1921).

17. Yu. Zederbaum (Martov), *Istoriya RSDRP* (Moscow, 1922), p. 28.

CHAPTER 4. The Making of a Hero

1. For a discussion of some of the psychological dynamics involved, see R. Landes and M. Zborowski, "Hypotheses concerning the Eastern European Jewish Family," *Psychiatry*, XIII, no. 4, 447–464.

2. Yu. Martov, *Zapiski sotsial demokrata*.

3. *Ibid.*, p. 16.

4. *Ibid.*

5. *Ibid.*, p. 27.

6. *Ibid.*, pp. 58ff.

7. *Ibid.*, p. 61.

8. *Ibid.*, p. 62.

9. *Ibid.*, pp. 93–94.

10. *Ibid.*, p. 97.

11. *Ibid.*, p. 109.

12. *Ibid.*, p. 148.

13. *Ibid.*, p. 188.

14. *Ibid.*, p. 225.

CHAPTER 5. The Path of Least Resistance

1. Martov, *Zapiski sotsial demokrata*, p. 263.
2. *Rabochaya Mysl'*, no. 4, quoted in L. Shcheglo, "Rabochaya Mysl'," *Katorga i Ssylka*, IV–V, 101–102 (Moscow, 1933).
3. *Ibid.*, p. 67.
4. *Rabochaya Mysl'*, no. 5, quoted in Takhtarev.
5. Letter of a Petersburg worker, 1897, quoted in Takhtarev, p. 71.
6. *Rabochaya Mysl'*, no. 1, October 1897.
7. Martov, *Zapiski sotsial demokrata*, pp. 316–317.
8. Dan, *Proiskhozhdenie bol'shevizma*, pp. 244–245.
9. *Ibid.*, p. 245.
10. Tugan Baranovskii, "Osnovnaya oshibka abstraktnoi teorii kapitalizma Marksa," *Nauchnoe Obozrenie*, May 1899; P. B. Struve, "Protiv Ortodoksal'-nosti," *Zhizn'*, October 1899. See also Struve's "Osnovnaya antinomiya teorii trudovoi tsennosti," *Zhizn'*, February 1900, and "K kritike nekotorykh osnov-nykh problem i polozhenii politicheskoi ekonomii," *Zhizn'*, May 1900.
11. Struve, *Na raznyya temy*, p. 314.
12. S. N. Bulgakov, "Osnovy problemy teorii progressa," in *Ot Marksizma k idealizmu* p. 155.
13. The text of the "Credo" is quoted in full in "Protest Rossiiskikh Sotsial Demokratov," in Lenin, *Sochineniya*, IV, 153–156.
14. P. B. Akselrod, *K voprosu o sovremennykh zadachakh i taktike rus-skikh sotsial-demokratov* (Geneva, 1898), pp. 19–20.
15. *Perepiska G. V. Plekhanova i P. B. Akselroda*, edited by P. A. Berlin, V. S. Voitinskii, and B. I. Nikolaevskii, vol. I (Moscow, 1925), 159.
16. *Ibid.*, vol. 2, 81.
17. P. B. Akselrod, *Pis'mo v redaktsiyu "Rabochego Dela"* (Geneva, 1899).
18. G. V. Plekhanov, *Vademekum dlya redaktsii "Rabochego Dela"* (Geneva, 1900).
19. Plekhanov, *Perepiska G. V. Plekhanova i P. B. Akselroda*, pp. 72–73.
20. *Ibid.*
21. Akselrod, *ibid.*, p. 107.
22. Akselrod, *K voprosu o sovremennykh zadachakh i taktike russkikh sotsial demokratov.*
23. Akselrod, *Pis'mo v redaktsiyu "Rabochego Dela,"* pp. 6, 17ff.
24. Plekhanov, *Vademekum dlya redaktsii "Rabochego Dela,"* p. 17.
25. "Protest Rossiiskikh Sotsial-Demokratov," in Lenin, *Sochineniya*, IV, 157.
26. *Ibid.*, pp. 162–163.

CHAPTER 6. Against the Stream

1. Krupskaya, *Memories of Lenin*, I, 3.
2. See article by Delanov, a member of the Second Duma, in *Sever* (Vologda, 1924), cited in Valentinov, manuscript on Lenin, p. 52; see also N. Lerner, "Otets Lenina," *Minovskie Dni*, no. 3, 1938.
3. This is the characterization of the young Alexander and Vladimir Ulyanov drawn in the memoirs of their older sister Anna. See A. I. Ulyanova,

"Vospominanii," *Proletarskaya Revolyutsiya*, no. 1, 1927; see also her "Detskie i shkol'nye gody Il'ycha," *Proletarskaya Revolyutsiya*, nos. 2, 3, 1927.

4. A. I. Ulyanova, "Detskie is shkol'nye gody Il'ycha."

5. *Ibid.*

6. A. I. Ulyanova, "Vospominanii," p. 83.

7. For further details on this conspiracy, see A. I. Ulyanova, "Delo 1 marta," *Proletarskaya Revolyutsiya*, nos. 1, 2, 3, 1927.

8. See Lalayants, "O moikh vstrechakh s V. I. Leninym," *Proletarskaya Revolyutsiya*, no. 1, 1929.

9. N. K. Krupskaya, in almanac *Udar*, 1927, quoted in Valentinov, p. 109.

10. Valentinov, p. 111.

11. Valentinov, p. 119.

12. *Leninskii Sbornik*, no. 9, p. 199.

13. *Ibid.*, p. 127.

14. *Ibid.*, p. 71.

15. Valentinov, p. 121.

16. N. A. Dobrolyubov, "Chto takoe Oblomovshchina," *Sochineniya* (St. Petersburg, 1911), II, 520ff.

17. "O mezhdunarodnom i vnutreniem polozhenii sovetskoi respubliki," *Sochineniya* (2nd ed.), XXVII, 177.

18. Valentinov, p. 152; see also Krupskaya, *Memories of Lenin*, I, 3.

19. Valentinov, p. 120.

20. "Kto takoe 'Druz'ya naroda'!" *Sochineniya*, I, 142.

21. "Ekonomicheskoe soderzhanie Narodnichestva v knige G. Struve," in *Sochineniya*, I, 315–484.

22. Struve, in *Slavonic and East European Review*, XII, 591.

23. "Vospominaniya P. B. Akselroda ob ego peregovorakh s V. I. Leninym Ulyanovym v 1895 g.," *Perepiska G. V. Plekhanova i P. B. Akselroda*, I, 270–271.

24. *Ibid.*

25. For Struve's own formulation of the propositions on which he and Lenin had agreed during this period, see Peter Struve, "My Contacts and Conflicts with Lenin" (II), *Slavonic and East European Review*, XIII, 66–71.

26. "Proekt i ob"yasnenie programmy SD Partii," *Sochineniya*, II, 80.

27. "Po povodu 'Profession de Foi,'" written at the end of 1899, *Sochineniya*, IV, 267.

28. P. B. Akselrod, *Istoricheskoe polozhenie i vzaimnoe otnoshenie liberal'noi i sotsialisticheskoi demokratii* (Geneva, 1898), pp. 13–14.

29. *Ibid.*, p. 13.

30. Plekhanov asserted in his 1891 essay: "The proletariat and the peasantry are real political antipodes. The historical role of the proletariat is as revolutionary as that of the 'peasant' is conservative" ("O zadachakh sotsialistov v bor'be s golodom v Rossii," *Sochineniya*, III, 388).

31. "Zadachi russkikh sotsial demokratov," *Sochineniya*, II, 311–312.

32. *Ibid.*, p. 312.

33. *Ibid.*, pp. 309ff.

34. Letter to Potresov, dated September 2, 1898, quoted in full in *Leninskii Sbornik*, IV, 15.

35. See "Popyatnoe napravlenie v russkoi sotsial demokratii," *Sochineniya*, IV, 239.

36. See letter to Potresov, dated September 2, 1898.

CHAPTER 7. "From a Spark a Flame Shall Be Kindled"

1. Krupskaya, *Memories of Lenin,* I, 39.
2. Martov, *Zapiski sotsial demokrata,* p. 412.
3. This particular phrase is to be found in V. I. Lenin, "Zayavlenie redaktsii 'Iskry'" (November 1900), in *Sochineniya,* IV, 329.
4. V. I. Lenin, letter to A. A. Yakubovoi, *Sochineniya,* 3rd ed., XXVIII, 64–65.
5. The substance of this argument is drawn from "Proekt zayavleniya redaktsii 'Iskry i Zari'" (Pskov 1900), in Lenin, *Sochineniya,* IV, 296ff and from L. Martov, "Pskov," in *Leninskii Sbornik,* IV, 296ff.
6. See the texts of "Proekt zayavleniya redaktsii 'Iskry' i 'Zari'" and "Zayavlenie redaktsii 'Iskry.'"
7. V. I. Lenin, "Nasushchnye zadachi nashego dvizheniya," *Iskra,* no. 1, December 1900, in *Sochineniya,* IV, 341–345.
8. V. I. Lenin, "S chego nachat'," in *Sochineniya,* V, 11.
9. B. Krichevskii, "Ekonomicheskaya i politicheskaya bor'ba v russkom dvizhenii," *Rabochee Delo,* no. 7, August 1900.
10. Martynov, "Sovremennie voprosy," *Rabochee Delo,* no. 9, May 1901.
11. B. Krichevskii, "Printsipy, taktika, i bor'by," *Rabochee Delo,* no. 10, September 1901.
12. *Ibid.*
13. Martynov, "Oblichitel'naya literatura i proletarskaya bor'ba," *Rabochee Delo,* no. 10, September 1901.
14. G. V. Plekhanov, "G–n P. Struve v roli kritika Marksovoi teorii obshchestvennogo razvitiya (Kritika nashikh kritikov)," in *Sochineniya,* XI, 262.
15. G. V. Plekhanov, Foreword to "Vademekum dlya redaktsii," in *Sochineniya,* XIII, 14ff.
16. For the substance of this argument, see "O taktike voobshche, o taktike Nikolaevskogo generala Reada v chastnosti, i o taktike g. Krichevskogo v osobennosti," *Iskra,* no. 10, November 1901.
17. P. B. Akselrod, "Pochcmu my ne khotim idti nazad," *Zarya,* no. 2, p. 57.
18. *Ibid.*
19. *Ibid.*
20. Akselrod, *Pis'mo v redaktsiyu "Rabochego Dela,"* p. 17.
21. *Ibid.,* p. 6.
22. Akselrod, *Bor'ba sotsialisticheskikh i burzhuaznykh tendentsii v russkom revolyutsionnom dvizhenii* (St. Petersburg, 1907), p. xvi (this particular section was written in 1902).
23. See in particular his articles "Issues of the Day" in *Iskra,* no. 4, and "On the Basis of Letters from Readers," in *Iskra,* no. 14.
24. Y. O. Martov, "Vsegda v men'shinstve. O sovremennykh zadachakh russkoi sotsialisticheskoi intelligentsii," *Zarya,* no. 2–3, December 1901, pp. 190–191.
25. Y. O. Martov, "Politicheskii razvrat i 'ekonomicheskoe' tupoumie," *Iskra,* no. 9, October 1901.
26. V. I. Lenin, "Beseda s zashchitnikami ekonomizma," *Iskra,* no. 12, December 6, 1901.
27. V. I. Lenin, "Chto delat'?" *Sochineniya,* V, 390.

28. *Ibid.*, p. 473.

29. *Ibid.*, pp. 347–348.

30. *Ibid.*, pp. 354–356.

31. *Ibid.*, p. 357.

32. *Ibid.*, p. 478.

33. *Ibid.*, p. 363.

34. *Ibid.*, p. 371.

35. *Ibid.*, p. 478.

36. *Ibid.*, p. 451.

37. *Ibid.*, p. 438.

38. *Ibid.*, pp. 437–438.

39. *Ibid.*, pp. 468–469.

40. *Ibid.*, pp. 421–422.

41. B. Krichevskii, "Printsipy, taktika i bor'by," *Rabochee Delo*, no. 10, p. 20.

42. V. I. Lenin, "Chto delat'?" *Sochineniya*, V, 433.

43. B. Krichevskii, "Printsipy . . ." *Rabochee Delo*, no. 10, p. 29.

44. V. I. Lenin, "Kak chut' ne potukhla 'Iskra,' " *Sochineniya*, IV, 309–324.

45. *Ibid.*, 317.

CHAPTER 8. A Program for Social Democracy

1. G. V. Plekhanov, "Kommentarii k proektu programmy RSDRP," *Zarya*, no. 4, August 1902, pp. 205–207.

2. Lenin's remarks about Plekhanov's first draft of the program are drawn from his "Zamechaniya na pervyi proekt Programmy Plekhanova" and "Proekt Programmy Rossiiskoi Sotsial-Demokraticheskoi Rabochei Partii," *Sochineniya*, VI, 3–17.

3. "Zamechaniya na vtoroi proekt Programmy Plekhanova," *Sochineniya*, VI, 32, 34.

4. "Dopolnitel'nye zamechaniya na komissionnyi proekt," *Sochineniya*, VI, 59.

5. "Zamechaniya na komissionnyi proekt Programmy," *Leninskii Sbornik*, II, 124–125.

6. Letter to Vera Zasulich, dated Geneva, March 19, 1902, quoted in *Leninskii Sbornik*, II, 95.

7. "Rabochaya Partiya i krest'ianstvo," *Iskra*, no. 3, in *Sochineniya*, IV, 400.

8. Letter dated Zürich, May 9, 1902, *Leninskii Sbornik*, III, 419.

9. "Zamechaniya na vtorom proekte Programmy Plekhanova," *Sochineniya*, VI, 36n.

10. "K derevenskoi bednote," *Sochineniya*, VI, 359.

11. *Ibid.*, p. 354.

12. "Agrarnaya programma russkoi sotsial-demokratii," *Sochineniya*, VI, 106.

13. *Revolyutsionnaya Rossiya*, no. 8, June 1902.

14. *Ibid.*, no. 32, September 1903.

15. *Ibid.*, no. 15.

16. "Otvet Zare," *Revolyutsionnaya Rossiya*, no. 4, February 1902.

17. "Dnevnik chitatelia," *Revolyutsionnaya Rossiya*, no. 47, 1904.

18. "Programnye voprosy," *Revolyutsionnaya Rossiya,* no. 11, September 1902.

19. *Revolyutsionnaya Rossiya,* no. 8, June 1902.

20. "Dnevnik chitatelia," *Revolyutsionnaya Rossiya,* no. 47, 1904.

21. "Ot krest'yanskogo soyuza," *Revolyutsionnaya Rossiya,* no. 8, June 1902.

22. "Novoe vino v starykh mekhakh," *Iskra,* no. 5, June 1901.

23. "Proletariat i krest'ianstvo," *Iskra,* nos. 32–35, January 15–May 1, 1903.

24. "Osnovnoi tezis protiv Eserov," *Sochineniya,* VI, 243–246.

25. *Ibid.,* pp. 244–245.

26. "Pochemu Sotsial-Demokratiya dolzhna ob"yavit' reshitel'nuyu i bes-poshchadnuyu voinu sotsialistam-revolyutsioneram," *Sochineniya,* VI, 151–154.

27. "Ot russkikh konstitutsialistov," *Osvobozhdenie,* no. 1, June 1902.

28. Martov's attitute toward his colleagues' negotiations with the Revisionist leader is discussed in his "Pskov," *Leninskii Sbornik,* IV, 51–60 (see also footnote on pp. 131–132 above); Lydia Dan, "Okolo redaktsii 'Iskry,' Iz vospominanii," and G. Aronson, "Kommentarii," *Protiv techeniya,* II (New York, 1954); and Struve, in *Slavonic and East European Review,* XIII, 66–84.

29. P. B. Struve, "Mirovaya i revolyutsionnaya bor'ba," *Osvobozhdenie,* no. 7, 1902.

30. See "Vsegda v menshinstve," *Zarya,* no. 2–3, p. 190.

31. "Conversation about Letters from Readers," *Iskra,* no. 14, January 1903.

32. "Na poroge dvadtsatogo veka," discussed above, p. 127.

33. "Chto zhe dal'she," *Zarya,* no. 2–3, December 1901.

34. The evolution of Plekhanov's attitude toward the negotiations with the Revisionist leaders can be traced in the following sources: "Kak chut' ne potukhla 'Iskra'; *Perepiska G. V. Plekhanova i P. B. Akselroda;* Lydia Dan, "Okolo redaktsii 'Iskry,' " and G. Aronson, "Kommentarii"; and Struve, in *Slavonic and East European Review,* XIII, 66–84.

35. Letter to Lenin, dated Geneva, July 14, 1901, in *Leninskii Sbornik,* III, 203–205.

36. "Zamechaniya na proekt programmy RSD, vyrabotannyi Kommissiei," *Leninskii Sbornik,* II, 110.

37. "Ortodoksal'noe bukvoedstvo," *Iskra,* nos. 41–43, June 1–July 1, 1903; *Sochineniya,* XIII, 373.

38. See "Istoricheskoe polozhenie . . ."

39. *Rozhdenie burzhuaznoi demokratii* (Zürich, 1902), pp. 5–6.

40. For further details, see Gérard Walter, *Lénine* (Paris, 1950), pp. 93–94.

41. Struve, in *Slavonic and East European Review,* XIII, 78–79.

42. *Leninskii Sbornik,* I.

43. "Zapis' 29 dekabrya 1900 goda," *Sochineniya,* IV, 356.

44. P. B. Akselrod, letter dated July 19, 1901, *Pis'ma P. B. Akselroda i Y. O. Martova,* p. 50.

45. G. V. Plekhanov, letter dated Geneva, July 14, 1901, *Leninskii Sbornik,* III, 200–204.

46. *Leninskii Sbornik,* III, 213–219.

47. "Goniteli zemstva i annibaly liberalizma," *Zarya,* no. 2–3, December 1901; in *Sochineniya,* V, 55–56.

48. *Ibid.,* pp. 64–65.

49. "Vnutrennee obozrenie," *Zarya*, no. 2–3, December 1901; *Sochineniya*, V, 276.

CHAPTER 9. Unification and Schism

1. Lydia Dan, "Okolo redaktsii 'Iskry,'" p. 68.
2. See "Programma 2–go s"ezda RSDRP," *Leninskii Sbornik*, VI, 57.
3. "Pis'mo k tovarishchu o nashikh organizatsionnykh zadachakh," September 1902, in *Sochineniya*, VI, 205–224. See also letter to I. I. Radchenko, dated July 16, 1902, *Sochineniya* (3rd ed.), XXVIII, 143–144; letter to Ch–U, dated August 2, 1902, *ibid.*, p. 96; and letter to E. Ya. Levin, dated November 1902, *ibid.*, p. 154.
4. Quoted in "Shag vpered, dva shaga nazad," *Sochineniya*, VII, 227.
5. *Ibid.*, p. 224.
6. "Programma 2–go s"ezda RSDRP," *Leninskii Sbornik*, VI, 65.
7. *Vtoroi ocherednoi s"ezd RSDRP, Protokoly* (Geneva, 1903), p. 109.
8. *Ibid.*, p. 115.
9. *Ibid.*, pp. 116–117.
10. *Ibid.*, p. 124.
11. *Ibid.*, pp. 169–170.
12. *Ibid.*, pp. 165ff.
13. See Liber's speech, *ibid.*, p. 219.
14. *Vtoroi ocherednoi s"ezd RSDRP*, p. 200.
15. See Popov's and Egorov's speeches, *ibid.*, pp. 154–156.
16. See Akimov's speech, *ibid.*, p. 157.
17. Speech by Goldblat, *ibid.*, p. 160.
18. See speeches by Martov and Akselrod, *ibid.*, pp. 238–239.
19. Speeches by Popov and Strakhov, *ibid.*, pp. 241ff.
20. Martynov's speech, *ibid.*, pp. 243–245.
21. Martov's speech, *ibid.*, pp. 245–246.
22. Plekhanov's speech, *ibid.*, p. 246.
23. Trotsky's speech, *ibid.*, 248–250.
24. Lenin, in *ibid.*, 250–252.
25. See Lenin's defense at the Congress of the Russian Social Democrats Abroad: RSDRP, *Protokoly 2–go ocherednogo s"ezda Zagranichnoi Ligi* (1903), pp. 48–49.
26. See V. I. Lenin, "Rasskaz o 2 s"ezde RSDRP," *Sochineniya*, VII, 13–14.
27. *Vtoroi ocherednoi s"ezd RSDRP*, p. 331.
28. *Ibid.*, p. 332.

CHAPTER 10. Bolshevism and Menshevism

1. Quoted in Wolfe, *Three Who Made a Revolution*, p. 250.
2. L. D. Trotsky and Y. O. Martov, "Resolution about our Current Tasks in the Intra-Party Struggle," *Leninskii Sbornik*, VI, 246–247.
3. Lenin, "Rasskaz o 2 s"ezde," written between September 1 and 15, 1903, *Sochineniya*, VII, 18; see also a letter to A. M. Kalmykova, dated September 7, 1903, *Leninskii Sbornik*, VI, 205.
4. Letter to "Kler" and "Boris" from "The Old Man," dated October 5, 1903, *Sochineniya* (3rd ed.), XXVIII, 299.

5. "Vtoroi s"ezd zagranichnoi ligi: doklad o 2 s"ezde RSDRP," in *Sochineniya*, VII, 57–67.

6. *Protokoly 2-go ocherednogo s"ezda zagranichnoi ligi*, pp. 61–62.

7. Letter to V. A. Noskov and G. N. Krzhizhanovskii in *Sochineniya* (3rd ed.), XXVIII, 307.

8. Letter to Krzhizhanovskii, in *Leninskii Sbornik*, VI, 218.

9. G. V. Plekhanov, "Chego ne delat'," *Iskra*, no. 53, November 25, 1903.

10. P. B. Akselrod, "Ob"edinenie rossiiskoi sotsialdemokratii i eya zadachi," *Iskra*, nos. 55 and 57, December 15, 1903, January 15, 1904; see also [Y. O. Martov], "Nash s"ezd," *Iskra*, no. 53.

11. G. V. Plekhanov, "Tsentralizm ili Bonapartizm" (Novaya popytka obrazumit' lyagushek, prosyashchykh sebe tsarya), *Iskra*, no. 65, May 11, 1904.

12. Y. O. Martov, *Bor'ba s osadnym polozheniem v RSDRP* (Geneva, 1904), p. 66.

13. Lenin, "Shag vpered, dva shaga nazad," *Sochineniya*, VII, 222–223.

14. *Ibid.*, pp. 356–357.

15. *Ibid.*, pp. 361–363.

16. *Ibid.*, pp. 238–239.

17. *Ibid.*, p. 246.

18. *Ibid.*, p. 249.

19. *Ibid.*, p. 254.

20. *Ibid.*, p. 253.

21. *Ibid.*, pp. 238, 254.

22. *Ibid.*, p. 241.

23. *Ibid.*, p. 239.

24. *Ibid.*, p. 360.

25. *Ibid.*, p. 362.

26. *Ibid.*, p. 360.

27. *Ibid.*, pp. 360–361.

28. *Vtoroi ocherednoi s"ezd RSDRP*, p. 248.

29. Rosa Luxemburg, "Organizatsionnye voprosy russkoi sotsialdemokratii," *Iskra*, no. 69, July 1904.

30. Vera Zasulich, "Organizatsiya, Partiya, Dvizhenie," *Iskra*, no. 70, July 25, 1904.

31. P. B. Akselrod, "K voprosu ob istochnike i znachenii nashikh organizatsionnykh raznoglasii," *Iskra*, no. 68, June 25, 1904.

32. Y. O. Martov, "Vpered ili nazad," *Iskra*, nos. 67–69, June, July, 1904.

33. Akselrod, "K voprosu . . ."

CHAPTER 11. The Party and Revolution

1. Martov, *Proletarskaya bor'ba*, pp. 129–130.

2. *Ibid.*, pp. 130–131.

3. G. V. Plekhanov, "K voprosu o zakhvate vlasti," *Iskra*, no. 96, April 1905.

4. Starover [Potresov], "Nashi zloklyucheniya," *Iskra*, no. 78 (November 20, 1904).

5. G. V. Plekhanov, "Vroz' itti, vmeste bit'," *Iskra*, no. 87, February 10, 1905; see also *O nashei taktike po otnosheniyu k bor'be liberal'noi burzhuazii s tsarizmom* (Geneva, 1905).

6. Y. O. Martov, "Rabochii klass i burzhuaznaya revolyutsiya," *Iskra*, no. 79, December 1904.

7. *Ibid.*; see also Martov's "Na Ochered'," *Iskra*, no. 75, October 5, 1904.

8. Y. O. Martov, "Na Ochered'," *Iskra*, no. 77; see also G. V. Plekhanov, "Pora ob'yasnit'sya," *Iskra*, no. 82, January 1, 1905.

9. Quoted in Y. O. Zederbaum [Martov], *Istoriya RSDRP*, p. 96.

10. Martov, "Rabochii klass i burzhuaznaya revolutsiya," *Iskra*, no. 79.

11. V. I. Lenin, "Zemskaya kampaniya i plan 'Iskry,'" *Sochineniya*, VII, 464.

12. *Ibid.*, p. 466.

13. *Ibid.*, pp. 470ff.

14. Plekhanov, *O nashei taktike po otnosheniyu k bor'be liberal'noi burzhuazii s tsarizmom.*

15. *Ibid.*

16. V. I. Lenin, "Zadachi revolyutsionnoi molodezhi," *Student*, no. 2–3, September 1903; in *Sochineniya*, VII, 32.

CONCLUSION

1. N. Berdyaev, "Filosofskaya istina i intelligentskaya pravda," *Vekhi*, pp. 44–46.

2. M. Gershenzon, "Tvorcheskoe samosoznanie, *Vekhi*, p. 79.

BIBLIOGRAPHY

It would be difficult to provide a complete and definitive bibliography for a subject as broad as the one discussed in the present work, and I shall not attempt to do so. The titles that are listed here are those of books and periodicals that, to a greater or lesser degree, actually influenced my analysis and conclusions. Very few secondary sources could be placed in this category as far as the core of the study is concerned. Only a handful of books have been written about the *early* development of Russian Social Democracy; of these, most are highly tendentious in their selection and treatment of available evidence, so much so that retrospective studies by participants in the political struggles discussed should be evaluated with the caution and care usually given to primary sources. Some exceptions to this general rule are: F. I. Dan's *Proiskhozhdenie bol'shevizma* (The Origins of Bolshevism), a survey which is amazingly objective and sensitive, on the whole, considering that its author was Martov's chief lieutenant during the long years of bitter struggle between Bolsheviks and Mensheviks; N. Volskii's superb, if somewhat long-winded manuscript account of Lenin's early development; and Bertram D. Wolfe's *Three Who Made a Revolution,* an impressive achievement, even if some of its interpretations appear swayed by sentiment. As for other works, most of the treatments of Lenin's revolutionary career that I consulted did not arouse much interest (with the exception of Edmund Wilson's highly stimulating essay in *To the Finland Station*), and no book-length biographies of Plekhanov, Martov, or Akselrod were available — although in the cases of Martov and Akselrod, this gap was filled somewhat by autobiographical accounts. Thus, in the examination of the early development and subsequent interaction of Lenin and his collaborators, I have had to rely heavily on the evidence to be found in primary sources — that is, in the polemical writings and available memoirs of these four men. It should also be pointed out that this almost exclusive emphasis on primary sources is due in part to the fact that my discussion of the early developments of Russian Social Democracy is focused on certain specific questions and is not aimed at a broad comprehensive survey of the era.

Secondary sources were far more heavily drawn upon for the historical introduction to the study and for its other background sections. Among these, I would like to single out the following works: Ovsianiko Kulikovskii's *Istoriya russkoi intelligentsii* (History of the Russian Intelligentsia) and Ivanov Razumnik's *Istoriya russkoi obshchestvennoi mysli* (History of Russian Social Thought), both of which are precious sources of insight into the ways in which members of the intelligentsia themselves viewed the turbulent evolution of their group; V. Y. Yakovlev's *Aktivnoe Narodnichestvo* (The Active [i.e., Revolutionary] Narodnichestvo) and his *Iz istorii politicheskoi borby v 70 kh 80 kh gg. XIX go veka* (From the History of the Political Struggle in the

1870's and 1880's), two extremely valuable histories of the Narodniki and Narodovoltsi; and finally, the various essays collected in the symposium *Obshchestvennoe dvizhenie v Rossii v nachale XX–go veka* (The Social Movement in Russia at the Beginning of the Twentieth Century), which, in spite of their general tendency to interpret events on the monistic basis of historical materialism, shed considerable light on the political, economic, social, and intellectual developments that were taking place on the Russian scene at the end of the nineteenth and the beginning of the twentieth century.

For the reader's convenience, bibliographical references have been divided into primary and secondary sources. I have departed from the usual practice in listing primary sources by generally including in this category those writings of the participants in the political struggle that are purported to be objective historical accounts. I have already alluded to the rationale for this procedure: even in the instances when these accounts were written many years after the event, they were usually so twisted by the author's prejudices and predilections that they throw as much, if not more, light on his psychology as they do on the character of events per se.

1. PRIMARY SOURCES

Newspapers and Journals Extensively Used

Chernyi Peredel. Organ of the Socialist-Federalists, Zemlya i Volya. Nos. 1–2, January to September, 1880.

Iskra. Organ of the Russian Social Democratic Labor Party. Published successively in Leipzig, Munich, London, and Geneva. Nos. 1–112, December 1900 to December 1905.

Osvobozhdenie. Edited by Peter Struve. Nos. 1–79, July 1902 to October 1905.

Rabochaya Mysl'. Organ of the St. Petersburg Union of Struggle for the Emancipation of the Working Class. Nos. 6, 9, 11 (St. Petersburg), April 1899 to April 1901.

Rabochee Delo. Organ of the Union of Russian Social Democrats (Geneva). Nos. 1–12, April 1899 to February 1902.

Revolyutsionnaya Rossiya (from 1902–1905, organ of the Socialist Revolutionary Party), nos. 1–76, 1900 to October 1905.

Zarya. Social Democratic scientific political journal; edited by G. V. Plekhanov, V. I. Zasulich, and P. B. Akselrod (Stuttgart). Nos. 1–4, April 1901 to August 1902.

Articles, Pamphlets, and Books

Akselrod, P. B. *Bor'ba sotsialisticheskikh i burzhuaznykh tendentsii v russkom revolyutsionnom dvizhenii.* 2nd rev. ed. St. Petersburg, 1907.

———— "Gruppa 'Osvobozhdenie truda'" (unpublished chapters of the 2nd volume of "Vospominaniia"), *Letopis' Marksizma,* no. 6, 1928, pp. 82–112.

———— *Istoricheskoe polozhenie i vzaimnoe otnoshenie liberal'noi i sotsialisticheskoi demokratii v Rossii.* Geneva, 1898.

———— *K voprosu o sovremennykh zadachakh i taktike russkikh sotsial demokratov.* Geneva, 1898.

———— *Ob"yavlenie o vozobnovlenii izdanii Gruppy "Osvobozhdenie truda."* Geneva, 1900.

———— *Perezhitoe i peredumannoe,* vol. I. *Letopis' revolyutsii,* no. 14. Berlin, 1923.

—— *Pis'ma P. B. Akselroda i Y. O. Martova.* Rus. rev. arkhiv: *Materialy po istorii russkogo revolyutsionnogo dvizheniya,* vol. I. Berlin, 1924.
—— *Pis'mo v redaktsiyu 'Rabochego Dela.'* Ed. Gruppa "Osvobozhdenie Truda." Geneva, 1899.
—— "Pochemu my ne khotim idti nazad," *Zarya,* no. 2, December, 1901.
—— *Rabochee dvizhenie i sotsial'naya demokratiya.* Ed. Gruppa "Osvobozhdenie Truda." Geneva, 1884.
—— *Zadachi rabochei intelligentsii v Rossii.* Geneva, 1893.
Baranovskii, Tugan. "Osnovnaya oshibka abstraktnoi teorii kapitalizma Marksa," *Nauchnoe Obozrenie,* May 1899.
Bulgakov, S. N. *Kapitalizm v zemledelii.* St. Petersburg, 1900.
—— *Ot marksizma k idealizmu.* St. Petersburg, 1903.
Chernyshevskii, *see* Tchernyshevsky.
Chicherin, B. "Zadachi novogo tsarstvovaniya," *K. P. Pobedonostsev i ego korrespondenty. Pis'ma i zapiski,* vol. I. Moscow, 1923.
Figner, Vera. "Zapechatlennyi trud," *Polnoe sobranie sochinenii.* 6 vols. Moscow, 1928–29. Vols. I–II.
Gruppa "Osvobozhdenie Truda." *Vademekum dlya redaktsii "Rabochego Dela."* Foreword by G. V. Plekhanov. Geneva, 1900.
Krasnyi Arkhiv, vol. I. 1934. (Contains important materials on Lenin).
Kremer, A. [Y. O. Martov, original editor]. *Ob agitatsii,* with a concluding statement by P. Akselrod. Geneva, 1896.
Krichevskii, B. "Ekonomicheskaya i politicheskaya bor'ba v russkom rabochem dvizhenii," *Rabochee Delo,* no. 7, pp. 1–22.
—— "Printsipy, taktika, i bor'ba," *Rabochee Delo,* no. 10, September 1901, pp. 1–36.
Iv–na, V. "Organizatsionnye voprosy russkogo rabochego dvizheniya," *Rabochee Delo,* no. 8, November 1900, pp. 1–22.
Lenin, V. I. *Sochineniya.* 30 vols. 3rd ed. Moscow, 1935. Vols. XXVIII, XXX.
—— *Sochineniya.* 35 vols. 4th ed. Moscow, 1941–1950. Vols. I–VII.
Leninskii Sbornik. 31 vols. Moscow, 1924–1938. Vols. I–XII.
Martov, Y. O. *Bor'ba s 'osadnym polozheniem' v Rossiiskoi Sotsial demokraticheskoi Rabochei Partii.* Geneva, 1904.
—— *Pis'mo k tovarishcham-propagandistam.* Geneva, 1902.
—— *Istoriya rossiiskoi sotsial-demokratii.* Moscow, 1923.
—— *Proletarskaya bor'ba v. Rossii.* Foreword by P. Akselrod. St. Petersburg, 1907.
—— *Rabochee delo v Rossii.* Geneva, 1899.
—— *Sovremennaya Rossiya.* Geneva, 1898.
—— "Vnutrennee obozrenie," *Zarya,* no. 4, August 1902, pp. 184–222.
—— "Vsegda v menshinstve. O sovremennykh zadachakh russkoi sotsialisticheskoi intelligentsii," *Zarya,* no. 2–3, December 1901, pp. 180–203.
—— *Zapiski sotsial demokrata. Letopis' revolyutsii,* no. 4. St. Petersburg, Berlin, Moscow, 1922.
—— "Zarozhdenie politicheskikh partii i ikh deyatel'nost'," *Obshchestvennoe dvizhenie v Rossii v nachale 20-go veka,* vol. I. St. Petersburg, 1909.
Martynov, A. "Oblichitel'naya literatura i proletarskaya bor'ba," *Rabochee Delo,* no. 10, September 1901, pp. 37–63.
—— "Sovremennye voprosy," *Rabochee Delo,* no. 9, May 1901.
Materialy dlya istorii revolyutsionnago dvizheniya v Rossii v 60kh godakh. St. Petersburg, 1906.
Mikhailovskii, N. K. "Pis'ma postoronnego," *Otechestvennyya Zapiski,* April 1883.

Popov, M. R. *Zapiski zemlevol'tsa.* Moscow, 1933.
Potresov, A. N. "Evolyutsiya obshchestvenno-politicheskoi mysli v predrevo-lyutsionnuyu epokhu," *Obshchestvennoe dvizhenie v Rossii v nachale 20-go veka,* vol. I, pp. 538–642.
Plekhanov, G. V. *Perepiska G. V. Plekhanova i P. B. Akselroda.* Edited by P. A. Berlin, V. S. Voitinsky, and P. B. Nikolaevsky. Moscow, 1945.
———— *Sochineniya.* Ed. D. Ryazanov. 24 vols. Moscow, 1923–1927. Vol. I–XIII.
Rabochee Delo. Otvet redaktsii 'Rabochego Dela' na 'pis'mo' P. Akselroda i Vademekum G. Plekhanova. Union of Russian Social Democrats. Geneva, 1900.
Redaktsiya "Rabochego Dela." "Nasha novaya programma," *Rabochee Delo,* no. 11, February 1902, pp. 1–14.
Rossiiskaya Sotsial-demokraticheskaya Rabochaya Partiya. *Vtoroi ocherednoi s"ezd RSDRP.* Protocols. Geneva, 1903.
Struve, P. B. "K kritike nekotorykh osnovnykh problem i polozhenii politi-cheskoi ekonomii," *Zhizn',* May 1900.
———— *Na raznye temy (1893–1901 gg.)* St. Petersburg, 1902.
———— "Osnovnaya antinomiya teorii trudovoi tsennosti," *Zhizn',* February 1900.
———— "Protiv ortodoksal'nosti," *Zhizn',* October 1899.
Tchernyshevsky, N. G. [Chernyshevskii]. *Que Faire? [Chto delat'?]* Lodi, 1875.
Tikhomirov, L. A. *Vestnik Narodnoi Voli,* no. 2, 1883.
Tkachev, P. N. *Izbrannye sochineniya na sotsial'no-politicheskie temy.* Ed. B. P. Kozmin. Moscow 1932–1933.
Trotsky, Lev. *Vtoroi S"ezd RSDRP.* Geneva, 1903.
Vekhi, Sbornik statei o russkoi intelligentsii. Moscow 1909.
Vorontsov, V. P. [V.V.] *Sud'by kapitalizma v Rossii.* St. Petersburg, 1882.
Zagranichnaya liga russkoi revolyutsionnoi sotsial-demokratii. *Protokoly 2–go ocherednogo s"ezda Zagranichnoi ligi russkoi revolyutsionnoi sotsial-demokratii.* Edited by I. Lesenko and F. Dan. Geneva, 1904.

2. Secondary Sources

Historical Background

Danielson, N. F. *Ocherki nashego poreformennogo khoziaistva.* St. Petersburg, 1893.
Ivanov-Razumnik, R. Y. *Istoriya russkoi obshchestvennoi mysli. Individualizm i meshchanstvo v russkoi literature i zhizni.* 2 vols. St. Petersburg, 1907.
Kravchinskii, S. *Podpol'naya Rossiya,* London, 1893.
Landes, Ruth, and Mark Zborowski. "Hypotheses concerning the Eastern European Jewish Family," *Psychiatry,* XIII, 447–464.
Masaryk, T. G. *The Spirit of Russia: Studies in History, Literature, and Philosophy,* trans. Eden and Cedar Paul. 2 vols. London, New York, 1919.
Milyukov, P. N. *Iz istorii russkoi intelligentsii.* St. Petersburg, 1902.
———— *Le Mouvement intellectuel russe durant les années trente.* Trans. G. W. Bienstock. Paris, 1918.
———— *Ocherki po istorii russkoi kul'tury.* St. Petersburg, 1904–1909.
Obshchestvennoe dvizhenie v Rossii v nachale 20–go veka. Edited by L. Martov, D. Maslov, and A. Potresov. 3 vols. St. Petersburg, 1909.
Ovsyaniko-Kulikovskii, D. N. *Istoriya russkoi intelligentsii. Itogi russkoi khu-*

dozhestvennoi literatury 19–go veka. 2nd ed. 4 vols. St. Petersburg, 1908–1911.

———, ed. *Istoriya russkoi literatury XIX veka.* Edited in collaboration with A. E. Gruzinskii and P. N. Sakulin. 5 vols. Moscow, 1908–1911.

Turgenev, Ivan. *Fathers and Children.* New York, 1948.

——— "Rudin: A Romance," *The Works of Ivan Turgenev.* Trans. Isabel F. Hapgood. New York, 1904.

Yakovlev, V. Y. *Aktivnoe narodnichestvo.* Moscow, 1912.

——— *Iz istorii politicheskoi bor'by v 70–kh i 80–kh godov XIX veka. Partiya "Narodnoi Voli," eya proiskhozhdenie, sud'by, i gibel'.* Moscow, 1912.

The Evolution of Social Democracy

Dan, F. I. *Proiskhozhdenie bol'shevizma.* New York, 1946.

Dan, Lydia. "Okolo redaktsii 'Iskry,' Iz vospominanii," and G. Aronson, "Kommentarii," *Protiv techeniya,* vol. II. New York, 1954.

Leibzen, V. M. *Leninskaya 'Iskra.'* Leningrad, 1939.

Martynov, A. *Vospominaniya iz epokh II s"ezda RSDRP,* Moscow, 1934.

Obshchestvennoe dvizhenie v Rossii.

Proletarskaya Revolyutsiya, no. 8, 1928; no. 2, 1933. (Both of these issues are devoted to the Second Congress of the RSDRP.)

Shcheglo, L. "Rabochaya Mysl'," *Katorga i Ssylka,* IV–V. Moscow, 1933.

Rubinstein, N., and G. Stopalov. *'Iskra.' 1900–1903 gg.* Moscow, 1926.

Takhtarev, K. M. *Ocherki Peterburgskogo rabochego dvizheniya 90–kh godov.* St. Petersburg, 1921.

V. I. Lenin

Alekseev, V. N. "Sem'ya Ul'yanovykh v Simbirske (1869–1887)." Ed. A. I. Ulyanova [Elizarova]. Moscow, 1925.

Fülöp-Miller, René. *Lenin and Gandhi.* Trans. F. S. Flint and D. F. Tait. London, 1927.

Gorky, Maxim [A. M. Peshkov]. *Days with Lenin,* New York, 1932.

Krupskaya, N. K. *Memories of Lenin.* Trans. E. Verney. 2 vols. New York, 1930.

Lalayants. "O moikh vstrechakh s V. I. Leninym," *Proletarskaya Revolyutsiya,* no. 1, 1929.

Lerner, N. "Otets Lenina," *Minovskie Dni,* no. 3, 1928.

Lunacharskii, A. V. *O Vladimire Il'iche.* Moscow, 1933.

——— *V. I. Lenin,* Moscow, 1924.

O Lenine. Moscow, 1927.

Pamyati V. I. Lenina. Ed. Academy of Sciences of the USSR. Moscow, 1934.

Shub, David. *Lenin, a Biography.* Garden City, N. Y. 1948.

Struve, P. B. "Moi vstrechi i stolknoveniya s Leninym," *Vozrozhdenie,* no. 9, Paris 1950.

——— "My Contacts and Conflicts with Lenin," *Slavonic and East European Review,* XII, XIII. London, 1934.

Trotsky, Leon. *Lenin,* New York, 1925.

Ul'yanova, A. I. (Elizarova). *Detskie i shkol'nye gody Il'icha,* Moscow, 1930.

——— "Vospominaniya ob Il'iche." Series *Vospominaniya starogo bol'shevika.* Edited by A. I. Elizarova and F. Kon. Moscow, 1926.

——— *Vospominaniya ob Il'iche.* Foreword by M. I. Ul'yanova. Moscow, 1934.

Valentinov (N. Volskii). Unfinished biography of Lenin (manuscript lent by the author). Sections of this biography have begun to appear in *Novyi Zhurnal* (New York).

Veretnikov, N. *Volodya Ul'yanov; vospominaniya o detskikh godakh V. I. Lenina v Kokushkine.* Moscow, 1941.

Walter, Gérard. *Lénine.* Paris, 1950. (Contains an exhaustive bibliography on Lenin.)

Wilson, Edmund. *To the Finland Station: A Study in the Writing and Acting of History.* New York, 1940.

Wolfe, Bertram D. *Three Who Made A Revolution.* New York, 1948.

G. V. Plekhanov

Deich, L. G. *G. V. Plekhanov, materialy dlya biografii.* Moscow, 1922.

———— "G. V. Plekhanov v 'Zemle i Vole,'" *Gruppa Osvobozhdenie Truda,* no. 3, 1925.

———— "Kak G. V. Plekhanov stal Marksistom," *Proletarskaya Revolyutsiya,* no. 7, 1922.

———— "Molodost' G. V. Plekhanova (Iz vospominanii)," *Molodaya Gvardiya,* no. 3, 1928.

———— "O sblizhenii i razryve s narodovol'tsami," *Proletarskaya Revolyutsiya* no. 8, 1923.

———— "Pervye shagi Gruppy 'Osvobozhdenie Truda,'" *Gruppa Osvobozhdenie Truda,* no. 1, 1924.

Frencher, A. A. "Na rodine G. V. Plekhanova," *Proletarskaya Revolyutsiya,* no. 8, 1922.

Kuzmin, D. "Kazanskaya demonstratsiya 1876 g. i G. V. Plekhanov," *Katorga i ssylka,* no. 42, Moscow, 1928.

Plekhanova, R. "Nasha zhizn' do emigratsii," *Gruppa Osvobozhdenie Truda,* no. 6, 1928.

Pozdnyakova-Plekhanova, V. V. "Detstvo i otechestvo G. V. Plekhanova," *Gruppa Osvobozhdenie Truda,* no. 1, 1924.

Smirnov, I. "G. V. Plekhanov v Voronezhskoi Voennoi Gimnazii," *Katorga i ssylka,* no. 61, 1929.

P. B. Akselrod

Akselrod, L. I. *Etyudy i vospominaniya.* Leningrad, 1925.

Potresov, A. *P. B. Akselrod (Sorok pyat' let obshchestvennoi deyatel'nosti).* St. Petersburg, 1914.

Y. O. Martov

Aronson, G. "Martov i ego blizkie (K 30–letiyu smerti Martova)," *Protiv techeniya,* vol. II. New York, 1954.

Ezhov, S., and K. I. Zakharova, *Iz epokhi 'Iskry' (1900–1905 gg.),* Moscow, 1924.

Levitskii, V. *Za chetvert' veka. Revolyutsionnye vospominaniya.* Moscow, 1926.

INDEX